The Dialectics of
Secret Society Power
in States

The Dialectics of
Secret Society Power
in States

STANTON K. TEFFT

Humanities Press
New Jersey ▼ London

First published 1992 by Humanities Press International, Inc.,
Atlantic Highlands, New Jersey 07716, and
3 Henrietta Street, Covent Garden, London WC2E 8LU

Library of Congress Cataloging-in-Publication Data
Tefft, Stanton K.
     The dialectics of secret society power in states / Stanton K. Tefft.
          p.   cm.
     Includes bibliographical references and index.
     ISBN 0–391–03734–X
     1. Secret societies—Political aspects—Case studies.   I. Title.
     HS150.T44   1992
     366—dc20   91–36743
                                 CIP

A catalog record for this book is available from the British Library.

Printed in the United States of America

To
E. A. Hoebel
who inspired me to undertake this research

and to
Roberta
whose encouragement was necessary for its success

Contents

Preface

Information control has always been an important sociopolitical strategy by which individuals and groups manipulate social relationships, and information control continues to be a significant mechanism by which social and political relationships are regulated. Information-control processes operate on all levels of sociopolitical organization, including interpersonal, inter-family, intercorporate, interclass, and interstate. Devices by which outsiders obtain information from insiders who deny the outsiders access to the information is *espionage*. *Secrecy* is the reverse of this strategy: procedures for the denial of information access. *Persuasion* involves the practices by which believable information is transferred to outsiders, and *evaluation* concerns the means by which outsiders test and appraise such information.

In a previous book (*Secrecy: A Cross-Cultural Perspective* [New York: Human Sciences Press, 1980]) I brought together a series of articles by various authors who investigated information-control processes both historically and cross-culturally. These studies showed that information control is a basic adaptive strategy employed by individuals, families, religio-political leaders in tribal communities, rebel secret societies, military conspirators, small and large economic organizations, and managers of political bureaucracies.

While *Secrecy: A Cross-Cultural Perspective* explored the dimensions of information control in varied historic circumstances, except for two articles, it ignored the political role of secret societies in early and modern states. However, even a casual review of the literature on secret societies suggests that such secret orders play an important role in the political dynamics of state systems.

While there has been considerable research on secret societies, there have been few systematic attempts to make a comparative analysis of the political role of secret societies in states. There have been some descriptive studies analyzing the history of secret society development in specific countries (e.g., Norman MacKenzie, ed., *Secret Societies* [New York: Collier Books, 1971]; F. W. Butt-Thompson, *West African Secret Societies* [New York:

Argosy-Antiquarian, Ltd., 1969]; J. Chesneaux, *Secret Societies in China* [London: Heinemann, 1971]; A. Daraul, *A History of Secret Societies* [New York: Citadel, 1961]; C. Heckethorn, *The Secret Societies of All Ages and Countries* [New Hyde, NY: Universal Books, 1965]; T. D. Williams, ed., *Secret Societies in Ireland* [New York: Barnes and Noble, 1973]; H. Webster, *Primitive Secret Societies* [New York: MacMillan, 1908]). But such studies do not offer a theoretical framework suitable for a comparative study of secret orders, especially a comparative analysis that aims at studying the changing role of secret societies in evolving state systems.

I hope this book, in part, fills this void by providing a more systematic analysis of the political role of a select number of secret societies within early and modern states. Using a dialectical theory framework I examine the power relations between secret societies and the state in Liberia, the Ottoman empire (Anatolia), eighteenth- and nineteenth-century China, early and modern Malaysia, and modern South Africa. The selection of these case studies was dictated in part by the availability of historical data on the particular secret societies chosen and in part by my desire to choose secret societies that played various political roles within the selected state systems. The Poro and Sande among the Kpelle of Liberia, the Bektashi among the Ottomans, the White Lotus sects within China, the Triads in Malaysia, and the Broederbond in South Africa met these criteria.

The dialectical analysis of secret societies within this book seeks to answer the following basic questions: How do the structural contradictions within states give rise to the conflicts in which the secret societies become involved? What is the nature of secret society involvement? How are the political dynamics of secret society–state relations channeled by information-control processes? Under what historic circumstances do secret societies undermine or help reinforce state authority? In what ways do secret society politics intensify or help resolve the crises produced by the structural contradictions within state systems? How do secret societies react to the attempts by central state authority to repress or destroy them?

WINSTON-SALEM, NC

Acknowledgments

Teachers, friends, and colleagues have assisted me at all stages of this book's conception and development. As a student of Professor E. A. Hoebel (now Regents Professor Emeritus) at the University of Minnesota I learned the value of clearly articulating the ontological and epistemological principles of scientific research. My studies with Professor Robert Spencer (now Professor Emeritus) at Minnesota made me better appreciate how the recursive analysis by individuals can generate a critical evaluation of institutions that may lead to movements for culture change.

I owe a great intellectual debt to several colleagues. Professor Christine Gailey's writings have clarified my understanding of state systems. I would not have adequately understood the nature of social power without the thoughtful analysis of this concept by Professors Isaac, Rus, and Collier. Without the insightful scholarship of Professor Israel on the dialectical process my theoretical paradigm for this book could not have been developed. And the work of Professor John Wilson has contributed immensely to my understanding of the principles of scientific realism.

My early interest in secret societies was stimulated by the writing of Professor Norman MacKenzie, Professor Gist, and Professor Heckethorn as well as many personal conversations with these noted scholars. Without their encouragement I might not have continued my research in secret orders.

Other colleagues have reviewed various chapters in this book. I especially want to thank Professor Robert P. Murphy of Northwestern University for his helpful suggestions for improvements in the chapter on the Poro of Liberia and Professor Mak Lau-Fong of the National University of Singapore for his useful criticisms of my analysis of the Triad secret societies of Malaysia.

I also wish to thank my typist, Jane Reade, for her excellent care with the manuscript and her helpful editorial suggestions.

Part of the research for this book was supported by a research and publication grant given to me by the Wake Forest University Graduate School. I greatly appreciate this support.

1

A Dialectical Framework for the Study of Secret Society Power in State Systems

THE NEED FOR A REALISTIC FRAMEWORK

Secret societies have long been a focus for social science research (Daraul 1961; Gist 1938a,b, 1940; Heckethorn 1965; MacKenzie 1967; Williams 1973; Wedgewood 1930; Simmel [1908] 1950; Hazelrigg 1969; Little 1965, 1966; Webster 1908). A secret society is a special type of association that has a set of well-defined norms, secret rituals and oaths, or similar declarations or demonstrations of loyalty that are intended to subjectively bind members to the secrecy required by the group's affairs.[1] Social scientists have studied the secret society as a special association, delineating its varieties and comparing this type of association with other forms of organization. But there have been few attempts to investigate the dynamics of secret society activities within the power structures of evolving state systems.[2] This book addresses this neglected dimension of secret society research.

In this book I want to demonstrate, through a comparative analysis of selected secret societies, how a dialectical method provides a useful source of propositions by which to explain the various trajectories of secret society development and their role within the changing power relations of state systems. To help the reader better understand the dialectical method employed in this book I will review the basic dialectical perspectives and principles used in my analysis, utilizing examples from the case studies discussed in greater detail in subsequent chapters. These examples will be drawn from my studies of the following states and secret societies: Liberia (Poro and Sande); Ottoman empire (Bektashi); Malaysia (Triads); Ch'ing China (White Lotus Society) and South Africa (Broederbond).

TOWARD A DIALECTICAL ANALYSIS OF SECRET SOCIETIES

The analysis of secret society power as a historical dynamic must be based on realist assumptions.[3] A dialectical method is based on such assumptions. It provides a useful analytical framework on which to build theories for the analysis of the secrecy processes.

The apparent appearance of stable, ordered social patterns mask more fundamental, essential processes. Dialectical models try to show how social networks (surface patterns) are produced by underlying structural mechanisms.[4] The reality that underlies these overt appearances is infected with conflict and opposition—that is, with contradictory forces containing the seeds of its own development and change (Sayers 1985:204).

It is these underlying structural contradictions that are the object of dialectical analysis. The dialectical method is concerned with how the underlying structure, through its dynamic contradictions, demonstrates its effects on the experience of particular individuals and groups (Israel 1979:113–14; Burawoy 1978:51).

Societal history is marked by a high degree of indeterminancy. It is a combination of changes in separate parts of the total system: political, ideological, economic, and environmental. Through contradictions these social aspects (or subsystems) overdetermine each other, thereby creating the historical dynamic that brings about change and transformation of the total system.

Thus, each social element or social practice is not a "thing-in itself." In reality the boundaries between such social elements are fuzzy ones. We must conceptualize such "things" or "social practices" relationally and historically as a dynamic network of relationships that change over time (Albert and Hahnel 1978:90–92). Resnick and Wolff point to the dynamic aspects of these dialectical relationships when they state that "the complex contradictions overdetermining any process serve as the basis for its complex influences upon all other processes" (1982:38).

Since human agents react to conflicts that result from some basic structural contradictions in different ways, depending on the historic instances, it is problematic through which trajectories of change a society will progress. Dialectical analysis does not seek to establish laws of social change but merely enlarge our capacity to perform specific historical analysis by identifying and analyzing the underlying structural processes responsible for social transformations.

From a dialectical perspective the focus of analysis should be on the totality that is "the whole set of social relationships and practices that characterize particular historic settings" (Wardell and Benson 1979:240). Dialectical analysis conforms to realist assumptions in that it rejects the idea that parts of the totality have prior independent existence as parts. There is an interpenetration of parts and the whole that result from the interchangeability of subject and object. Put more concretely, the total system is based on intrinsic relations that cannot operate independently of the totality (Levins and Lewontin 1985:273–74; Warren 1984:190; Israel 1979:60–67; Jakubowski 1976:102).

A dialectical analysis of the social totality, then, investigates the ways in which social complexes overdetermine one another. Social complexes (or subsystems) both overdetermine and are overdetermined by one another. A social complex is overdetermined when its existence, properties, or qualities are constituted by each and every other social complex. An overdetermined subsystem exists as a site of a particular interaction of all influences originating from other social complexes or subsystems comprising the social totality (Resnick and Wolff 1987:2,24). Thus, each complex both helps produce the whole and is produced by it, determines the whole and is determined by it (Kosik 1976).

The internal nature of social practices (moments) and their relation to one another are mutually interpenetrating opposites within a social totality (Sumner 1979:209). Because of the mutual constitutedness of the moments or social complexes, movement and change in one subsystem will bring change in other complexes which, in turn, will react back on the first subsystem bringing further change (Resnick and Wolff 1987:24). Thus the objective forms of all social phenomena change constantly in the course of their unremitting dialectical interaction (Lukacs 1968:13).

In studying secret societies, then, we must recognize that secret society activity is not solely constituted by the class-related interests of the secret society membership but by other economic, religious, and political practices or moments. And, in turn, secret societies overdetermine other social complexes within the social totality.

The surface relationships within the totality are composed of patterned relationships between actors and/or collectivities across space and time (Giddens 1981:26). But such patterned relationships are instances of a dialectical process. There are interdependencies between such instances (moments). These moments constitute regularized practices or activities. Such interrelations between moments may reproduce the relation or, as a result of contradictions, the instances change one another, thereby superseding the relation between them (Carchedi 1987:78–79; Israel 1979:112; Wardell and Benson 1979:233). Therefore transformation in a moment or social practice actually consists of changing social relationships between these moments, which already exist but cease to be the same practices. The relationships between these moments (or subsystems) evolve within the social totality and therefore the social totality itself changes (Gledhill 1981:14).

Relations that reproduce themselves over long time-space distances I will call "structural moments," and relations subject to supersession (either radical or nonessential or both) I will call "conjunctive moments" (Jessop 1982:252–53). Thus, "structural moments" involve "relatively enduring social relations between agents in their performance of definite social practices" (Isaac 1987:57). Success in reproducing these relations depends on the social actors' success in repairing the inconsistencies that result from the structural contradictions (Archer 1988:81). The resolution of conflicts produced by systemic contradictions may bring change, but the particular character of this change can reproduce certain social complexes over and over again (Albert and Hahnel 1978:93).

Governmental policies may produce changes that merely reinforce existing political hierarchies. The Ch'ing dynasty in China relied on scholar-officials to run the governmental bureaucracy. But these officials were paid very low salaries in spite of the fact that their official duties required them to spend a large amount of money, which their meager income did not cover. This potential source of conflict between the Ch'ing rulers and their bureaucrats was mitigated because the former tolerated the efforts of the middle- and low-level officials to supplement their incomes, within the bounds of customary practice, through graft and corruption (Ch'u 1962).

Conjunctive moments are overt manifestations of structural contradictions within the social totality. A dynamic concept of the social totality is based on the assumption that all social phenomena are subject to inner conflict and tensions. All things are contradictory, constituting a unity of opposites (Sayers 1985:35–36; Mirkovic 1980).[5]

Contradictions refer to those oppositions which are inherent within a system at a particular state in its history and yet destructive of particular structures or entities (Heilbroner 1980; Zeitlin 1980). Such contradictions are irresolvable within existing rules or conditions (Habermas 1975). Structural contradictions occur when interrelated structures become functionally incompatible (Giddens 1979). Or, looked at in more concrete terms, contradictions occur when sooner or later social practices reach a point at which the goals of the practice can no longer be obtained in the trouble-free way they once were (Suchting 1983:168–69).

Primary contradictions occur when subsystem *A* becomes dependent on subsystem *B* but where *B* operates as a hostile environment in which *A* is enmeshed (thus, *B* contravenes *A*) but from which *B* cannot be removed if *A* is to continue to operate (Archer 1988:198).[6]

Political relationships may involve such structures of mutual dependency as well as opposition. During the Ch'ing dynasty in China the Ch'ing relations with the gentry constituted a relationship of both mutual dependency and antagonism. The gentry depended on the state to provide it with a means to attain wealth and prestige. The government examination system gave members of the gentry class an opportunity to obtain high government posts. Individuals occupying such government positions were exempt from labor service and land taxes. Such offices provided opportunities for the gentry to accumulate great wealth through various corrupt practices. On the other hand, the state needed the gentry officials to maintain order and to collect taxes in the local villages and towns. However, the Ch'ing rulers' economic, military, and political demands on the gentry put the latter in opposition to the central leadership of the Ch'ing state. The gentry found ways to subvert the government policies and laws when they found it to be in their interest (Lapidus 1973; Wakeman 1975b; Feuerwerker 1976).

The Ottoman rulers of Anatolia faced similar crises that were the result of primary contradictions within the imperial system. In order to establish and maintain control within their empire, the Ottoman sultans created an efficient military corp, the Janissaries, who were equipped with modern weapons of the time. The Ottoman posted members of this corp to newly conquered areas to serve as a police force. The Janissaries also formed units within the Ottoman armies. But soon the Janissaries acquired so much power that they came to constitute a threat to the Ottoman leadership. In some provinces they consolidated enough power to appropriate the tax revenues that were destined for the state treasuries. But since the early Ottoman sultans depended on the Janissaries to maintain local control within the empire, these Ottoman leaders could not effectively repress them (Shaw 1976; Birge 1937).

In more specific terms, contradictions occur when social agents come into conflict as they pursue solutions to problems produced by the primary contradiction. The conflicts are fought out within opposed economic, political, legal, and ideological frameworks that reflect the contradictions (Allen 1975; Sztompka 1979). The opposing thought-systems (or ideological frameworks) generated by these conflicts may identify or clarify for the actors the nature of the social contradictions on which the conflicts are based (Sumner 1979:15; Marx and Engels 1975:182). Thus, "contradiction and conflict are intimately united; conflict is the active realization of contradictions" (Parker-Pearson 1984:62).[7]

Such long-term or short-term conflicts tend to cluster around intersections of contradictions in social reproduction. These contradictions supply the "fault lines" along which conflicts are generated (Giddens 1981:232–38). The "fault lines" manifest themselves as divisive issues that provoke the conflict between groups. These are the social conflicts that produce the "conjunctive moments" that transform the "structural moments." Structural contradictions, then, generate the social conflicts that produce the crises in social systems. Such crises are manifest in the processes of destruction and construction, challenge and response, and subversion and defense of existing norms. There is an interpenetration of economic, social, and political crisis tendencies (O'Connor 1987:137).

Thus, in the long run, primary contradictions produce crises that threaten the reproduction of the social totality. Social agents attempt to solve these crises. But the solutions to such problems produce consequences that negate the original solution-producing secondary contradictions (Allen 1975:264).

To maintain ruling-class support, governments may execute policies that create new problems rather than resolve the basic systemic contradictions. The Ch'ing rulers in China maintained expensive armies and poured a great deal of state wealth into court extravagances and a royal pension system. These policies depleted the government treasury. Ch'ing efforts to increase state revenues through taxation and new fees led the gentry and the peasants to adopt defensive strategies to avoid these new tax burdens. This resistance prevented the Ch'ing from increasing state revenues in sufficient amounts to fill the depleted state treasury (Wakeman 1966; Atsushi 1984).

Thus the dynamic aspects of the social totality stem from the contradictions in which subsystems or social practices (moments) work toward opposite goals. Viewed in this way the social totality is a concrete unit of interacting contradictions (Allen 1975:254; Meszaros 1972:63–64). The conjunctive moments that operate to resolve secondary contradictions bring change in certain subsystems. Changes in these subsystems have an overdetermined impact on other social complexes. The social complexes of a social totality move from structuration, destructuration, and restructuration (Basserman 1968:102).

Primary contradictions may produce the fault lines that produce conflicts between governments and subordinate political groups. Conflict between the state and secret societies in Malaysia provides one example. By the early twentieth century the British colonial government in Malaysia came into direct conflict with the Triad secret societies. The "fault lines" produced by contradictory economic interests between the government and the Triads led to these conflicts. The Triads recruited overseas Chinese labor for the benefit of their own ethnic groups, which had control over farms, mines, gambling dens, and prostitution establishments. Secret society monopoly on labor supply deprived the European-operated companies of an adequate labor force. Warfare among Triad secret orders over the control of various enterprises discouraged Western business investment in the colony. The British found these conditions completely unsatisfactory and took measures to suppress these secret organizations by deporting their leaders and jailing many members. In reaction the secret societies decentralized their organizations, making it more difficult for the British to control them (Mak 1975b, 1981; Andaya and Andaya 1982; Jomo 1988).

A dialectical perspective assumes that as humans we utilize our power, individually or in cooperation with others, to change our environments and, in so doing, change ourselves as well. As humans we are "beings of praxis"; thus, we consciously make changes. We are both subjects and objects of history (Albert and Hahnel 1978:98).

The conjunctive moments, generated by social crises, result from the conscious efforts by social agents to resolve structural contradictions or to deal with their consequences. The problems precipitated by these contradictions demand and require human solutions. Such interventions may, through radical means, resolve the original primary contradiction by means of basic institutional change. More often, however, the changes merely perpetuate the existing primary contradiction though tempering the level of conflict it produces.

The basis for social analysis must include the human subject but not an autonomous, isolated subject. The basic systemic relations specify an array of advantages and disadvantages accruing to certain social actors, which provides them with a particular range of opportunities for shaping the production of material and organizational content in society. While any social structure will limit and restrain production of future alternatives, some structures contain openings through which social actors may develop innovative alternatives to the current limitations (Israel 1979:63; Wardell and Benson 1979:235; Albert and Hahnel 1978:54). Thus, how social agents reproduce or transform society is determined by the totality of social relations in which they stand, not by the agent's individual personal character or intentions (Collier 1989:92; Resnick and Wolff 1982:37).[8] As Marx observed, "men make their own history but they do not make it just as they please; they do not make it under circumstances chosen by themselves but under circumstances directly encountered, given or transmitted from the past" (1970b:96).

There is a dialectic between structure and practice such that the evolving moments do not always take place the way people suppose they will and over time what appears to be reproduced is transformed. Marx (1964, 1971 [1857], 1975) conceptualized this idea as a dialectical interaction between the concrete-real and the thought-concrete. Marx viewed the concrete-real as the actual, material, natural, and social totality. The products of the thinking process (thought-concrete) bring change in the concrete-real or, more specifically, in the component processes of the social totality. But these changes in the concrete-real react back on the thinking process, changing it in turn (see also Resnick and Wolff 1987:56). Thus, dialectical analysis assumes that consciousness "is determined by the transformation of being; but as the consciousness of acting men, it in turn transforms the being" (Jakubowski 1976:60).

Viewed in this way the structures involved in the production and reproduction of social systems are both the medium and outcome of social practices. As Marx and Engels suggested, "circumstances make the man just as much as man makes the circumstances" (1970:59). Knowledgeable social actors can consciously utilize and manipulate social structures to attain particular ends (Giddens 1981:25).[9] Yet such manipulations may produce unintended consequences that thwart the agents' efforts and subvert their aims. These undesirable effects may not result from a clash of agent interests or from ensuing conflicts (Boudon 1986:13–14). The consequences may be the result of "composite effects," the result of the aggregate of individual or group acts (Giddens 1984:10; Boudon 1979:59). The forces, tendencies, or moments released by human praxis may, in many instances, be incomprehensible to the social actors (Lukacs 1978:43–44). Such "composite effects" may occur more or less in the distant time-space (Giddens 1984:14). Even so, because they lead to secondary contradictions, such long-term difficulties can undermine the goals of particular practices, forcing social agents to change the circumstances of their action (Suchting 1983:169; Elster 1985:8).[10]

Political leaders may initiate policies whose long-term consequences can threaten their power base. The history of the Kpelle people in Liberia illustrates this historic dynamic. Early Kpelle chiefs encouraged immigration into their chiefdoms. By so doing the chiefs expanded their economic and military power. But in the long term the immigrants began to threaten the economic power of the chiefs' descent groups. Descendants of the immigrants tried to establish claims to land controlled by the chiefs' kin groups. The chiefs, as we will see, used their positions as leaders of the Kpelle secret societies to resist these land claims (Bledsoe 1980; Murphy 1980).

The dialectical framework outlined here assumes that between structures of a given social situation and the actions of agents or collectivities lie belief systems through which actors "interpret, identify and evaluate the significance of events, objects and interpersonal encounters in their social world" (Tilley 1981:139). Human social activities manifest a recursive quality whereby human agents monitor the ongoing flow of social life (Giddens 1984:2–3). Ulin makes a similar observation when he suggests that "the human subject [can] grasp the objective, social and historical conditions woven into human activity in the world" (1984:154). Benton (1984:212) argues that the decision-making by collectivities is also recursive. However, Roseberry rightly qualifies these conclusions when he states that "people do not simply act in terms of objective limits and positions but also in terms of apparently subjective evaluations of limits, positions and possibilities" (1984:5). Acting on these subjective evaluations social actors can also initiate "conjunctive moments." Bhaskar captures the essence of this societal model when he states "men do not create society. It pre-exists them. Rather it is an ensemble of structures, practices and conventions that individuals reproduce or transform but which would not exist unless they did so" (1979:120).

Social formations and the encompassing social systems within which they are enmeshed are human-made, but as historic entities they act back upon the social agents. Conceptualized as an entity separate from the human agents responsible for its origin and modification, a social formation "contains constraints [but also] . . . it embodies new possibilities and it introduces new problems through the relationship between the emergent entitics themselves and between these and the physical environment and between these and the human actors" (Archer 1988:107).

In my analysis I will conceptualize the social totality as a social formation whose social complexes or subsystems, which are moments of the whole, are founded on the production of material life but must interact not only with one another but with the economic base (Jakubowski 1976:40). In conceptualizing a social totality as a social formation I will differentiate among economic, political, and cultural/ideological subsystems.

A social formation refers to a complex whole made up of a mode of production or several modes of production with one dominant. Each mode of production consists of an economic base and the apparatus necessary to its reproduction. Thus, the mode of production consists of relations of exploitation-appropriation plus relations of realization, circulation, plus the forces of production (Friedman 1976). Such infrastructures are interrelated in complex ways to the dominant superstructure (government, ideology, religious systems, etc.). Superstructures react back upon and influence the economic base. While changes in the dominant mode of production ultimately bring changes in the overall social formation, the economic forces are not always absolutely primary nor are the political and ideological complexes absolutely secondary (Sayers 1980a:93; Porpora 1985:230).[11] At any point in time the interacting subsystems that make up a social formation are mutually overdetermining and overdetermined. These subsystems consist of the means and processes of production, the forms and distribution of products, and the relations of these forms to the conditions of reproduction and production, class relationships, state and other political apparatus, special cultural and ideological forms, and relationships with other social formations (Hindess and Hirst 1977:50).

Legal and ideological forms act as organic elements within the mode of production (Sumner 1979). Thus, the economic base consists of interwoven material elements and mental elements. In this way aspects of the prevailing political ideology becomes an organic part of the economic base (Poulantzas 1973:199–224; 1983:63–93). The Nationalist government in South Africa, for example, has, up to recent years, subscribed to a Christian-Nationalist ideology that proclaims the cultural and racial superiority of white Afrikaners and that their God-created mission in South Africa, as the chosen people, is to civilize the non-white races. This belief system has provided the Nationalist government with the ideological justification for its labor policies. White Afrikaners have controlled and staffed every branch of the state civil service apparatus, judiciary, police, and army. In the business sector white Afrikaners, regardless of ability, have been placed in higher-paying and more prestigious jobs than Africans (Bunting 1964; Ume 1981). Today, of course, this ideology is being radically changed by the South African government. How these reforms will increase nonwhite employment opportunities in government and the private sector is yet to be demonstrated.

The conceptualization of base (infrastructure) as separate from the superstructure is a methodological device to simplify dialectical analysis. Both constitute part of an indivisible whole of social life. These parts are constantly changing and interacting with one another. (Jakubowski 1976:56).[12]

Structural contradictions within social formations generate the conflicts at the "fault lines" that produce opposing ideologies among groups of social actors (Sumner 1979:218). Such conflicts may force social actors to adopt practical ideologies that challenge the prevailing cognitive systems based on ruling class ideology (Bloch 1977). Under these circumstances the social actors assess the "rationality" of the ruling-class ideology. If the dominant ideology requires social actors to pursue actions that prove detrimental to their well-being, social actors may begin to question its rationality (Therborn 1980:33–35; Miliband 1990). But these ideologies of resistance are not uniform ones. The structural positions of opposition groups (e.g., class and class factions, sex and racial divisions) differ, and therefore their economic and political concerns do likewise. These differing interests produce different anti-elite ideological frameworks.

For example, the negative impact of apartheid policies on South African blacks (and other non-whites) have led them to develop anti-apartheid ideologies. But even within the African population there is no uniformity of belief regarding the future system that should replace apartheid. Young black radicals want to limit white rights while the black middle class prefers a multiracial system that protects white rights (Davies, O'Meara, and Dlamini 1988).

Bloch has suggested that a characteristic of dominant ideologies is their "power to remain unchanged when other things are changing" (1985:45). This is also a characteristic of some belief systems that challenge the dominant ideology. They have a recoverability despite the dissipation or destruction of dissident groups that advocate them.

While the South African government, for example, has had success in destroying specific anti-apartheid groups, the ideological basis of the anti-apartheid movement has survived, to reappear in new organizational forms. Thus, black nationalism and multiracialism, as distinct political belief systems, have survived the demise of the specific political groups who have support these anti-apartheid ideologies (MacShane, Plant, and Ward 1984).

Superstructural forms may both affect the movement of the economic base and be, in turn, affected by economic movements (Sumner 1979). Superstructures establish the operating conditions on the basis of which the reproduction of the productive system rests. But being overdetermining as well as overdetermined superstructures can, in fact, be very disruptive with regard to reinforcing the objective conditions of the economic base. Legal and political structures may create blockages in the system of continued reproduction, thereby acting as negative forces on the existing mode of production (Meszaros 1987:62–63). The reproduction of the conditions necessary for the perpetuation of the political hierarchy may force changes in the economic base which, in turn, may lead to further changes at other structural levels, such that, the totality of the social formation relationships are changed (Gledhill and Rowland 1982; Gamble 1981). Thus, the emergent and evolving relationships among structures should be understood as dynamic effects of the relationships within the whole social totality (Zeitlin 1980; Allen 1975; Althusser 1970; Lukacs 1968).

A social formation forms only a partial, localized part of the historic setting. Analysis is not confined to boundaries of autonomous political units but is directed toward studies of the dialectical articulation between the local unit and their "encompassing context," the larger interaction system, hereafter called the social system (Gledhill and Rowland 1982; Ekholm 1981; Comaroff 1982; Giddens 1984:244; Friedman, 1976; Ekholm and Friedman 1979).[13] Thus, a social formation need not contain within itself all the necessary practices sufficient for its own reproduction. It is usually dependent on external factors whose impact is mediated by internal structures and relationships (Ellen 1982:255). Internal events have external consequences and external events are internalized (Kaufman 1988:224).

Crises in the reproduction of state economic systems may be produced by a combination of internal and external contradictions. In South Africa the apartheid system has blocked economic development by creating a poorly educated black population on whom South African whites must depend in the future to provide a skilled labor force if South Africa's industrial base is to be expanded. But this economic crisis has been magnified by the withdrawal of foreign-controlled companies whose investments generate foreign exchange necessary for the import of machinery and equipment, essential for economic development (Battersby 1987b).

An analysis of secret society dynamics, then, must rest on a dialectical model that relates the emergence and operation of the secret society to the conflicts produced by structural contradictions within the social formation. Following the identification of the structural contradictions, the analyst must show how the conflicts generated by these contradictions at the structural fault lines impinge on the experiences of the secret society members, or, at least their leaders, in a way sufficient to motivate them to employ the secret order as a political force to implement conjunctive movements, aimed at resolving the crises that they define as threatening to themselves and their constituency.

State Systems

States[14] are fragile polities subject to the dangers of fragmentation (Yoffee 1988:13, Eisenstadt, Abitbol, and Chazan 1988; Gailey 1987:28). The nature and patterns of state power are constantly changing (Schatzberg 1988). Both archaic and modern states manifest unstable configurations of dominant and subordinate groups in which dominant classes attempt to impose their power while subordinate classes attempt to neutralize and negate it (Patterson 1990:4). As Gailey observes, state institutions are "tense and contingent accommodations" (1985:77). States are born out of the crises that afflict pre-state polities and once established create new crises of their own.

States arise as pre-state elites successfully centralize power over delimited territories (Vincent 1987:19; Mann 1986:173). The specific crises that generate these centralizing tendencies vary with the historic circumstances (Bodie and Birnbaum 1983:50). But in all instances the crises result when "structural moments" regulating actions of the political leadership come into conflict with the "structural moments" regulating actions of the dominated class(es). The resulting structural contradictions produce the conflicts that threaten the economic and political position of the ruling elite (Brumfiel 1983). The "conjunctive moments," initiated by the pre-state elite to deal with the crises, if institutionalized, become the basis for state structures. The particular trajectories leading to state development depend on the options available to the pre-state leadership. Such options, though not completely determined by the nature of the pre-state social formations (or its structural moments), are, at least, circumscribed by them.

The crises in pre-state social formations are the result of both internal and external structural contradictions. In pursuing their economic and political interests, the emerging ruling class (or a ruling-class faction) comes into conflict with the "peripheral elite" (the traditional foci of pre-state power) over which they must establish control (Zegarell 1986; Yoffee 1988:12; Gailey 1987). In a like fashion, attempts by pre-state leaders to establish control over uncertain external environments by means of warfare or other political strategies place their polities in conflict with neighboring groups. To deal with these external crises the pre-state leaders will devise ways to expand their administrative power (Carneiro 1970, 1978; Webb 1975; Webster 1975).[15]

The expansion of the Liberian state illustrates these processes. Internal and external contradictions created crises that Liberian state expansion tried to solve. Founded by freed slaves, the Americo-Liberian state expanded its control over indigenous African polities to help solve severe economic problems, mainly a large foreign debt, and to counteract the threat by the British and the French to claim parts of Liberian territory. To gain control over the hinterland chiefdoms, the Liberian government subdued chiefdoms by military force and, later, co-opted chiefs through a system of indirect rule, while at the same time imposing control over secret societies that had become centers of opposition to state rule (Fulton 1968; Bowen 1973).

Thus, a state emerges when the central leadership accumulates sufficient resources to force the "peripheral elites" to submit to central control. The form of this centralization will vary with the historic circumstances (Bodie and Birnbaum 1983:34). However, in all cases it involves the development of "extensive power," the ability by the state to organize large numbers of people over fairly extensive territories in such a way that they give the government, at the very least, minimal cooperation (Mann 1986a:7). Being fragile polities, states develop special mechanisms to maintain and reproduce themselves. These mechanisms include political apparatus and legal frameworks, information processes, ritual and symbolic devices, and structures of control located in the centers of society (Eisenstadt, Arbitol, and Chazan 1988; Krader 1968:108).

At no time in its development is the state *a priori* a neutral or a completely autonomous arbitrator. States are foci of social conflict and are more or less dependent on certain classes or class factions[16] (Bodie and Birnbaum 1983:55). In South Africa, when the Afrikaner whites took power, middle-class interests dominated the government's agenda. However, the National Party's support for apartheid policies earned its support from white farmers and Afrikaner workers. However, with the growth of monopoly capital in South Africa the influence of the large corporations in government has grown. Monopoly capital considers apartheid policies to be detrimental to its economic interests. With the National Party now seeking to revoke apartheid laws, the South African state has become a locus for new conflict between big business, on one side, and pro-apartheid classes on the other, including rural whites, petty bureaucrats, and white labor (Adelman 1985).

To expand and consolidate their power the dominant class (or class faction) gains control of the production and/or procurement of basic resources (Haas 1982). To reproduce this structure of production the rulers must expand the administrative hierarchy. Through such bureaucratic organizations the political leadership communicates to local populations, mobilizes resources and labor, gathers information, and institutes surveillance in order to detect noncompliance with policies or laws (Kaufman 1988:227). By institutionalizing the legal process the state aims at establishing routine mechanisms by which conflicts can be repressed or compromised. Under these circumstances resistance to state authority is channeled through institutionalized forms of redress (Mann 1986:132).

By the time the Manchus, for example, had completed their conquest of China in 1681 and replaced the Ming dynasty, they had established a unique bureaucratic system. At first they set up feudal-type banner military structures. Under this system an imperial clan leader governed an estate worked by prisoners of war. But as the Manchu (Ch'ing dynasty) expanded control over all China they set up a bureaucratic hierarchy under centralized ministerial bodies. Beneath these ministries was a hierarchy of gentry-scholars (Michael 1965).

Rulers, such as the Manchu, had to evolve various strategies to protect themselves against potential usurpers. To achieve this end some state leaders fused the traditional but loyal ruling class with that of the conquerers, thereby cutting off the disloyal traditionalist leaders from the new, emerging government bureaucracy (Dowse and Hughes 1972:100). This was the strategy used by the Ch'ing (Manchu) monarchs. The Ming officials who had deserted to the Manchu were placed in influential state positions. These ex-Ming bureaucrats provided the core of higher- and middle-level government officialdom (Wakeman 1985, vol. 1).

State rulers recruit to government posts individuals who pose little political threat to the existing leadership. Within the Ottoman empire sultans gave important military and government posts to the slaves. The Ottoman military corps, the Janissaries, which the sultans situated in key provincial garrisons, were recruited from prisoners of war. But this corps was under the direct control of the sultan rather than lower-level officials. This arrangement gave the sultan direct control over a powerful military unit (Anderson 1974; Shaw 1976; Itzkowitz 1980).

However, ruling-class attempts to monopolize coercive power are not sufficient to maintain their dominance. They must also establish hegemony—legitimate authority.[17] To justify the surplus extraction of labor and material resources the state must legitimize such levies on the general population. One way of establishing the legitimacy of such extractions is through legal institutions by which the state guarantees internal peace and public welfare (Yoffee 1988:97).

However, ideologies as legitimizing frameworks are also used by state elites to transform the rule by coercion into government by moral authority, a less expensive mechanism than the rule by force (Fiori 1970:238; Gramsci 1971:182; Carnoy 1984:66–73; Dowse and Hughes 1972:112). Such ideologies have allowed some state leaders to justify their authority by doctrines that proclaim the natural superiority of the ruling elite over the rest of the society. In other cases, monarchs, for example, have justified their right to rule on religious or other moral grounds (De George 1985:147–48).

To successfully rule, the political leaders must "mould the personal convictions, norms and aspirations of the masses" (Vincent 1987:168). This "suprastructural" power enables the state leadership to implement political decisions throughout the polity (Mann 1986:113; Skalnik 1978:64). Within Ch'ing China, political authority was legitimized by Confucian values, the so-called three bonds (*San Kang*). These bonds called for the subordination of subject to monarch, child to parent, and wife to husband.

To spread these Confucian values throughout the governing bureaucracy the Ch'ing reestablished the traditional examination system (A.D. 1644–79) as well as special schools to train the gentry in the classical literature necessary for the successful completion of their exams. The Ch'ing also instituted a local lecture system by means of which they hoped to indoctrinate the peasantry in Confucian ethics. The state also encouraged the performance of state rituals through which the government hoped to buttress Confucian ideals (Hsiao 1960; Arkush 1990).

Candidates for state examinations went through long periods of training in schools and academies in which they were supposed to read and understand the Confucian classic literature. But in many cases such schools, being poorly run, gave the students only a superficial exposure to the Confucian classics (Hsiao 1960:250–52).

The state examination system was established in order that the Ch'ing could assure themselves that governmental officials were schooled in the classic Confucian values and political standards (Fairbank 1967:47–48). But fraud and deception were involved in many exams. Many officials passed the exams who did not understand the Confucian classics but received government posts anyway. Some scholars passed the exams but were unable to obtain government posts because there were not enough positions available relative to the number of the candidates. Such frustrated candidates turned to rebellion or other disorderly activities (Hsiao 1960:246–48). Thus, the examination system did not create a body of gentry-officials with a genuine faith in Confucian political values nor totally loyal to state concerns.

At the local community level the Ch'ing hoped that through lectures given to the peasantry by respected Confucian scholars the populace would learn the Confucian beliefs in obedience to the state and virtues of lawful conduct. However, for the most part, these lecturers considered their duties a mere formality, giving little serious consideration to the Confucian classics (Hsiao 1960:202–3).

At state-sponsored sacrificial ceremonies the Ch'ing rulers hoped that through ritual reinforcement the common people would come to appreciate the power of the state and the religious basis for its legitimacy. In most cases, however, the worshippers attended these rites in order to enhance their own prestige and influence and that of their families (Hsiao 1960:226).

The Ch'ing rulers achieved only limited success in the indoctrination of the gentry-officials and even less ideological control over the peasantry. The general observations by Arkush about peasant acceptance of state ideological orthodoxy is applicable to the situation in Ch'ing China. He observes that the "peasant acceptance of orthodox values and beliefs was limited, somewhat grudging and mixed with feelings of cynicism about Confucian moralism" (1990:331).

The Ch'ing example suggests that state ideologies can only be partially effective in unifying the state when many people suffer under state rule. Under these conditions some of the populace at least will come to see the cause of their suffering and take action to alleviate their misery (Donham 1990:3).

The inability of states to effectively indoctrinate the masses with moral dogma that reinforce state authority places limits on the government's ability to penetrate the total society and effectively implement its decisions (Mann 1986:169–70). The discrepancy between the state's hegemonic message and the populace's actual experiences results in popular resistance to government indoctrination. The state is therefore forced to find new ways to manufacture consent (Miliband 1990).

Ultimately popular support for a regime rests on its ability to produce benefits sufficient to satisfy the material needs of the population. Without such basic rewards compliance to authority is superficial at best (Godelier 1986:610). Under the conditions where centralized authority fails to provide for basic welfare of the populace discontented segments of the population may find an ideological justification for rebellion or revolt. Orthodox beliefs contain sufficient ambiguities and contradictions to allow for various interpretations that can justify political attacks on the state (Aronoff 1980:6; Toland 1987).

In Ch'ing China, for example, while prevailing Confucian values called for the subordination of subject to the monarch, increased economic hardship convinced the peasants (and other class factions) that emperors had lost their "Mandate of Heaven." According to this belief a ruler maintained the right to rule only so long as he did not engage in bad conduct. Environmental disasters and economic crises demonstrated to the people that the monarch had lost this Mandate of Heaven. Accordingly the people were then justified in overthrowing the corrupt dynasty if they could (Fairbank 1967:50–53). Under these circumstances Chinese peasants and other disaffected class segments were receptive to Buddhist beliefs that interpreted these crises as evidence that the fall of the dynasty was imminent and predicted that a new, more propitious era was at hand.

State leaders must also conceal their own deviations from proclaimed values and norms to maintain the legitimacy of their administrative power. Strategic considerations may force state leaders to violate the well-established political codes. The ease or difficulty with which leaders guard state secrets will depend on the relative openness of the communication networks within the state and the degree to which opposition elements have access to information sources within the state agencies.

State administrators may secretly subvert constitutional regulations in order to more effectively use violence against their political opponents. The South African government, for example, apparently secretly funded a military force called the Civil Cooperation Bureau, which directed a network of assassins whose goal was to kill anti-apartheid activists (Battersby 1990g).

There are also circumstances in which state agents (and others) secretly collude with criminal organizations for profit. Malaysian government efforts to control secret society activity have been undermined by police, other public officials and influential businessmen who have tried to protect the secret societies from government harassment for a price (Mak 1975b).

Once established, state power becomes an arena for contention by newly organized political forces that challenge the existing state leadership (Bodie and Birnbaum 1983:58). Efforts by the dominant class (or class faction) to exercise their political power consistent with their economic interests results in conflicts of interests. The objectives of allied classes or class factions and/or the dominated class(es) do not coincide. Neither do the interests of the state and those of other polities. To meet the crises generated by these structural contradictions state leaders initiate "conjunctive moments" that usually exacerbate the prevailing structural contradictions with the result that there is an increase of conflict at the structural fault lines.

The continued failure to effectively resolve the political and economic crises often lead to dissension within the governing class, weakening the central authority (Kaufman 1988:226). Such divisions within the ruling class make it more difficult for the state to engage in those activities necessary for the reproduction of the relations of production.

Such conflicts have emerged within the South African state and well illustrate the political consequences of such confrontations. Once in power, the Afrikaner middle class initiated policies that gained them the support from white farmers, labor, and government workers. These apartheid doctrines became the rationale for this interclass unity. But recent political and economic crises has stimulated increased Afrikan (and other nonwhite) opposition to apartheid laws and has also brought new pressure from South African monopoly capitalists for radical reforms in the government's apartheid policies. Under this pressure the Nationalist government has begun the process of abolishing the apartheid system. These reforms have produced fissures within the ruling party and the Afrikaner population itself. White laborers, rural farmers, and lower-level government officials adamantly oppose these apartheid reforms because they see their traditional privileges being destroyed (Charney 1987; Magubane 1984).

To meet these new internal and external crises the state leaders devote new resources to support and expand those institutional structures necessary for the maintenance of internal and external order (administrative, military, religious, etc.). These new state expenses require new taxes and other levies (Tainter 1988). Because these new economic demands fall largely on the dominated class(es), new tension arises between the producing class(es) and the nonproducing class(es) (Kaufman 1988; Cowgill 1988). Concurrent natural disasters may force overtaxed families into debt and eventually, for some, into various types of anti-state activity.

The expansion of political, military, and religious hierarchies may create potential new foci of opposition to state authority. Lower-level officials may find opportunities to divert resources from state control, which enables them to create localized centers of power. In so doing they become less dependent on state support and, thus, less accountable to state leadership (Skalnik 1978:611). Such bureaucratic proliferation, along with increased corruption, rigidity, incompetence, extravagance, and inefficiency makes for waste of existing resources, necessitating further tax burdens on the producing class(es) (Cowgill 1988:263). An eventual drop in productivity may force new attempts by the state to make up lost revenue with new taxation, furthering the tensions between administrators and producers.

As we have seen, such structural contradictions created crises within China during the Ch'ing rule. As a result there was increased discontent. The prevalence of banditry, military revolts, and heterodox religious sects reveals the widespread nature of this dissatisfaction. These frequent threats to local order forced the Ch'ing rulers to rely more and more on the local gentry to organize and finance militia to maintain public order. But to acquire the resources to support such military operations the gentry imposed new taxes on the peasants and others. These tax levies went beyond rates that custom dictated as fair. Thus, these increased tax burdens created new centers of resistance to the government, making it more difficult for the Ch'ing rulers to finance their efforts to suppress rebels and secret societies.

The centralized state authority may try to weaken the opposition forces by co-opting some groups to their cause. They may give certain dominated class factions more political power as well as material privileges (Zagarell 1986). The South African government has used this strategy against the anti-apartheid forces. It has tried to divide the opposition by changing apartheid laws to the advantage of middle-class black Africans, Asians, and

Coloureds (people of mixed ancestry) and by creating a group of Bantustan chiefs dependent on the government for their power on the rural reserves (Thompson 1990).

SECRET SOCIETIES AND STATE POWER

Historic circumstances determine conditions under which secret societies play a significant role in the dynamics of state development. Whether they serve the interests of the state managers by protecting ruling-class concerns or serving as foci of opposition to state rule, secret societies employ the same power strategies as the state to neutralize opposition, guard against repression or destruction, and to maintain internal discipline. State power strategies are merely centralized versions of power found in secret society organizations or other social structures (Mann 1986:172). To understand the nature of secret society power strategies we must study the dialectical relationships between states and secret societies and how these dialectical interactions affect the emerging power structures of both the state and the secret society itself.

Secret society politics are merely surface manifestations of deep-seated conflicts growing out of structural contradictions. Secret societies appear at the "structural fault lines." The conflicts in which secret societies become involved reflect these basic contradictions within the state systems. The success or failure of the secret societies in pursuing their objectives in these conflicts is a consequence of their ability or lack of ability in actualizing the potential power available to them as secret organizations.

Debate over the concept of power has polarized into specific conceptual oppositions. It has been either conceived as a property produced by the actions of individuals or as a feature of collectivities. It has been regarded as an intentional, operationalized capacity of individuals to attain certain ends or a structural feature of social systems. Power may be viewed as a negative, repressive force or as a positive, productive feature of all social relationships (contrast Weber 1968:926 with Foucault 1977, 1980). Power may be either illegitimate or legitimate, with people obeying orders of power agents[18] either out of fear or respect. One line of analysis has been to develop elaborate typologies of various types of power (Lasswell and Kaplan 1950; Wrong 1979).

Following Isaac, I conceptualize social power as "those capacities to act possessed by social agents in virtue of the enduring relations in which they participate" (1987:80). However, I am more concerned in my secret society studies with those social relationships in which there is an asymmetrical distribution of social power—that is, power that enables individuals or collective agents to get other agents (individual or collective) to do (or to not do) something they would otherwise not do (or do). It is through these direct or indirect means of controlling the behavior of others that agents alter the conditions and outcome of their life (Miller and Tilley 1984; Bacharach and Baratz 1963; Lukes 1974, 1979; Wong 1979).[19]

The very asymmetry of such power relations makes conflict coincident with, a condition of, and an outcome of power. The study of power structures involves an investigation of the dynamic interaction of dominance and resistance (Rus 1980; Turk 1982; Miller and Tilley 1984). As Rus has pointed out, power "is more or less a durable dialectical process in which induction and resistance are only two poles of an otherwise uniform contradictory process" (1980:6). Power agents not only respond to the actual imposition of power or its resistance but also to the *anticipation* of induction and resistance (Turk 1982). And in the dialectical interplay between induction and resistance the power relations between power agents are changed (Rus 1980; Giddens 1982).[20]

Thus power relationships do not consist of stable relations of autonomy and dependence. They allow for a variety of means for "leverage, maneuvering, and strategic bargaining between agents" (Isaac 1987:91). For as Nyberg suggests, the "relative dimensions of power and powerlessness are continually being rearranged and readjusted" (1981:60). The stability of power relations, then, is problematic, a circumstance to be explained not assumed. Power is a contingent social relation. Its exercise is determined "both by the structural distribution of power and by the subjective understandings, preferences and wills of concrete social agents" (Isaac 1987:97).

Such a dialectical power process is illustrated by the dynamic interaction between the Triad secret societies and the British colonial state in Malaysia. Initially the British colonial government tolerated the Triads because these secret orders organized the procurement and control of Chinese laborers necessary for the reproduction of the colonial infrastructure. However, once open conflict between the secret societies threatened foreign investments and the secret society monopoly over labor supply threatened European businesses, the British moved to suppress the Triad secret organizations. When Japanese rule replaced British rule in Malaysia during World War II, secret societies were subject to even harsher regulations. After the British returned to Malaysia with the defeat of Japan, they relaxed enforcement of anti–secret society ordinances in order to give the anti-communist Triad groups a free hand in action against the communist rebels in Malaysia who were fighting against British rule. But with the defeat of the communists the British and the post-colonial governments reinstated the tough measures against Triad groups. However, one unanticipated consequence of this repression was a proliferation of small, criminal secret societies that were hard to control. Thus, in the case of Malaysia, the ebb and flow of Triad-state relations has been determined by the extent to which the Triads have helped or hindered the government in reproducting the relations of production and the political structures on which they are based (Comber 1957; Douglas and Pedersen 1973).

Power, then, is a dialectical moment in interaction between power agents. It therefore draws upon and creates resources (Foucault 1980). These resources may be material (e.g., technology or raw materials) or nonmaterial (e.g., knowledge or skills). They are produced through the material and symbolic praxis of power agents (Miller and Tilley 1984). Resources constitute the structural constraints on power whether it is exercised as induction or resistance (Jessop 1982; Giddens 1981; Hindess 1982; Cartwright 1965).

Ch'ing China again provides us with an example showing how resource limitations prevented the Ch'ing from effectively eliminating the dangers of secret society–led rebellions while a similar lack of power assets prevented the White Lotus secret society–led rebellions from successfully challenging the central authority in Peking. The ability of the Ch'ing rulers to prevent repeated secret society–led uprisings was made difficult because their armies were dispersed in garrisons that lacked the mobility that would enable them to unite against large but localized rebellions. The gentry-led militias were also weak and ineffective. The government found it costly to regroup its military forces in order to fight large, regional rebellions organized by the secret societies. The costs of such military operations drained the government treasuries. With depleted government funds the Ch'ing rulers were forced to impose new taxes on the population, thereby re-creating the conditions that produced the earlier insurrections (Kuhn 1970; Wakeman 1966; Feuerwerker 1975).

However, efforts by secret societies, such as the White Lotus, to lead successful revolts against the Ch'ing rulers also failed. The White Lotus leaders lacked sufficient organizational resources to carry out a successful insurrection by defeating the government armies. The people who joined the White Lotus–led rebellions in the last stages of the revolt usually did not have as strong an ideological commitment to the movement as did the small core of loyal members. Motivated to join the rebellion solely out of personal self-interest they were more likely to desert the rebel army if it suffered defeats or setbacks. For this reason the rebel armies lost their potential power to defeat the government forces.

Power resources involve more than the capacity of agents to secure compliance through punishments, threats of punishments, rewards, or the promises of rewards. Power involves more indirect forms of control. The capacity to suppress public awareness of certain issues or to conceal activities is also a power resource (Bachrach and Baratz 1963, 1970). Power agents may conceal decisions or the information on which their public decisions were based, or simply refrain from taking actions contrary to their interests but in the vital interest of other social actors.[21] Bachrach and Baratz describe this source of power in the following way:

> power is exercised when A devotes his energies to creating or rein-
> forcing social and political values and institutional practices that limit
> the scope of the political process to public consideration of only
> those issues which are comparatively innocuous to A. To the extent
> A succeeds B is prevented from bringing to the fore any issues
> that might in their resolution be seriously detrimental to A's set of
> preferences. (1970:7)

I have already given specific examples showing how government leaders act in secret, often illegally, to carry out policies that the general public would usually oppose if they were aware of them. But secret societies also control the dissemination of information to protect their organizations by concealing potentially damaging information from newly inducted members until the loyalty of these new recruits has been tested. The Ottoman Bektashi sect used dissimulation to coverup their unorthodox beliefs by publicly claiming to adhere to the Sunni orthodoxy of the Ottoman leadership. Only the most trusted members of their monastic order learned the true nature of their Sufist religion. Before a novitiate learned the true doctrines of the order his loyalty was tested in many ways (Garnett 1912; Birge 1937).

To protect themselves from their enemies both the state and secret societies adopt espionage strategies through which they obtain information from persons or groups who might otherwise deny them useful intelligence information. The Afrikaner secret society, the Broederbond, has functioned as a secret force supporting the Nationalist government of South Africa. The Broederbond has been able to infiltrate its members into a variety of political, religious, social, educational, professional, and commercial organizations. Through its secret influence within these groups it is able to spread its racial and nationalistic doctrines. To make sure that their members faithfully carry out this mission the Bond leaders have established watchdog committees through which they check on the activities of Bond members in these various groups. In this way the Broederbond makes sure its beliefs are being accurately propagated by the membership (Wilkins and Strydon 1979; O'Meara 1947).

However, effective secrecy strategies do not eliminate dissatisfaction with state rule. Resistance may occur when social actors are punished by the unfavorable consequences of such concealed decisions or non-decisions. This is especially true when such concealed decisions help perpetuate a system of inequality. Under these conditions some people "will question whatever legitimizations are offered, some will be moved to resentment and some will resist" (Turk 1982:254). Counter-power movements, though not directed at specific decision-makers, may undermine the leaders ability to control the situation, thus modifying the power relation. The Broederbond's secret influence over the South African government's racial policies has not prevented the emergence of strong anti-apartheid movements among the nonwhite populations and even segments of the white minority.

By shaping and determining the values, wants, and needs of power subjects, power agents exert another power resource (Lukes 1979; Parenti 1978). By successful indoctrination of this sort power agents assure themselves that subordinates aspire to the same goals, thereby being more compliant to the power agents' commands. In doing so, the power agents are able to "define the agenda of issues . . . [and] thus win the battle without having to fight" (Parenti 1978:41).

This analysis assumes that state populations are exposed to no alternative values or definitions of need other than those of the power agents. But of course this is not true. Within a society social actors find alternative reference groups advocating points of view contrary to the dominant leadership group. Effective repression of such groups by power wielders is not always possible, thus leading to sources of resistance to prevailing values and beliefs of the leadership.

As I have already indicated, it has been largely through the activities of the Broederbond that the South African Nationalist government has attempted to disseminate its Christian-Nationalist ideology in order to unify the Afrikaner population. Up to recent times, at least, this portrayal of the Afrikaners as the chosen people with a social mission to civilize black Africa has enabled Afrikaner leaders to cement the various Afrikaner classes and class factions behind a common mission and objective regardless of the fact that different class interests exist (Bloomberg 1989).

Challenges to these racist doctrines have provided alternative belief systems for some whites as well as blacks. New political groups have emerged which are working for the development of a multiracial society and a democratic political structure. Such groups as the African National Congress and the United Democratic Front have provided not only the black African and nonwhite populations but South African whites as well with sources of anti-apartheid ideology that have legitimized political movements which undermine the government's power.

Thus, essential to the maintenance or extension of both state and secret society power is the ability of governments and secret societies to successfully employ information-control strategies: espionage, secrecy, persuasion, and evaluation. Strategies for obtaining information from persons or groups who would deny outsiders access to their secrets is espionage. Secrecy is the reverse of this strategy, procedures for the denial of such access. Persuasion results in the transfer of believable information and evaluation concerns the testing and appraisal of transmitted information (Wilsnack 1980; Scheibe 1979).

It is through such information control strategies that secret society leaders develop and maintain a focus of intensive power (Mann 1986a:7). Unlike many governments, secret society leaders have the ability to organize tight systems and command a high level of mobilization and commitment from members.

The effectiveness of secret society information control processes will, for the most part, determine the nature of power relations within secret societies and between them and hostile social agents or groups within the state. To understand the nature of these power relations we must identify the structural contradictions that give rise to the conflicts at the "fault lines" in which the secret societies become involved. To do so it is necessary to trace the evolution of the social formation, identifying the primary structural contradictions and the relation of these contradictions to the crises that have generated the conflicts. It is important that we study these evolving conflicts and the role that the secret society plays in the interaction that takes place. A key point in the analysis must be to determine the extent to which the information-control process enables secret societies to transform their relations with other collectivities and/or social agents in such a manner as to bring about a "conjunctive moment" by superseding the existing relations, thereby resolving the basic contradictions, or, more likely, merely intensifying the existing relations.

The case studies of secret societies to be compared in this book were chosen to illustrate the different systematic contradictions that give rise to secret society activity. Each secret society represents the product of different patterns of dialectical interaction, some perpetuating "structural moments" and others being responsible for "conjunctive moments."

2

The Poro and Sande Secret Societies among the Kpelle of Liberia

The study of the Poro and Sande provide a case study of secret societies whose power has been shaped by the nature of their dialectical relations with the political leadership of, first, Kpelle chiefdoms and, second, the Americo-Liberian state. The nature of these power relations has been, in part, determined by the role the secret societies have played in dealing with the crises produced by the contradictions in the social system within which the Kpelle chiefdoms and, later, the Americo-Liberian state were enmeshed. Such crises were the result of reciprocal internal and external contradictions. The responses of the political leadership to the conflicts that these contradictions produced had an overdeterminant impact on the other societal subsystems (or structural moments), which, in turn, affected secret society interests. The enlargement and contraction of secret society power has been determined by the historical dynamics at the structural fault lines created by the structural contradictions.

To understand the changing role that the Poro and Sande secret societies have played in Kpelle society, it is necessary to understand how the Kpelle chiefdoms have evolved and how their political structure has been modified by their incorporation within the Americo-Liberian state. The Poro and the Sande provided the Kpelle with a political and religious structure by means of which the dominant Kpelle lineages within each chiefdom could maintain their power as each chiefdom grew in size to meet the military threat of its

26

rivals. But once the Kpelle became incorporated within the America-Liberian state, the co-opted chiefs (paramount and clan chiefs), whose primary responsibility was to represent the interests of the central government, relied on the Poro and Sande to help them maintain an influence at the local level. The Liberian government considered that the maintenance of the Poro, or, at least, a Poro organization subject to some governmental restrictions, was in its interests. Yet the Poro and the Sande, in contradiction to the interests of the Liberian state, have functioned to reinforce the ethnic identity of the Kpelle by the ritual enculturation of tribal boys and girls. Such Poro and Sande initiations have stressed traditional values. However, more and more the Kpelle have been subject to the influences of Christianity and Western education. They have been drawn away from their towns and villages by jobs in urban areas and on cash-crop plantations. Gradually the intensity of Poro and Sande influence on the Kpelle youth has been undercut by these forces as well as by the government restrictions on the length of initiation ceremonies. To understand the changing role of the Poro and Sande in Kpelle society a brief overview of Kpelle history and a description of the changes brought to the Kpelle by the growth of the Liberian state are necessary.

OVERVIEW OF KPELLE HISTORY

The Kpelle are the largest tribal group in Liberia with a membership of around 200,000 (20 percent of the total population). They reside in the central interior of the country, largely in Bong County (Fulton 1968:8). The Kpelle are descendants of the Mande-speaking migrants who moved into the area in the fifteenth and sixteenth centuries from the north and northwest. The Kpelle reached their present location shortly before 1600. From there they dispersed westward to the St. Paul River and by the nineteenth century were moving westward across the river and southwest along the river (Stakeman 1986:5).

Employing an ironworking technology, the Kpelle were able to carve out farms in the forest by means of shifting cultivation methods.[1] Rice was the major crop grown and remains so today.[2] However, the Kpelle have supplemented rice with leafy vegetables, cassava, okra, plantains, sweet potatoes, and oil palms. Today Kpelle cash crops include peanuts, sugarcane, rubber, and coffee (Fulton 1969; Gibbs, Jr. 1965; Stakeman 1986).[3] Freshwater fishing along the St. Paul and its tributaries provide the Kpelle with protein sources.

In their earlier history the Kpelle were divided into village groupings or chiefdoms. By the end of the nineteenth century the Kpelle had formed thirty to fifty of these chiefdoms in central Liberia (Stakeman 1986:22). Each chiefdom usually consisted of a central village, surrounded by satellite hamlets, in which the dominant group was the landowning patrilineage made up of the descendants of the founder of the community. Sublineages were ranked according to their distance from the family ancestor (Fulton 1969:46).

The size of each chiefdom varied over time. Most traditional chiefdoms had fewer than 5,000 people. Usually the maximum unit corresponded roughly to the clan unit (Kaplan 1985:112). Discontented members sought new land in the forests or allied with more powerful chiefdoms (Liebenow 1987:421; Fulton 1972:1220). The heads of the founding (or core) lineages tried to attract followers. The more important "latecomers" were those that could bring prestige and military support to the founding lineage (Stakeman 1986:71–75). But immigrants that could offer only labor became "clients" or even slaves, entirely dependent on the protection and patronage of the founding lineage (Murphy and Bledsoe 1987:126). The powerful latecomers helped the landowning lineages to secure their territory by building settlements within it. These important immigrant leaders were allowed to establish a separate quarter in the paramount chief's town or to build a new village. While consulted by the head of the founding lineage, the latecomer chief was required to pay tribute in goods and services. The marriage of a latecomer leader with a woman of the founding lineage established affinal relationships that reinforced the political ones between the two groups (Murphy and Bledsoe 1987:128).[4]

These assimilation policies of the dominant lineage leadership were to have "composite effects," not immediately recognized by the chiefs, which threatened the economic and political power of the founding lineages when the immigrant kin groups made property claims against them. This primary contradiction in the relationship between the founding lineages and the immigrant populations resulted in "structural fault lines" along which conflicts between some immigrant kin groups and the dominant lineages appeared.

KPELLE POLITICAL STRUCTURE

As founder of the new territory the *Loi-Kalon* (or *Loi-Namu*) was considered its landowner and it was this head of the founder family or lineage who allocated the farmland, accepted or rejected new immigrants, banished wrongdoers and rivals, and generally oversaw the chiefdom's secular and ritual administration (Murphy and Bledsoe 1987:126). Thus, the *Loi-Kalon* was a steward of the lineage land and the keeper of the village medicine. The

Loi-Kalon's powers were held in check by the lineage elders, Poro leaders, and strong war chiefs.

The war chief (*Ko-Kalon*) was responsible for the military affairs of the chiefdom, including the supervision of the mercenary forces, if present, and the division of war spoils. The *Ko-Kalon* formulated the overall military strategy while his generals (*Ko-Kuluba*) conducted the actual raids.

Opposition by the *Loi-Kalon* to a raid could prevent it from taking place, since the chief provided food and other resources for the military effort. However, by offering such resources to a war chief, the *Loi-Kalon* or any other wealthy man could gain a share of the war spoils (Fulton 1968:11). On the other hand, war provided opportunities for some war chiefs to acquire enough wealth and power to challenge the authority of the *Loi-Kalon*. Under these circumstances the *Loi-Kalon* might become a figurehead with the real power in the hands of the *Ko-Kalon*. But normally a balance of authority was struck between these two chiefs (Fulton 1968, 1969, 1972).

As a paramount chiefdom grew it developed into a hierarchical polity with a paramount or district chief (*Loi-Kalon*), a village chief (*Taa-Kalon*), and quarter chief (*Koli-Kalon*). The incumbents of the positions of "owner" and "administrative" chief were often the same person (that is, chiefdom or district landowner was *Loi-Namu*; village-owner, *Taa-Namu*; and quarter-owner, *Koli-Namu*). However, a "landowner" might appoint a relative to be "chief." The chief, rather than the landowner, would engage in the actual administration of the polity (Murphy and Bledsoe 1987:126–27).

OVERVIEW OF LIBERIAN HISTORY

The state of Liberia grew out of a colony established in the 1820s by the American Colonization Society, which resettled freed slaves in the coastal areas.[5] About 18,000 New World blacks settled in Liberia between 1822–1905. These groups required land to establish settlements and trading posts (Akpan 1985). These first settlers either looked on farming as degrading or found farming in the Liberian environment too difficult. Therefore, many turned to trade for a livelihood. They bartered such items as tobacco, gunpowder, firearms, salt, cotton cloth, and iron pots for African palm oil, rice, camwood, ivory, hides, and gold (Stakeman 1986:80; Wilson 1980). For the most part the early immigrants depended on purchases from indigenous African growers for their food supply (Rinehart 1985:17). Later Americo-Liberians became absentee landlords, growing cash crops such as sugarcane, rice, and coffee on plantations worked by poor immigrants or African recaptives from slave ships (the so-called *Congoes*).[6] But these cash crops for most settlers were merely sidelines. The blacks' primary interest was in trade and administrative occupations (Rinehart 1985:17). As the populations of America-Liberians expanded, many also gravitated into ministry, teaching, and politics in addition to commerce (Liebenow 1987:22).

By 1838 a commonwealth had been established, and in 1847 the Republic of Liberia was formed under a new constitution (Bowen 1973; Wilson 1980). The new constitution set up a House of Representatives and a Senate. The head of state became the president. Suffrage was given to all the male citizens over twenty-one years of age, but within this group of potential voters stiff property requirements restricted the number of eligible voters (Rinehart 1985:19). In reality, power was concentrated in the presidency. Approval of the president's program by the bicameral legislature became pro forma (Tartter 1985:197).

The 1847 constitution did not recognize native tribal peoples as citizens. African chiefdoms were represented in the Liberian legislature by "delegates" who could not vote and only spoke on issues through interpreters. Such restrictions on the political rights of Africans were defensive strategies employed by the America-Liberians to maintain their power. These settlers were afraid that any substantial extension of the franchise to the African people, who greatly outnumbered them, would enable the Africans to take over the government (Akpan 1985:9). It was only in 1904 that tribal populations were given citizenship (Liebenow 1987:47).

The True Whig Party (TWP) came into power in 1877. From this point on one-party rule became the norm in Liberia. Because the TWP represented the interests of the wealthy and powerful America-Liberians until the 1980 military coup, the leading America-Liberian families monopolized the executive, legislative, judicial, and ambassadorial posts (Liebenow 1987:67).[7] The representatives of the hinterland populations acquired only lower-level positions in the government.

Corruption became a characteristic feature of the TWP government. To obtain ordinary services Liberians had to give officials bribes or gratuities. There was a diversion of funds from development projects, the padding of payrolls with nonexistent employees, and the sale of government-owned supplies (Tartter 1985:207). These conditions created the widespread dissatisfaction which led to the 1980 coup.

A military coup by seventeen noncommissioned officers and eight other enlisted men under the leadership of Master Sergeant Samuel Doe toppled the First Republic on 12 April 1980. The conspirators killed President Tolbert and twenty-seven members of his security guard. They suspended the constitution, banned political parties, released political prisoners and, later, executed fifteen of the defeated government ministers. To govern, the coup leaders formed the Peoples Redemption Council, which was assisted by a cabinet composed of members of the opposition parties and a few of President Tolbert's remaining administrators (Rinehart 1985:68).

After a new constitution was approved by popular vote, presidential and legislative elections were held in October 1985. The vote count indicated that the presidential victor was the head of the Liberian Action Party. Samuel Doe then appointed fifty people from his own party and ethnic group (the Krahn tribe) to recount the votes. This group certified that Samuel Doe and his National Democratic Party of Liberia (NDPL) was the winner.

Following the 1985 election there was great political instability in Liberia with political repression, restrictions on press freedom, strikes, and several coup attempts (Harsch 1989; James 1986a; Smith 1987; Tartter 1985). These political troubles came at a time when Liberia faced an economic crisis with a declining per capita income, a falling gross domestic product (GDP), widespread business closures, and high levels of unemployment (Harsch 1989). By mid-1989 the Doe government was 7.1 million dollars in arrears on the repayment of a United States loan (Huband 1990).

On Christmas day, 1989, a small group of insurgents, the National Patriotic Front of Liberia (NPFL), under the leadership of Charles Taylor, crossed the Ivorian border and established a military base in Nimba country, Liberia. Doe's Krahn-dominated army attacked these rebel forces but failed to dislodge them, yet killed many civilian members of the Gio and Mano tribes living in the area, who were the Krahn's traditional enemies. This brutal action by Doe's military force led to more support for the insurgents. Later a co-leader of the rebel force, Prince Johnson, split with Taylor and formed his own army. Both rebel armies soon trapped Doe and his remaining Krahn fighters in the presidential palace at the capital in Monrovia, but the Johnson and Taylor armies fought each other as well.

Because the continued conflict between these armies was leading to anarchy, extreme loss of life (5,000 killed), large population displacements (over one million in Liberia alone), and danger to the nationals of other African countries, a joint military force from Nigeria, Mali, Guinea, Sierra Leone, and Ghana was organized by the sixteen-nation Economic Community of West African States (ECOWAS) to bring an end to the fighting in Liberia. ECOWAS hoped that the multinational force could restore normalcy and evacuate foreign nationals from the battle zones.

In early September 1990, Prince Johnson's army killed Doe as he and a portion of his fighters were on their way to visit the ECOWAS army headquarters in Monrovia.

At this writing, the ECOWAS army has put in place a provisional president, but there is no representative government (Huband 1990; Lardner, Jr., 1990; Wells 1990; Press 1990). Charles Taylor's National Patriotic Front of Liberia now controls 90 percent of the country's territory. Efforts by ECOWAS to get the warring parties to agree upon procedures to form a provisional government have so far failed (Best 1991).

LIBERIAN EXPANSION INTO THE HINTERLAND

There were various phases during which the Liberian government extended control over the Liberian ethnic groups. From 1822–75 Liberia expanded its foothold along the coast and established protectorate relations with the nearby chiefdoms (e.g., Vai, Kru, Grebo). Then from 1875 to 1904, because the government faced bankruptcy, Liberia minimized its intervention in the affairs of the native peoples. But between 1904 and 1925 the Americo-Liberian leadership instituted a system of "indirect rule," eventually subjugating the remaining independent native polities. During the next phase, between 1925–74, the government tried to stimulate economic development by encouraging foreign expatriate companies to invest in agriculture, mining, and manufacturing. These economic changes had an impact on African peoples by providing them with new job opportunities outside their tribal areas. Between 1974–80 the government expanded educational opportunities for Africans. Among the African groups this was also a period of increased political activity, including strikes and political agitation (Abasiattai 1987).

By 1900 the Liberian government had become increasingly dependent on foreign credit, obtaining loans from American and European banks and financiers in 1871, 1906, 1912, 1926. In 1922 the Liberian government went into international receivership and into all-American receivership in 1926 (Abasiattai 1987:57–58). These serious economic problems forced the Liberian government to seek new sources of revenue through taxation of the hinterland tribes. There were also the French and English[8] threats on Liberian territory. The French and English, who controlled colonies adjacent to Liberia, coveted Liberian land. By the end of the nineteenth century, France and Britain occupied almost three-fourths of the land that Liberia claimed in 1866 (Stakeman 1986:91; Rinehart 1985:33–34). At the beginning of the twentieth century the Liberian government was forced, through an agreement with Britain and France, to delineate its boundaries and to prove that it could effectively control these areas (Fulton 1968:114; Bowen 1973; Wilson 1980).

These external contradictions, then, forced the Liberian state to initiate "conjunctive moments" (extension of state control into the hinterland), which produced new secondary contradictions that were manifested as conflicts between the chiefdoms and the government forces at newly formed "fault lines." Initial attempts by the government to extend control into the hinterland regions met with frequent resistance by the African chiefdoms (Fulton 1968:104).[9] Such rebellion is not surprising considering the fact that once the central government took control in tribal areas the Africans lost title to their land,[10] lost their political sovereignty, and found that the central government began to intervene in the affairs of their chiefdoms.

To help pacify the area the government moved in the newly organized Liberian Frontier Force (LFF), but because of limited government funds the LFF was often not paid. As a result the LFF stole food and other resources from the villages and towns (Stakeman 1986:95). Corrupt government administrators used the LFF to raid and pillage villages and to round up men for forced labor on road building, government farms, and for porterage (Rinehart 1985:38).

These conditions led to tribal revolts, some of which were probably led by the secret societies. By 1912 the Northern Kpelle chiefdoms had begun to organize resistance. But the Southern Kpelle groups, who now were trading with the Americo-Liberian settlements along the St. Paul River and providing labor for them as well, were reluctant to fight the government forces (Stakeman 1986:96).

To secure a more firm control in the hinterland areas, the government set up a system of indirect rule between 1907 and 1920. Provincial and district commissioners were appointed by the government. The district commissioners investigated various legal cases including murders; they also collected taxes, ensured a supply of contract labor, and kept out foreigners (Fulton 1968; Jones 1973; Bowen 1973; Rinehart 1985:36).

Under indirect rule the hinterland was divided into sixteen tribal clusters each of which was placed under the supervision of a paramount chief. Through this system of indirect rule the Liberian government co-opted the chiefs into government service (Rinehart 1985:36–38).

The government dismissed many chiefs selected by traditional procedures and only approved those candidates that came from families friendly to the government (Jones 1973). The government supported paramount and clan chiefs who were former *Loi-Kalons*, *Ko-Kalons*, or members of wealthy families. The paramount chief answered to the district commissioner. Each paramount chief had several district (or clan) chiefs under his authority. Within each district important towns had town chiefs as heads, and in the large towns the quarter chiefs continued to administer the localized family clusters. The quarter chiefs reassigned available land, organized community projects, and settled disputes within each quarter while the town chief settled disputes between contesting kin groups within the town. By grouping various clans, which were essentially territorial units rather than kin groups, into paramount chieftaincies, the Liberian government undermined the power of the clan chiefs (Liebenow 1987:40–41; Stakeman 1986:119).

The chiefs that were co-opted by the government were freed from some of the traditional checks on their power. The chiefs could claim a percentage of all taxes collected, fees from recruiting labor, and a portion of the court fees (Fulton 1969).

The government decrees in 1921 required that the Africans pay a hut tax, provide labor on government projects, become porters for government officials and provision district commissioners. The paramount chiefs had considerable power in determining who and who did not provide these services. The chief could pass over a favored village when the government imposed labor quotas and force a village in which his political opponents lived to supply labor (Stakeman 1986:113).

Many chiefs collected more hut tax than the government levied or collected it more often than required; and chiefs allied to the Americo-Liberians acquired large estates (up to 20,000 acres) for as little as fifty cents an acre (Liebenow 1987:155; Stakeman 1986:116). Labor demands by the chiefs for farm labor along with those by the District Commissioner and the Americo-Liberians disrupted Kpelle subsistence farming because men were often absent from their own farms (Liebenow 1987:57).

Later, government slavery policies prevented the wealthy Kpelle landowners from obtaining farm labor through traditional devices. Government legislation abolished tribal slavery and pawning in the 1930s. Domestic slavery, pawning, and forced labor had been a means by which the prominent Kpelle families, and even government officials, had obtained labor for their farms (d'Azevedo 1969; Lowenkopf 1976).[11] However, the chiefs continued to use their power to impose labor quotas as a device to obtain farm labor for their own needs.

Once the Americo-Liberian government had established firm control over the hinterland groups, it could initiate projects aimed at economic development. The Open Door Policy of President William Tubman was designed to encourage foreign investment to develop the mineral resources of Liberia and diversify agricultural production (Liebenow 1987:59). As a result of this policy, foreign companies provided the economic entrepreneurship in agriculture, mining, and industry. Export of rubber, logs, coffee, cacao, palm oil, coconuts, and iron-ore increased rapidly (Whitaker 1985:143). Americans, Germans, Scandinavians, Swiss, and other non-Liberians owned and operated the mining and other concessions. By the early 1960s there were twenty-five major foreign firms operating in Liberia (Rinehart 1985:52).

While lower-status America-Liberians and Africans provided the un-skilled and semi-skilled labor for these organizations, the America-Liberian elite profited by buying shares in the companies, serving on their boards of directors or as corporation lawyers. Educated America-Liberians lacked the technical training necessary for the performance of skilled jobs. Thus, ex-patriate personnel occupied most of the managerial and technical positions in the foreign companies (Rinehart 1985:52).

In a very short time the African populations were integrated within the evolving modern economy. In 1970 only one-fourth of the tribal popula-tions were involved in some phase of the modern Liberian economy but by 1980, one-third to one-half were so involved (Liebenow 1987:80–81, 157).

The government concession that had an early economic impact on the Kpelle was that given the Firestone Company. The 1926 agreement granted Firestone a ninety-nine-year lease on one million acres of land. Firestone paid an annual rent of six cents per acre and a 1 percent tax on gross income (Rinehart 1985:42). In addition Firestone arranged a loan for the govern-ment that was used to finance road and communication projects. The Fire-stone plantation, located as it was near the edge of Kpelleland, provided the Kpelle with a great demand for unskilled labor (Fulton 1969). Eventually Firestone employed 20,000 Liberians (Rinehart 1985:42).

The spread of governmental control over the hinterland and development of modern industry increased the need for Western-educated tribesmen to fill political and economic positions that the small number of America-Liberian elite did not have the manpower to fill. Until the administration of President William Tubman formal education at mission-run schools and the University of Liberia remained the monopoly of the America-Liberian elite. Today in Kpelle districts the Lutherans, Methodists, and Episcopalians are training a second generation of modernized Kpelle youth. While the America-Liberian youth gain most of the foreign fellowships, this elite monopoly works to the advantage of the tribal youth for more of them are now being admitted to the University of Liberia (since 1950) and mission-run schools (Liebenow 1969). However, until the Doe government took power there was still evidence of discrimination against tribal members in favor of America-Liberians in the process of gaining scholarships (Lowenkopf 1976).

DEVELOPMENT OF THE SECRET SOCIETIES

The development and extension of Poro power and, to a lesser extent, Sande power was directly related to the adaptive challenges facing Kpelle chief-doms as a result of warfare, tribal migrations, slave trade, and, later, by the foundation and expansion of Liberian state power. The movements of European populations into the area in the seventeenth and eighteenth century provoked more or less continuous warfare which, in turn, led to the formation of numerous competing confederations. Later these confederacies fought for control of the slave trade routes between the coast and the interior (d'Azevedo 1962a, 1969). Competition over the control of the slave routes gave way to struggles to maintain a monopoly on trade with the Americo-Liberian settlers when the slave trade began to dwindle in the nineteenth century (Lowenkopf 1976). By 1822, Gola expansion had cut off the inland and coastal peoples, largely Vai and Dei, from direct trade with the Atlantic coast or with Sudan. These obstructions to trade were the major cause of the intertribal wars in the Liberian hinterland during the nineteenth century (Akpan 1985:7). The resulting warfare led to further political disruption in the hinterland.

These conditions constituted the "encompassing context" in which the Kpelle chiefdoms operated and which posed the challenges that chiefdoms faced in trying to replicate themselves. Thus, these reciprocal internal and external contradictions had both external and internal repercussions. The new "conjunctive moments" that the chiefdoms evolved to meet these crises had, in the long run, "composite effects" that had the potential of undermining the political and economic dominance of the founding lineages and, thereby, the chiefs' power.

This early warfare created a political environment in which the amount of land controlled by a lineage did not alone determine its power. Its power also came to depend on the ability of lineage leaders to maintain a military force sufficient to protect its economic and political interests. The Kpelle chiefs established a military force to protect the chiefdoms' political autonomy as well as its trading interests. By attracting more followers the chiefs could also increase production by taking over more land through military means (d'Azevedo 1962a,b; 1969). Yet by this very process of increasing their political power and wealth, the dominant lineages of expanding chiefdoms often saw their control over lineage land weakened by the fictional claims advanced by the descendants of the immigrants. Older lineages were in danger of becoming completely absorbed by these newly arrived populations (Bledsoe 1980:69; d'Azevedo 1962a,b).

The abolishment of the slave trade, imposition of the control by the Americo-Liberian state, legislation against tribal slavery, policies of indirect rule, and the development of the rubber plantation, as well as the expansion of modern educational opportunities, have created new contradictions within Kpelle society. The principle Kpelle secret societies, the Poro and Sande, have played a major role in dealing with the power conflicts that these series of contradictions have generated.

The Poro and Sande secret societies date back to at least the eighteenth century. Of the sixteen major ethnic groups in Liberia, ten have Poro and Sande societies (Kaplan 1985:114).[12]

Kpelle secret society control over their members and, indeed, within the chiefdoms themselves has been based on secret society control over the power resources of information control, indoctrination and both positive and negative sanctions. Secrecy has enabled secret society leaders to deny nonmembers as well as low-ranking secret society initiates knowledge of medicine power and important historical information. Secret society initiates are also indoctrinated with political and social values that stress the virtues of obedience to the religious and political leaders of the chiefdoms. The secret societies have also had a major role in enforcing community laws and punishing outsiders who have trespassed on the sacred secret society bush precincts. Since access to desired statuses within each chiefdom can only be acquired through Poro or Sande membership, the secret societies have maintained their power by controlling the rewards that only secret society membership can bring.

The Poro, the male secret society, in alliance with the Sande, the female secret organization, has served and continues to serve the interests of the wealthy, dominant lineages within chiefdoms. Both the Poro and the Sande constitute the sacred ruling structure of the community. They are responsible for the maintenance and control of the town's protective and offensive medicines. However, while the Poro shares religious authority with the Sande, the Poro remains the dominant political force. Nonetheless the Sande does keep secrets from the men and men fear the potential harmful power of Sande secrets (Murphy 1976).

The Poro and Sande societies initiate nearly all the men and women, respectively, in a chiefdom. In earlier times the Poro conducted initiations for four years and then controlled the bush for an additional four years, ritually turning over control to the Sande, which conducted initiation of the girls for three years and controlled bush for another three years (Gibbs, Jr., 1965; Bellman 1979, 1984; d'Azevedo 1973). During the period of Sande control, however, the Poro council of prominent lineage elders continued to make important political decisions (Murphy 1980).

In the past, each Poro lodge enjoyed local autonomy. There was no central leadership governing all the Kpelle lodges.[13] Some small chiefdoms had no Poro lodges, so their members were initiated into the lodges of nearby chiefdoms until they could afford to establish a bush school or grove

(Stakeman 1986:131). When provided with appropriate fees a ritual leader would introduce Poro rituals into new areas (d'Azevedo 1969). Prominent Poro and Sande leaders all belong to the wealthy and powerful lineages. Usually the Poro leader's eldest son succeeds his father (Bellman 1984:49). And the Poro leaders, the *Zoes*, give constant reinforcement to the common belief that only *Zoes* from such prominent lineages can make societal medicine work for the benefit of the community (Bellman 1984:48). The Kpelle believe that it is this secret knowledge that gives lineage leaders the power and wealth that they enjoy (Murphy 1980). The Poro and Sande perpetuate this idea by giving prominent secret society positions to members of the prominent lineages including the chiefs. Thus the Poro *Zoes* integrate the interests of the Poro with those of the prominent lineages (Bledsoe 1980). The *Zoes*, who claim knowledge of profound secret medicine powers (*Sale*),[14] are ranked according to their responsibility in initiation rituals.[15] One *Zo*, the *Namu*, serves as the speaker of the Poro council and chief administrator of the Poro initiation activities. The *Namu* is also the messenger for the bush devil (*Ngamu*), the chief spirit of the Poro lodge (Bellman 1984).

Other *Zoes* act as liaisons between the priesthood and the town, some are doorkeepers who protect the Poro village and others are in charge of various categories of initiation rituals. Certain *Zoes* adjudicate disputes within the Poro or between the Poro and other secret societies (Bellman 1984:25). Each *Zo* represents the power of the whole spirit world and its representative on earth, the Poro (Fulton 1969:72).

Leaders of the Sande lodges also inherit their secret society titles as a result of their membership in the prominent lineages of a chiefdom. The titled head of a Sande lodge, the *Zogbe*, controls the lodge's magical power, which gives women fertility. She is assisted by three to four female elders (d'Azevedo 1973; Bledsoe 1980).

Sande and Poro leadership cooperate in the management of community affairs. They share some reciprocal secrets, thus assuring the cooperation of the opposite secret order (d'Azevedo 1973; Bellman 1979). Nonetheless the Sande is dependent on the Poro to punish men who have transgressed the rights of women (Bellman 1984).

The power of the Poro has stemmed from its control over male access to adult status, its ability to indoctrinate Poro members in the values and normative rules consistent with the interests of the Poro leadership, and its authority to impose sanctions against those who violate Poro rules and certain community laws (Gibbs, Jr. 1965; Sibley and Westermann 1928; Stakeman 1986). The Poro's complete control over the care and welfare of the community's young men when they undergo initiation in the bush schools has enabled Poro leaders to make economic demands (money, food, etc.), on the parents who, at least till recently, feared that noncompliance might endanger the lives of their sons (Murphy 1980).

When boys reach the age of puberty and the time is appropriate for a bush school session, the boys are "captured" by the priest representing the *Ngamu* (in symbolic terms "killed" by *Ngamu*) and taken into a Poro grove. The initiates are required to take ritual oaths, swearing they will not disclose information on activities within the bush school. While living in the bush the boys are considered dead by the town. During their period of isolation they are washed with special medicine, go through a scarification ritual, are taught the laws of the town's protective medicine, and are given military instruction as well as instruction about Poro rituals. In the course of their training they learn respect for the elders in all matters. At the end of the initiation the boys are given symbolic rebirth by the head priest in the "womb" of the *Ngamu*'s wife, or *Zoes*, representing bush devils, ritually regurgitate children they have "eaten." They are now considered adult men and can return to their families (Bellman 1979, 1984; Murphy 1980).

Access to normal adult status for the Kpelle girls is controlled by the Sande. Kpelle women cannot make satisfactory marriages until they have gone through the Sande initiation. Sande leaders are influential in arranging suitable marriages for members of these lodges. But these marriages usually further the interests of the dominant lineages by enabling them to establish ties to other families important to leaders' economic and political power (Bledsoe 1980).[16]

All girls join the Sande after puberty and at the time that the Poro turns over the bush to the Sande control. Initiates are said to be "eaten" by the Sande "bush devil," the *Zegele*. In the bush village the girls are instructed in women's knowledge, laws of the town, and are given knowledge about medicines and poisons. They go through a scarification ritual. Before being "reborn" their clitorides are cut, they receive new names and thus full adult status (Bellman 1979; Murphy 1980).

During initiation both Poro and Sande leaders reinforce prevailing authority structures by stressing the importance of obedience to the wishes and commands of the Poro and Sande leadership. The cultural training initiates receive seems less important than the "political" indoctrination (Bledsoe 1980; Murphy 1980). It is significant that the children from the families of the *Zoes'* lineages are not required to spend the entire initiation period in the bush but only participate in closing ceremonies at the end of the initiation period (Bellman 1984). This suggests that the Poro believes that children of prominent families do not require the same intense political indoctrination that the children of commoner lineages do.

The opportunity for initiation into the most powerful tribal medicine societies is dependent on Poro and Sande membership. It is assumed that initiation into the Poro and Sande has conditioned them to the practices of secrecy (Bellman 1984). Such prior membership is necessary before initiation in such secret societies as the *Moling* (Spirit Society) and *Mina* (Horn Society). The *Mina* Society protects the town from witches and the *Moling* protects the sanctity of the Sande bush among other tasks (Bellman 1984:40).[17]

The Poro punish the violators of their own rules as well as the violators of the Sande norms, when Sande leaders request such help; they also enforce community laws. The Kpelle are convinced that Poro leaders have authorized the killing of Poro members who have revealed Poro secrets or outsiders who have learned Poro secrets (Murphy 1980). It certainly has been in the interests of the Poro to spread stories about such punishments. The occasions when the costumed figure of the *Namu* makes public appearances serves no other purpose than to frighten and impress the women and children (Welmers 1949). Women who are not deceived by such dramatizations may nonetheless fear Poro power over the lives of their sons while the boys are in the bush initiation schools.[18]

In precolonial times the Poro council judged cases referred to them by the chiefs, such as murder, arson, rape, or other severe transgressions of community law. The Poro played an important role in the enforcement of market rules and the preservation of scarce resources through an imposition of trade restrictions during times when certain goods were in scarce supply (Gibbs, Jr., 1965; Harley 1941). With the backing of the Sande the Poro could punish husbands who transgressed Sande laws (Bledsoe 1980).

During the early period of regional instability and warfare, the Poro provided a mechanism by which the dominant lineage leadership in each chiefdom could maintain power through confederation and alliance with other chiefdoms. The pan-tribal training in obedience to Poro codes contributed to resolution of disputes between political units and helped reinforce agreements among the various Poro officials in different chiefdoms (Fulton 1972; Richards 1973). The Poro distribution throughout Liberia suggests that it "is a manifestation of the peculiar politico-economic relations among people brought into close proximity under conditions requiring mutual adjustment and thus represent an adaptive mechanism of societies in an emergent region" (d'Azevedo 1962b:516).[19] The role of the Sande in arranging marriages for Sande initiates must have further helped the chiefs in transacting alliances.

However, the political strategies employed by Kpelle chiefs to protect their power in an environment of political instability led to the development of structural contradictions within the chiefdoms. By encouraging immigration into their chiefdoms the politically dominant lineages incorporated into their community populations from diverse backgrounds whose descendants eventually tried to usurp power from them by fictionalizing relationships to these wealthy lineages. By so doing they tried to get controlling rights in more land (Murphy 1980; Bledsoe 1980). In this way the political subsystem had a overdeterminant impact on the relations of production.

Thus, a political structure emerged within which the dominant lineage leadership depended on the "newcomers" for political survival but, at the same time, faced political threats from the descendents of these very same immigrant populations. This primary contradiction led to the formation of "structural fault lines" that divided the interests of the dominant lineages from those of the immigrant descent groups. The chiefs had to contain this conflict in order to protect the interests of the dominant lineages.

Through their control of the Poro, the leaders of the dominant lineages fought off such threats. Elders of the Poro are the proprietors of knowledge concerning the specific history of individual families that settled in a particular area. Such knowledge bears on the questions of property rights and political position. Crucial decisions regarding such matters are made covertly by the Poro leadership. Oaths of secrecy prevent any members of these ruling councils from divulging the basis for public decisions. Important facts concerning genealogy, land rights, and local history can be made public in such a way that the interests of the community leadership are not threatened. Thus, knowledge made public by Poro elders about land disputes may not be a correct version but deceptions used to protect the interests of the dominant lineages. As Murphy points out "the Poro and the Sande societies provide the elders of the dominant lineage not only with mystical legitimation but also with a social veil behind which they can manipulate the important decisions affecting the community" (1980:203). Since secret society socialization imbues the male members of low status lineages with fear and respect toward the Poro leaders, they are less likely to challenge Poro elders' versions of genealogical histories. Thus, by monopolizing such crucial information, the dominant lineages can exert control because weaker families whose ancestral records are sketchy are always at a disadvantage in pursuing their interests (Bledsoe 1980; Murphy 1980; d'Azevedo 1962c). In this way the Poro leadership, while not eliminating the contradiction, minimized its disruptive effects.

Fearful that the Kpelle secret societies might serve as a foci of anti-state power, the Americo-Liberian leadership and their successors in the Doe government have attempted to regulate the Poro and to a lesser extent Sande activities but, at the same time, preserve these local organizations as a structure through which the state can exert some influence in the local community. However, there are contradictory aspects to the state-Poro relationship, for the secret society serves to perpetuate traditional values that undermine government modernization efforts.

The structural moments established by the state, as well as the new economic and religious subsystems, have had an overdeterminant impact on the secret societies. New industries and new religions compete with the secret societies for the Kpelle youths' time and loyalty.

In combination, the overdeterminant impact of new political, economic, and religious subsystems have eroded some of the traditional power resources of the Kpelle secret orders. The Poro leaders rely less on coercion to control the secret society membership than they have in the past and their ability to conduct intensive indoctrination of Kpelle youth during initiations has been circumscribed by the government rules limiting the initiation period.

The expansion of the central authority of the Americo-Liberian government into the hinterland areas and its establishment of direct authority over secret society organizations has significantly undermined the autonomy of the Poro and in a like fashion the Sande. Beginning with President William Tubman's administration, both the Poro and the Sande became regulated by federal laws and administrative regulations. The direct supervision of such organizations was assigned to the minister of local government. President Tubman and subsequent presidents were made the honorary heads of all Poroes. This gave the Liberian presidents an added popular power base as well as supervisory control (Liebenow 1987:84).

The government has sponsored a national Poro organization (Bellman 1984; Liebenow 1969; Lowenkopf 1976). Such arrangements give Poro leaders channels of communication with the government, but also enable officials to infringe on secret society autonomy. However, government interference with the Poro and Sande societies has largely involved placing limits on the length of their initiation ceremonies. At the local level the Poro still plays a role in mediating cases of intertown fighting and land-tenure disputes (Bellman 1984:26).

Once the Americo-Liberian government had established control in the hinterland, it made sure the paramount and clan chiefs owed primary loyalty to the government. Now literacy as well as a European education has become essential for Kpelle political leaders who wish to advance their political as well as economic careers. Western-educated Kpelle leaders find

Poro influences less vital to their acquisition of political power than their European education. While older chiefs (co-opted paramount and clan chiefs) still rely on their Poro connections to protect their lineage interests, modern Kpelle political leaders have exploited their positions in the state bureaucracy to defend their lineage interests as well as to increase the power of their lineages (Liebenow 1987:259; Stakeman 1986). Many Western-educated Kpelle leaders have turned to inter-ethnic political organizations to further their political and economic goals (Abasiattai 1987).[20]

Modern chiefs serve as "cultural brokers." The local perception of the central government in Monrovia, the capital, is that of an arena of political activity which is privileged, powerful, and dangerous. The chief ("broker") uses his claims, real or imagined, to privileged access to powerful people at the national level to enhance his local power. The local community comes to view the chief as a person who can protect them from the impositions of the national government as well as secure for them government benefits (Murphy 1980).

Thus, today the interests of many of the Kpelle chiefs and the Poro and Sande no longer coincide to the extent they did in the past. While earlier accounts stressed the power of the Poro over the chiefs (see Sibley and Westermann 1928; Harley 1941), recent research has suggested that the power of the Poro over the secular Kpelle leadership has declined (Fulton 1969, 1972). The Zo's power, to some degree, has been undermined by the rise of the new political brokers on whom the local people depend in their transactions with the national leadership.

The ability of the Poro and the Sande to indoctrinate initiates has also been seriously undermined by the presence of modern schools, plantations, and industry. These institutions compete with the secret societies for initiates' time and allegiance. Initiation now takes place only over a few weeks during periods of public school vacation (Bellman 1979, 1984; Gibbs, Jr., 1965). Even so, workers for modern corporations near the rural towns continue to send their children to secret society initiations. Employees of Firestone and Liberico-American Swedish Minerals Co.,[21] located near some Kpelle towns, send their children to secret society schools (Lowenkopf 1976:98), but the children's contact with Poro and Sande influence is a brief one.

The modernizing influences on Kpelle youth have led some of them to question the basis of the elders' leadership and control. Murphy (1980) stresses the role of the Poro in preventing or deflecting youthful challenges to Poro elders' monopoly of knowledge. This defensive role for the Poro and Sande has apparently become more important as young villagers are exposed to new values and beliefs on the basis of which they might question the authority of elders in matters of political and religious control.

There seems to be less coercion during Poro initiations now that parents have potential access to the modern state, whose laws hold Poro leaders accountable for any harm inflicted on their children (Murphy 1989).

Over the years Christian missions have continued to challenge the authority of the Poro and other secret societies. The Lutherans, for example, forbade converts from participating in secret society rituals. If a convert joined the Poro they were suspended from the church (Stakeman 1986:172). Converts themselves have even made physical attacks on the Poro and Sande members (Liebenow 1987:54).

Although the autonomy of the Poro has been undermined, it still functions as an organization within which secret political decision-making can take place at the local level. Many legal disputes are also disposed of in secret deliberations by the Poro councils (Murphy 1989). The *Zoes* continue to exercise power as religious brokers, utilizing their secret knowledge of the supernatural forces to claim ability to cure or prevent illness (Murphy 1981). The Poro and Sande also play a role in the selection of local chiefs and in the mustering of opposition to unpopular local officials (Tartter 1985:230).

Conclusions

The rise and fall in the power and influence of the Kpelle Poro and Sande secret societies has been determined by the extent to which the elders of the dominant lineage within each Kpelle chiefdom and the political leaders that represent these lineages depended on the Poro and Sande to protect lineage interests and help expand lineage power. The nature of the threats to the powerful and wealthy lineages were manifestations of structural contradictions that emerged within and among the Kpelle chiefdoms. Kpelle secret societies constituted the site at which conflicts generated by these contradictions became manifest. The Poro, for example, has been active at the "structural fault lines" produced by contradictions in the social formation as a counterdeterminant moment, either reinforcing existing political authority or undermining it.

The Poro and the Sande emerged in a highly mobile and fluctuating political environment to defend the interests of the dominant lineages within each chiefdom. Wars generated by trade rivalries forced the chiefdoms to attract new supporters and clients in order to maintain a strong military posture, but these political practices had long-term "composite effects." In maintaining and expanding their political interests in this fashion, the dominant lineages were faced with the threats to their control over their lineage land by fictional claims advanced by the descendants of the immigrants, whom the chiefs had attracted as supporters. These inherent structural contradictions led to conflicts at these fault lines between dominant lineages and immigrant claimants. The Poro and Sande served to legitimize the power of the dominant lineages. As members of the inner council of the Poro the elders of the dominant lineages were able to maintain a monopoly over critical historical knowledge that the less-powerful lineages needed access to in order to challenge the elite lineage land claims. Decisions on such claims were made in secret by the Poro council. This made it impossible for the "upstart" lineages to evaluate the merits of the decisions. Any opposition to Poro authority was limited since most men and women had been trained during secret society initiations to obey Poro and Sande leaders without question. These secret society leaders, of course, were members of the powerful and wealthy lineages within each chiefdom. Thus, by employing secret society power resources, the Kpelle chiefs were able to repair the inconsistencies that resulted from the structural contradiction. Using information-control strategies and indoctrination they deflected the potential challenges to their economic and political control.

The interrelated contradictions within the emerging Americo-Liberian state and the wider social system of which it was a part (interstate relations) motivated its leadership to seek solutions to the economic and political crises that the state faced by expanding state control over the hinterland populations. However, in setting up indirect rule over the hinterland polities, the central authorities needed the cooperation of the chiefs and the secret societies, especially the Poro, which helped the dominant lineage maintain its local power. On the other hand, the Americo-Liberian leaders were fearful of secret society power because many Poro societies had helped the chiefdoms organize military resistance to state efforts to establish hinterland political control. Given these circumstances the Liberian government decided to regulate the secret societies but not destroy them. While these state policies have placed limits on the traditional powers of the Poro and Sande, they have, nonetheless, left in place organizations that can still promote local ethnic loyalties that work against state efforts to create a well-functioning nation-state system. These Liberian state–secret society relationships again illustrate the dialectical interplay between induction and resistance in power relations whose evolution can produce new structural contradictions.

The Americo-Liberian state, forced by the British and French threat to its territories and by the need to find new finances to support its ruling class, took measures to expand control over African polities in the hinterland after subduing the coastal tribes. By pursuing such policies the state's political interests came into contradiction with those of the chiefdoms. African chiefdoms, including some of the Kpelle, put up a fierce resistance. It is likely that the Poro played some role in organizing these revolts.

Once the hinterland was subdued, the Liberian government set up a form of indirect rule: the co-opted chiefs. The paramount and clan chiefs now owed primary loyalty to the government, but to govern effectively the chiefs still needed support of the Poro and the Sande. The Liberian government also recognized that the Poro would be useful to them. By becoming honorary members of the Poro, the presidents of Liberia extended their popular base of support but also exerted some influence over Poro affairs. Nonetheless, the government has placed restrictions on Poro activities. The Poro and Sande are part of a state system, thereby subject to the laws and regulations of the government.

The legitimatization of the Poro and Sande led to unanticipated consequences: the Americo-Liberian government has thus enabled some of the co-opted chiefs to employ Poro initiations to reinforce Kpelle ethnic identity through the transmission of traditional values during initiation rituals. To the extent to which the Poro and Sande are successful in these efforts they undercut efforts by the government to develop a pool of Western-educated Kpelle leaders more loyal to the state bureaucracy than to their local ethnic groups.

The state has found ways to limit some of the traditional secret society powers, but secret society power resources have also been undercut by the overdeterminant impact of modern industries and new religions. These compete with the Poro and Sande as alternative reference groups and sources of new values for Kpelle youth.

The ability of the Poro and Sande to indoctrinate Kpelle youth according to traditional values and norms and, thereby, exercise control over them, has been undermined by the emergence of competing institutions such as modern industry, the Christian missions, and state schools. The Poro and Sande continue to conduct initiations, but for shorter periods than in the past. The spread of modern medicine and the opposition of Christian converts has further weakened the power of the secret society *Zoes*.

As Western-educated Kpelle political leaders achieve more influential positions in the state bureaucracy, they will utilize their government connections, as many already have done, to advance the interests of their lineage groups. This will profoundly affect the political role of the Poro.

At the local level, however, the Poro continues to play important political and religious roles. As adjudicators, religious brokers, and politicians Poro leaders continue to exercise influence within Kpelle society. However, the long-term powers of the Poro and Sande are likely to diminish.

In conflicts that have emerged at the structural fault lines the Poro and the Sande have represented the interests of the chiefs within the Kpelle chiefdoms. However, within the modern state, the power resources of the secret societies have become limited. When the Kpelle chiefdoms were independent polities the secret societies had more power resources. Not only could the Poro conceal information but it could also indoctrinate members and employ coercion when necessary. The Sande had similar though more limited power resources.

Today the overt exercise of secret society power against the state is illegal, and the Poro and Sande no longer have as complete and intense control over the socialization process of community members. Within the modern Kpelle community its members, as we have seen, have found alternative reference groups advocating points of view that challenge Poro and Sande values and norms. Study of Kpelle secret society dynamics merely reinforces the concept of power as a fluctuating relationship that is continually being rearranged and readjusted. It seems that today the Poro leadership relies less on coercion and indoctrination and more on information control (e.g., secret knowledge of medicine powers and lineage histories) as power resources. In this way it continues to perform an important political role for the powerful local lineages and local politicians.

3

The Ottoman Bektashi

HISTORY OF THE OTTOMANS

The evolution of a religious order into a secret one often reflects the nature of its dialectical relation with the state and its relation with the groups within the state on which the government depends for the exercise of power. These relations, in turn, are conditioned by contradictions within the social formation and the wider social system of which the social formation is a part. Government strategies that evolve to meet the crises produced by the structural contradictions can bring change in state relations with a religious order: a shift from tolerance to repression. These conjunctive moments initiated by the state can bring corresponding changes in the structures of the religious order. In resisting government action against it the religious order may employ secrecy as a power resource in order to survive. The Ottoman Bektashi order illustrate this kind of historic dynamic.

The Bektashi order was one of the mystic sects that were found among the Turkoman tribes during Seljuk rule in Anatolia. Later persecution of the Bektashi by the Ottomans forced members of the order to form, in effect, a secret society limiting knowledge by outsiders about the sect.

To understand the role of the Bektashi in Ottoman society and the ultimate demise of the sect, we must gain an understanding of the origins of the Ottoman empire and how the contradictions within the later Ottoman state and the larger social system of which it was a part led to the internal and external conflicts that ultimately resulted in a suppression of the sect. Conjunctive moments initiated by the Ottoman rulers to solve the crises produced by these structural contradictions had an overdeterminant impact on the religious, political, and economic subsystems. Eventual changes in these subsystems had a counterdeterminant effect on Ottoman central authority, resulting in the erosion of state power and further weakening Ottoman control of the economy.

To comprehend Ottoman origins we must trace the rise of Ottoman power during the period of the decline of the Seljuk empire in Anatolia. The Seljuks, descending from Turkestan into Persia and Mesopotamia, established their empire at Baghdad in A.D. 1021 (Anderson 1974:362). Thirty-five years later the Seljuk state was founded in Anatolia following the Seljuk victory at Manzikert over the Byzantine forces in the highlands of Armenia (Turan 1970:231).

The Seljuk invasion of western Asia opened up the area for various immigrants, among which were the Turkoman tribes. The Seljuk success in their military campaigns, at least in part, came from the support they received from these nomadic Muslim tribes, driven by a quest for plunder as well as their devotion to *jihad*, a holy war against the infidel (Turan 1970:232; Inalcik 1970a:269; Wittek 1958:18).

To govern the frontier districts, the Seljuks placed generals (*emirs*) whose positions became hereditary in family lines. But the main strength at the frontiers lay with the Turkoman tribes who were governed by their own hereditary leaders, *beys* (Inalcik 1970a:263–64; Shaw 1976:9–10).

To enable the Turkoman tribes to acquire land and subsistence the Seljuks encouraged them to redirect their energies in holy war (*ghaza*) against the Christian provinces of Byzantium (Itzkowitz 1980:6). But in these conquered areas the Turkoman felt themselves to be more or less independent of Seljuk rule, and they resisted central government interference and taxation (Wittek 1958:18).

Even when the Mongols invaded Anatolia in the thirteenth century, establishing their governing superstructure, the *beys* retained power on the frontiers (Turan 1970:251; Wittek 1958:30). The disruption caused by the Mongol invasion around A.D. 1234 resulted in the formation of numerous *ghaza* emirates in Anatolia whose military leaders set up various independent dynasties.[1]

The Mongol invasions displaced peasants, artisans, and religious leaders, who moved into Anatolia from central Asia in the eleventh through thirteenth centuries (Turan 1970:232, 251). Within these migrant groups were the holy men or *shaykhs* who sought security in the frontier districts among the Turkoman tribes (Wittek 1958:30). These *shaykhs* spread heterodox forms of Islam among the Turkomans and promoted resistance to the Mongols (Griswold 1966:38). Mystic Sufist sects helped cushion the local nomads against the political and military turmoil of their times. Mystic leaders arose all over Anatolia, establishing orders whose teachings were a mosaic of both mystic and heterodox Islamic, Christian, and tribal beliefs (Shaw 1976:10; Turan 1970:256). The founder of the Bektashi order was one such wandering holy man named Haji Bektash (Birge 1937:50). The Seljuks were fearful of the revolts led by such Sufi dervish sects. The last powerful Seljuk leader, Ghiyas Ud-Din II (1236–59) ordered a general massacre of the Sufis to prevent a major revolt (Brown 1968:xix).

The emirate of Osman I was one of the independent provincial dynasties formed during the period of disruption caused by the Mongol invasion of Anatolia, but unlike the other emirates it soon became a dominant power. Being situated on the Nicaean Plains, close to Byzantium, the Osmani maintained a cohesive emirate strongly motivated by *ghaza* ambitions (Itzkowitz 1980:10); Anderson 1974:363). Because of population pressure as well as holy-war motives, the Osmani, like other *ghazi* tribes, began to expand, but they were more successful than most (Inalcik 1970a:267–69).

By the fifteenth century the Ottomans incorporated all the emirates of Anatolia into an empire (Wittek 1958:461). The Ottoman rulers eventually extended their power into Europe, Persia, the Mediterranean, and Arabia (Shaw 1976; Itzkowitz 1980:38).

OTTOMAN POLITICAL ORGANIZATION

As the Ottomans extended their power over this vast domain, the complex tasks of governing a large empire forced them to establish a more elaborate governmental bureaucracy. Bayezid I was the first Ottoman ruler to introduce the classical Turkish Islamic system of central government. Centralized decision-making took place through a council of state (*divan*). State officers contacted the sultan through the Chamber of Petitions. The grand vezir drew up and enforced general orders in the sultan's name. The *mufti* of Istanbul was the supreme religious leader, who was given the job of interpreting the sacred laws of *Sharia* (Inalcik 1970b:302–3; Anderson 1974:369).

The empire was divided into provinces (*eyalets*), which were subdivided into units called *sancaks*, policed by *sancak beys*, the military chiefs appointed by the grand vezir. The *sancak beys* enforced the laws within the *sancak* and under the orders of the provincial governors, the *beylerbeys*; the *sancak beys* called up local troops for campaigns. When on military expeditions the *beys* were temporarily replaced by *kadis*, who were officials appointed by the central government. *Kadis* reported cases of unrest, held court, and organized food and supplies for the army when it crossed their districts (Griswold 1966:17–18; Alderson 1956:17). Thus, the line of administrative authority more or less ran from the sultan (and his royal council) to *beylerbey* to *sancak bey* (Itzkowitz 1980:47).

Kadis along with *katibs* (secretaries) and *defterdars* (treasurers) were trained in *medreses* (schools attached to mosques). For the Muslim students, or *softas*, these *medreses* opened doors to successful advancement within the governmental structure (Griswold 1966:40).

One source of political instability was related to the problem of succession to the throne. The Ottomans had no fixed rule of succession. There was a struggle among brothers over access to the throne. A new sultan assigned provinces to each of his sons or princes (*celebi*) to govern. Each prince established a miniature court at the chief town of the province and began to build a power base in order to compete with his brothers for the throne (Griswold 1966:35; Alderson 1956:18). Mehmud II tried to solve the problem of succession in A.D. 1453 when he gave legal sanction to the law of fratricide, which allowed a newly enthroned sultan to murder other male heirs. However, in 1603 a new system replaced the fratricide law. Heirs presumptive were placed in detention in a cagelike room within the palace to prevent royal bloodshed (Griswold 1966:35; Alderson 1956:12, 25).

To exert effective rule the sultans had to create a loyal political and military administration. In order to establish a basis for economic support of officials and military leaders, the Ottoman continued the Seljuk system of land tenure, but the Ottomans also gave important military and government posts to slaves, or *ghulam* (Itzkowitz 1980:21). Under the Ottomans all agricultural land passed to state ownership (*miri*). Like the Seljuks the Ottomans gave land grants to state officials. These grants were called *timars*. Such grants gave the landlords a share of income produced through taxation in kind (*aosur*, or product tax), one-half to one-eighth of the peasant crop. Infidel subjects (non-Muslim *rayah*) were burdened with special taxes (Anderson 1974:370).

The Ottoman government was in a constant struggle with the *beys* of the Balkans who often operated in an autonomous fashion. Slave appointees to such offices were more easily controlled since their life and property were under total government control. *Beylerbeys* were moved from province to province to prevent them from establishing strong local roots (Griswold 1966:21; Karpat 1973:20–21).

The *sipahi*, cavalry officers and soldiers, who received such *timars* had to perform military duties for the state as well as provide their own equipment (Itzkowitz 1980:14; Islamoglu and Keyder 1981; Anderson 1974:363). To fulfill their obligations of supplying horses and arms, the *sipahi* sold their farm surpluses to get cash to acquire these military supplies. By law the *timar* grants only gave usufruct rights to *sipahi*. In reality the *timars* were treated as private property since the eldest son of the father might inherit his father's *timar* if he showed bravery in battle (Griswold 1966:15–16).

The *timar* system encouraged an orderly cultivation of the land. But the *timar* system also stimulated the growth of population without being able to absorb the increase. It restricted land expansion and discouraged the introduction of new farming methods (Karpat 1974:89).

In their attempt to establish and maintain effective political control over their growing empire the Ottomans instituted a political structure that led to unanticipated political and economic problems. Such "composite effects" led to new contradictions between the structures necessary to the reproduction of the social formation and the capacities of the existing economic base to provide the ruling class with sufficient resources to maintain this political system.

THE JANISSARIES

The *timariot* system also created a military force potentially independent of Ottoman control and able to challenge the authority of the sultans. To counter the potential disruptive political power of the *timariots*, Sultan Murad I organized a powerful military force from prisoners of war called Janissaries (Shaw 1976). The Janissaries became the major channel through which the sultans effectively extended their authority into the provinces (Karpat 1974:87). They were expected to give one-fifth of their booty to the sultan. Later Mohammed II equipped the Janissaries with modern weapons and situated them in provincial garrisons (Itzkowitz 1980:26; Inalcik 1970b:301; Parry 1970:837). By the time of Suleiman the Magnificent (1520–68) the Janissary corps had increased to twelve to fifteen thousand. The Janissaries constituted a military force loyal to the sultan. Even the grand vezir could not issue orders directly to the commander of the Janissaries.

The *devsirme*, or child-tribute system, was instituted by the Ottoman rulers to provide the sultans with a cadre of military personnel and administrators totally dependent upon them and therefore extremely loyal to them (Shaw 1976). This institution had been established by Murad II in 1430 (Wittek 1958:49). A certain number of male children from Christian Balkan families in areas under Ottoman control were sent to Anatolia. Here they underwent a strenuous seven-year period of training including hard physical labor and instruction in Islam and the Turkish language. Those individuals who excelled in martial arts were selected as cadets for the Janissary corps, while others who were adept at book learning, mathematics, and calligraphy became royal pages from which many future administrators were chosen (Severy 1987:574–75; Itzkowitz 1980).[2] About four to five thousand war prisoners and slaves that had been purchased were given similar training (Anderson 1974:366).

The Janissaries had special ties to the Bektashi sect to whom they vowed complete loyalty. Most Janissaries were incorporated into the order. Bektashi holy men accompanied the Janissaries on campaigns as chaplains (Brown 1968:163; Shaw 1976:123; Birge 1937:74).

OTTOMAN ECONOMIC POLICIES

Reflecting the Ottoman economic doctrines, the Ottoman political superstructure was closely integrated within the economic base. The state regulated all craft and mercantile activity. Speculative profiteering was prohibited. Urban craft production was undertaken by guilds under strict state regulations (*hisba*). The state controlled the allocation of raw material for craftwork and the quantity and quality of manufactured goods, and also fixed market prices. The Ottomans imposed a strict control over internal and external trade. The internal trade provided the state with a source of market taxes as well as revenues from customs dues. The market taxes (*bac pazar*) were determined in proportion to the business transacted (Islamoglu and Keyder 1981).

The power to collect taxes was given to recipients of land grants or farmed out to other officials. Large merchants collected the custom duties (Islamoglu and Keyder 1981:303). The state also sold concessions to the merchants who agreed to purchase and sell only those goods which were officially sanctioned by the government. By granting such concessions the state provided itself with revenue, and by giving only officially sanctioned merchants the right to purchase goods in local markets, the government ensured that goods would move toward the important major cities, particularly Istanbul. In turn the state ensured the safety of merchants and their wares, protected trade routes, and closely monitored the business transactions in the marketplace (Islamoglu and Keyder 1981:302–4).

External trade was not limited to luxury items. During the sixteenth century the Ottomans monopolized the silk and spice trades. Bursa was an important entrepôt for this east-west trade. Silk from Iran and spices and dyes from India were exchanged for European woolens at Bursa. Black Sea entrepôts served as centers of trade with Russia, Poland, and the Crimea. Products from the East, Anatolia, and the Mediterranean were exchanged for wheat, furs, and iron goods from the northern Italian cities, which were intermediaries in trade with Western Europe (Islamoglu and Keyder 1981:305).

Thus the Ottoman ruling class spread an ideology that justified its extensive control over the state political economy. The peasants came to accept the idea that all land belonged to the sultan and that the state did not permit the accumulation of land. The *hisba* regulations placed on urban guilds were justified in similar ways. Though merchants received protection from the state the Ottomans prohibited speculative profiteering, which was considered sinful. Ottoman political and economic authority was sanctioned by Sunnite religious doctrines. Nonetheless, the Ottomans did tolerate heterodox religious elements within the empire for strategic reasons. Being far removed from the masses, the Ottoman religious leadership, the *ulema*, depended on the local influence of the dervish orders to strengthen the state's religious control over the populace, even though this practice entailed obvious risks. By fine-tuning the political and economic subsystems with modest structural reforms and by justifying these policies through an orthodox religious ideology, the Ottoman rulers, at least initially, were able to reproduce the social formation by mitigating the intensity of the conflicts produced by basic contradictions within the empire. However, such conjunctive moments initiated by the state were to produce long-term crises apparently not anticipated by the central authority.

THE BEKTASHI

The Bektashi was one of the dervish orders that emerged during the fifteenth century, a period of Ottoman history when the Ottomans extended their hegemony over a vast area in the course of founding their empire. However, unlike other heterodox sects, the Bektashi had close ties with the powerful military body, the Janissaries.

Being a Shiite brotherhood, they therefore supported the claims of Ali, Muhammed's son-in-law, to the caliphate. Unlike the Sunni Muslims, they believed that the twelve *imams* were the rightful religious leaders, Ali being the first (Brown 1968:76; Gibb and Kramers 1953:61–63).[3] They also claimed that the spiritual ancestors of Haji Bektash could be traced back to Ali (Shaw 1976:154). They denied the Sunni claim that Abu Bakr was the legitimate heir to the caliphate (Gibb and Kramers 1953).

For the Sunni, conformism and obedience were basic commandments that the Prophet himself proclaimed. Failure to observe these sacred injunctions was considered a sin as well as a crime. From the Shiite perspective, however, obedience to existing Sunni rulers was merely a temporary necessity, to be given only as long as it could not be avoided. Believing that the Sunni leaders had strayed from the true path of Islam, the Shiites felt no inherent necessity to obey them (Lewis 1985:7).

The Bektashi dervishes sought the essence of reality. The physical world, and the evil in it, according to the Bektashi, were illusions. They believed that God (Allah) is everywhere and appears in many manifestations, and that humans, under appropriate conditions, could become the mechanism for the divine revelation of God (Birge 1937:87). Thus the Bektashi accepted the Hurufist belief that man himself could become a divine revelation of the deity (Birge 1937:54). Because of their beliefs the Bektashi held the orthodox religion of Islam in scorn (Birge 1937:93).

Hadji Bektash (the *pir* or founder) established a "path" consisting of seven nominal but four essential degrees through which an aspirant might gradually seek union with God (Shaw 1976:154; Garnett 1912:95). Union with Allah gave a Bektash so much sanctity that he had superior powers. Thus he achieved the state of *qutb*, an intimate union with the deity. This state could be achieved only after long periods of fasting and prayer. Only a few *shaykhs* and important dervishes seem to have achieved such sanctity (Garnett 1912:32). Ranking below the *qutb* were twelve other officials with varying degrees of sanctity (Garnett 1912:84).

During the novitiate of 1,001 days, the aspirant (*mursit*) was led by degrees to abandon the Islamic beliefs necessary for the unenlightened but not acceptable for a Bektashi. Under the guidance of the *shaykh* (or *baba*), who imparted his mystical philosophy to the novitiate, the aspirant came under the spiritual influence of the *pir* or founder of the order (Bektash), acquiring his attributes and power of performing supernatural acts. Eventually a successful few might gain spiritual communion with Allah himself, into whose soul the aspirant became absorbed (Garnett 1912:97, 147). Having attained this highest degree, the individual became endowed with various spiritual and superhuman powers (e.g., the gift of prophecy, power to influence events).

Thus, the *shaykhs* maintained power over their followers through a gradual conversion process, whereby novitiates became resocialized to heterodox religious values. The *shaykh*'s followers believed that by subjecting themselves to his authority they would learn the secrets necessary for enlightenment and spiritual communion with God. The source of the *shaykh*'s power, then, was not coercive authority but his ability to transmit knowledge to sect members that would eventually bring them rewards.

Obviously the popularity of such heterodox and mystic religions among the Ottoman tribesmen created concern for the orthodox Sunnite leadership. For by indoctrinating sect members with values and beliefs that questioned the religious and moral justification on which the Ottomans based their state authority, the Bektashi subverted the central authority's ability to effectively spread the Sunnite religious doctrines among potentially dissident groups, which justified Ottoman control of the state.

The Ottoman rulers were Sunnites, yet they tolerated the Bektashi sect (as well as other dervish groups) in spite of the Sunni priesthood's (*ulema*) hostility to these Shiites. The early sultans' sufferance of the Bektashi sect was, it would appear, largely for pragmatic reasons. The Ottoman rulers depended on the Janissaries to maintain control in the provinces, and since the Janissaries were members of the Bektashi order the sect was less vulnerable to state suppression. Moreover, while the state leaders were suspicious of the Bektashi, they were not always certain about the sect's religious beliefs because the Bektashi were able to disguise some of their unorthodox doctrines behind a veil of secrecy (Garnett 1912:182).

Some sultans even hoped to win support from the Turkoman tribes, within which heterodox religions were strongly entrenched, by supporting the Bektashi and the other dervish sects. For example Sultan Orhan Gazi created *waqf* endowments, lands bequeathed to the sects *tekkehs* or monastic establishments in order to finance these Sufi mystic orders (Shaw 1976:13). The *waqf* endowments could not be sold, mortgaged, or taxed (Garnett 1912:64). Each *tekkeh* was administered by the *shaykh* (*baba*) who managed the estates and was responsible for the general religious and social activities of the monastery (Garnett 1912; Birge 1937; Brown 1968). The sect was open to both men and women (Birge 1937:163). Associated with the *tekkehs* were tombs (*turbehs*) for the saints (Garnett 1912:64).

CRISIS WITHIN THE OTTOMAN STATE

The attempt by the Ottoman rulers to develop a political superstructure through which they could maintain their imperial control, and thus reproduce the Ottoman social formation, not only created political crises, once their imperial expansionism ceased, but also had an overdeterminant and negative impact on the Ottoman economic base. The crises (or secondary contradictions) that resulted produced conflicts at various structural fault lines along which the state came into violent opposition to groups that formed the foci of resistance to state authority. These unresolved conflicts gradually began to undermine state power.

The crises, which eventually led to the repression of the Bektashi order, were the result of the basic contradictions within the social formation and social system of the Ottoman state. The crises produced by these contradictions affected different groups in different ways. In part, Ottoman hostility toward the Bektashi was the result of the latter's close association with the Janissaries, who opposed new reforms initiated by the later sultans, thus provoking state hostility toward themselves and the Bektashi who supported them. However, the erosion of Ottoman support for the Janissaries also gave the Sunnite priesthood an opportunity to move against these Shiite enemies.

Contradictions between the economic and political interests of the Ottomans and other social formations led to contradictions within the wider social system in which the Ottoman state was integrated. The erosion of Ottoman imperial power as well as state trade monopolies led to negative impacts on the internal economy of the Ottoman social formation, seriously undermining the economic position of certain groups. The state's response to these new economic and military crises put the central government on a collision course with class factions who had lost power, intensifying the conflicts with such groups. On the other hand, shifts in power to new emerging class segments (e.g., Janissaries, *ayans*) began to undermine state authority.

As I have indicated previously, the Ottoman military organization, civil administration, taxation system, and land tenure laws were geared to a state that was expanding by conquest into the lands of the "infidel." By the sixteenth century the Ottoman empire had reached the limits of its expansionism. Further advance to the east was barred by Persia and the eastern waters were dominated by the Portuguese navy, which swept Muslim ships from the Indian Ocean. Russia blocked Ottoman access to the Crimea and the lands beyond. The maritime power of the West cut off access to the Mediterranean (Lewis 1970:218–19). During the seventeenth, eighteenth, and early nineteenth centuries the Ottomans lost parts of their empire as a result of a series of treaties with their enemies (Lewis 1970:232–331).

The halt in this territorial expansion resulted in the slow stagnation of Ottoman economy (Anderson 1974:378–79). The shrinking economy had to support a costly superstructure at a time when the population was increasing so rapidly that it exceeded the available farmlands (Inalcik 1970c:343). Now that war booty was limited and traditional forms of taxation could not cover the increased costs, the Ottoman state resorted to levying new taxes, selling public offices, debasing the coinage, and expropriating the wealth of ethnic minorities to get more capital (Griswold 1966:14–15).

Ottoman economic problems were accentuated by the influx of silver from America and the loss of its trade monopoly to European powers. European nations exported silver to the Ottomans, receiving gold in exchange. This trade arrangement increased prices of goods. The inflation resulted in the adulteration of currency, counterfeiting, speculation, high interest rates, and usury. Inflation hurt groups with fixed incomes, particularly the Janissaries and the *sipahi* (Inalcik 1970c:344; Karpat 1973:49; Lewis 1970:223–24; Anderson 1974:280–81).

The entrance of the English and Dutch into the Asian trade undermined the Ottoman trade monopoly. The spice trade was diverted from Ottoman territories when English and Dutch entered the Indian ocean during the latter part of the seventeenth century. At the end of the sixteenth century the French, Dutch, and English began to compete with the Ottomans for the Levant trade, displacing Venice as chief supplier of silk via Allepo. Having established their hegemony in the Indian Ocean, the Dutch and the English came to supply Europe with silks from Persia, Bengal, and China. Changes in these trade relationships resulted in a significant loss of sources of Ottoman revenue. It also resulted in a decline in the Ottoman trade centers, such as Bursa and Allepo (Islamoglu and Keyder 1981:305; Heyd 1970:368).

Declining government revenues led the Ottomans to turn against classes that wasted state resources. The Ottoman rulers turned against the *sipahi timar* holders. The introduction of European weapons into the Ottoman military forces had made the *sipahi* military role obsolete. The Ottoman state began to assign *timars* to Janissaries and nonmilitary officials or, on death of *sipahi* holders, absorb their lands back into state control (Anderson 1974:385; Griswold 1966:16). In place of the *sipahi* there now emerged a class of absentee landowners that had become recipients of *timar*-grants. These fief holders gained control of great latifundia (Lewis 1970:225).

Many Janissaries became part of this landed aristocracy. The size of the Janissary corps increased so dramatically that by the end of the sixteenth century there were 100,000 registered members of the corps. Inflation made it difficult for the government to support this large force, so *timar* grants were given to the Janissaries. Some Janissaries had to supplement their incomes through craft production and commerce (Islamoglu and Keyder 1981; Itzkowitz 1980; Anderson 1974:381–82). The Janissaries came to constitute a wealthy class independent of the sultan's control and more interested in pursuing an aristocratic lifestyle than fighting (Itzkowitz 1980:91; Shaw 1976:174). The Janissaries became the dominant element in most towns and cities often in alliance with, and sometimes a part of, the large wealthy estate owners (*ayans*). In the more distant provinces they came to form the dominant class with enough political power to appropriate most of the state revenues for themselves (Shaw 1976:174). Thus, by the seventeenth century the Janissaries constituted an elite group, only a fraction of which had military training. Yet their control over modern weapons enabled them to terrorize sultans and make and unmake the grand vezirs (Birge 1937).

High prices for goods and food produced in Europe encouraged the merchants to subvert state control by selling products in contraband operations rather than in local markets or to the state. Even state officials holding land grants engaged in smuggling. Shortages of products led to higher guild prices and thus higher palace expenditures for craft goods, further depleting the treasury (Islamoglu and Keyder 1981).

By the 1580s the English were importing mohair, yarn, cotton, and silk from the Ottoman empire and were exporting wool broadcloth, tin, and steel to them. Later France increased its trade with the Ottomans by importing cotton and cotton thread and exporting cloth. Gradually the Ottoman economy became integrated into a world economy in which the Ottomans acted as suppliers of raw material and imported expensive manufactured goods. These imports resulted in declining guild production and the devastation of rural craft industries (Islamoglu and Keyder 1977:43–44).

New extraordinary taxes (*avariz*) were imposed. And the Ottomans also expanded an old system of collecting such new revenues, tax-farming. This tax-form system (*iltizam*), involving the farming out of specified revenues to the highest bidder, had been used to collect custom dues, poll taxes and sheep taxes. In the seventeenth century it was expanded to cover traditional agricultural taxes as well as those now on *waqf* estates and former *timar* land (Islamoglu and Keyder 1981:312). Some tax-farms were life farms (*malikane*) made to friends of the court in which the holder had unfettered control over peasant labor and control over expected revenue (Lewis 1970:225; Griswold 1966:20; Anderson 1974:386; Inalcik 1970c:342).

Tax-farming accelerated the development of commercial estates (*ciftlik*) in the eighteenth century. Tax-farmers (especially the *malikane*) grew cash crops such as wheat, maize, cotton, and tobacco for European markets. Because of their wealth, tax-farmers were able to build up their local political authority. The tax-farmers became part of landed aristocracy of local notables called *ayans*.

Under the new tax-farm system, the peasant's position deteriorated seriously. The displacement of the *sipahi* class left the peasants with no one to defend their interests. The *ciftlik* system drove many peasants into debt bondage. In addition to *osr* payments (product taxes) the *ciftlik* holders demanded half the peasants' produce, along with labor service (Islamoglu and Keyder 1981:314; Griswold 1966:16). To pay their taxes the peasants used liens on their farmland. In this way peasants lost the security of tenure. Some impoverished peasants were driven from the land (Lewis 1970:227).

As a result of these economic conditions many peasants became members of bandit gangs. Others drifted to cities of the Anatolia, Balkans, Persia, and Crimea. Some of these displaced peasants took advantage of free education provided by the *medreses*. This, of course, swelled the class of *softas* (students). To support themselves the *softas* went to rural villages to aggressively collect alms from already impoverished peasants or turned to brigandry, striking at travelers, merchants, peasants, and landowners alike (Griswold 1966:41).

The disappearance of the *sipahis* from the provinces made the job of governing these areas more difficult in face of the increase in political disorder. The *sancak beys* now had no regular force of warriors to rely on to enforce the law. They were forced to hire troops and often hired landless peasants, dispossessed *timariots*, or nomads. These irregular infantry forces were called *levends* (Griswold 1966:19; Parry 1970:846). The irregulars served in the provincial armies and later, when the military campaigns were over, as a police force for the *beys*. To support these military forces the governors had to increase the tax on the peasants (Itzkowitz 1980:93).

These political and economic changes led to a breakup of the Ottoman empire and a devolution of state power. Being far removed from Ottoman control, the *pashas* and officers in Egypt and Syria and the *mamluk* governors of Baghdad and Basra rebelled. In Rumelia, by the end of the eighteenth century, the *ayan* class took over control of local government, establishing its own armies, treasuries, and courts of law (Lewis 1970:232).

By the beginning of the eighteenth century the *derebeys* (valley lords) in Anatolia were virtually autonomous. An irregular infantry gathered around such rebel provincial officials, helping them to exact taxes and tribute (Griswold 1966:226).

Some subordinates of the *beys* broke away from their leadership and formed brigand gangs, which preyed upon villages, caravans, and travelers. These groups were sometimes joined by *sipahis* and landless peasants.

Such brigand bands formed the raw material out of which the larger *celali* armies were formed. Military deserters, dissatisfied with military pay or lack of promotion, provided such diverse groups with the type of leadership necessary to wield them into a large fighting force capable of attacking cities. Such armies constituted a serious military threat to the government. Often sultans controlled these rebel leaders by giving them areas to govern rather than by fighting them (Griswold 1966:193).

Thus, certain classes and class factions found that, by conforming to state demands, they were at a serious economic and political disadvantage compared to other classes or class factions. Depending on their position in the social structure, members of these classes or class segments initiated social practices (conjunctive moments) by which they hoped to actualize their political and economic self-interest in more realistic ways. By so doing, however, they began to subvert state authority, producing new fault lines between themselves and the centralized authority.

This political instability provided the appropriate climate in which heterodox sects and orders could thrive. The Turkomans, always resentful of the central government's efforts to extend control in areas where they enjoyed autonomy, were attracted to the heterodox religious doctrine that gave support to political separation and anti-Sunni sentiments (Shaw 1976: 86–87). Mystic cults provided leadership in earlier revolts or separatist movements among the nomads.[4] For example, under the rule of Mehoud I (1413–20), Seyd Medreddin Mense organized a secret mystic cult among the Turkomans which enabled him to build his power (Shaw 1976:43). Between 1301–1447 Shiite rulers of Persia, members of the Safavid order, sent Shiite preachers among the Turkoman (Shaw 1976:78). The Safavids were responsible for Turkoman revolts in 1511 and 1519 and between 1526 and 1528 (Shaw 1976:92).

By the sixteenth century, the Ottomans, fearful that these revolts would further undermine their shaky control over their empire, made greater effort to suppress the heterodox sects. Preparing to campaign against the Safavids in A.D. 1512, Selim I utilized a state spy system to hunt down suspected Shiite supporters in eastern Anatolia, and is said to have ordered between forty and seventy thousand killed or imprisoned (Itzkowitz 1980:32; Shaw 1976).

REPRESSION OF THE BEKTASHI

Class segments that have an overdeterminant impact on state policies because the rulers depend on them to provide essential services necessary for the preservation of the social formation may come to constitute a threat to state authority if they begin to consolidate wealth and political power. Once such class factions fail to perform these necessary state functions (i.e., to help rulers perpetuate their power) then the ruling class may resolve this contradictory relationship by destroying or repressing such class factions (an ultimate form of counterdetermination). The Janissary-Ottoman relationship evolved along such lines, and, in a corresponding way, so did the state-Bektashi connections, since the fate of the Bektashi were closely interwoven with the political fortunes of the Janissaries.

Given the Janissary history of participating in intrigues against sultans (and their *vezirs*), together with the fact that they were influenced by the heterodox Shiite beliefs of the Bektashi, it is not surprising that the orthodox Ottoman leaders began efforts to eliminate the Janissaries and their religious allies. Moreover, the Janissaries had become a less effective fighting force for the government, and they stood in the way of the reforms. Sultan Selim III (1789–1807) and Sultan Mahmud II (1808–39) wanted to make military reforms (*tanzimat*) in order to modernize the army as part of the overall program to Westernize decaying Ottoman institutions (Heyd 1970; Shaw 1976:262).

Selim III organized new military regiments, called *Nizam-i-Cedid*, which numbered about 25,000 by the end of his reign. Armed with modern weapons and trained by European officers, this new military force was superior to that of the Janissaries and other elements of the old Ottoman army. But the Selim did not effectively use this new army because the Janissaries and their class allies opposed its integration within the existing military units. As a result of this opposition Selim eventually dissolved the *Nizam-i-Cedid* (Shaw 1965).

When Mahmud II came to power in 1808 he began to organize an army patterned after Western military prototypes. To win the loyalty of the *ulemas* for his modernization policies he gave *ulema* leaders economic support and appointed them to high government posts. Lower-ranking *ulemas* (*softas*) were given posts in the military companies where they were employed to instruct the troops on the principles of Islam.

While Mahmud encouraged the Janissaries to join the new army, they felt threatened by these military reforms and on 15 June 1826, Janissaries in Istanbul revolted. But the people of Istanbul, including the *softas*, gave their support to the sultan, who was able to suppress the revolt. On June 17, Mahmud disbanded the Janissary corps with support from the *ulema* leadership (Levy 1971). This destruction of the Janissaries resulted in the deaths of four thousand members of the corps in Istanbul and probably thousands in other cities (Birge 1937:76; Shaw 1976).

At the same time, Mahmud ordered the Baktashi order suppressed. The principal *shaykhs* of the order were executed and some of their *tekkehs* were razed (Birge 1937:77). Between July and October 1826 the government also confiscated Bektashi property, turned these holdings into mosques, schools, and religious trusts, and gave them to the *ulema* (Levy 1971). Mahmud, like previous sultans, sought support for his repression of the Bektashi from the *ulemas*, the Sunni religious leaders. The *ulemas* justified the suppression of the sect as a means of defending Islamic orthodoxy. In reality, of course, the *ulemas* merely wanted to maintain their spiritual supremacy and the power that went with it.[5]

Once the new army was organized and effectively under his direct control, Mahmud was less dependent on the *ulemas* for support of his modernization plans. He began to reduce their influence within the army units. Because of these new government policies the *ulema*, mainly from the lower ranks, withdrew their support from the sultan and some of them incited popular revolts against the government (Levy 1971).

The Bektashi orders were officially reestablished twenty-three years later (in 1849) and continued to exist until the Republic of Turkey abolished all dervish *tekkehs* in November 1925 (Barnes 1974). How were the Bektashi able to survive the intense period of government repression under the later sultans so as to be able to surface again in 1849? The Bektashi avoided total destruction by extending and strengthening the secrecy strategies already employed by the sects. Through the strategy of dissimulation (*takiye*) the Bektashi covered up their heterodox beliefs by claiming adherence to orthodox ones (Birge 1937:17), and only the most trustworthy members of the *tekkeh* learned anti-Sunnite doctrines.

As we have indicated, each novitiate was required to learn certain paths, special action, and behavior necessary to achieve mystic union with Allah. Such mystic knowledge was structured into levels. The novitiate was led by degrees to reject the orthodox religion of Islam and accept the mystic beliefs of the Bektashi order. These beliefs, which were not in accord with orthodox teachings, were taught to the novice (*murid*) with great care. The loyalty of the novice was tested: he was taught false secrets to test his powers of reserve and reticence (Birge 1937:98; Garnett 1912:97; Brown 1968:208). Such secrets, told to the novitiates by the *shaykh*, were transmitted to them under a fearful penalty for betrayal (Garnett 1912:101; Brown 1968). Only novices that had passed the tests to their power of reticence learned the "darker" secrets of the order (Garnett 1912; Birge 1937). At all meetings guards were posted at the doors to prevent outsiders from intruding (Brown 1968:206).

By relying on such strategies for secrecy the Bektashi (and other dervish orders) have prevailed, even to the present, against the attempts by the Turkish government to destroy them.

Thus, the nature of the power relations between the Bektashi and the Ottoman state depended, in part, on the strategic interests of the state in tolerating or suppressing the sect but also, in part, on the ability of the sect to deter government attacks either through alliances with other power groups (e.g., Janissaries) or by means of information-control strategies. However, as these historic dynamics unfolded, the power relations between the Bektashi and the state were rearranged and readjusted.

SUMMARY

As the Ottoman empire expanded, internal and external contradictions worked on each other. There were two unresolved primary contradictions that constantly threatened state stability: First, Ottoman control over a large empire required the development of a political hierarchy loyal to the centralized authority but financed in such a way that the tax burdens on the peasantry would not alienate them or give local administrators the power to amass their own wealth and independent political authority. Second, to maintain a steady source of state revenue the Ottoman rulers had to control the economy in the face of the growing power of merchant capitalists and commercial agriculturalists who began to pursue their own economic objectives independent of government authority and contrary to state interests.

Efforts by the Ottoman sultans to deal with the economic and political crises generated by these basic contradictions led to state-sponsored conjunctive moments that ultimately produced secondary contradictions manifested as intra- and interclass conflict at various structural fault lines. The displacement of the *sipahis*, the mainstay of the early Ottoman agrarian system, and their replacement by tax-farmers and others only interested in immediate short-term tax revenues, and with no long-term commitment to peasant welfare or land conservation, ultimately led to a decline in farm production. The peasants were either forced into the hands of money lenders and speculators or driven off the land entirely. Local administrators began to amass wealth and political power. The central government ceased to exercise any check or control over agriculture and village affairs, which were left to the powers of the local potentates.

The process of state-power decentralization had an overdeterminant effect on the state functions. The decline in revenues collected by the central authority threatened the ability of the state to reproduce their power. The state's political and ideological functions could not be carried out effectively and localized power centers emerged to challenge state authority.

The Janissaries, together with their Bektashi associates, represented one of many structural foci at which these crises manifested themselves. An unanticipated composite effect of the Ottomans' creating the Janissary corps was the development of a powerful military force on which the sultans depended for the maintainance of political order, but which increasingly undermined state authority by its involvement in court affairs. Janissary alliance with the Bektashi sect, whose Shiite religious doctrines challenged the orthodox Sunnite religion of the Ottomans, also caused state rulers concern. Although the Bektashi were Shiites and thus hostile to the Sunni doctrine of the Ottoman rulers, the early sultans tolerated the Bektashi order. This acceptance was largely due to the circumstances under which the Janissaries were incorporated into the Bektashi order. Since the early sultans depended on the Janissaries to extend their power into the provinces, they were forced to accept the Bektashi, whom the Janissaries relied on for spiritual leadership. This basic contradiction was ultimately resolved when, because of historic circumstances, the Janissaries and their Bektashi associates became expendable to the Ottoman state.

To maintain control over their large empire the Ottoman sultans needed to establish a political and military organization whose officers were loyal to the sultans alone. However, the early political and military structures that the Ottoman empire established led to developments unanticipated by the rulers—circumstances that began to undermine their power.

Contradictions emerged between the Ottoman interests and those of the *timariots*. By appointing slaves to posts in the bureaucracy and military, the Ottoman sultans acquired more direct control over their political officials. Among these appointees were the *sipahi* who, unlike the Turkomans, were dependent on the government for the land which supported them. By giving *timars* to the *sipahi* the sultans were able to create a military force more loyal to the state than found among the nomads of the *ghaza* frontier districts. The *sipahi* was a military body that provincial governors could use to keep order within their provinces.

However, the creation of the *sipahi* class under direct control of the governors gave the *beylerbeys* a potential power base from which to challenge state control. To deal with this problem the sultans needed a strong and efficient military corps to which they alone could issue orders. The Janissaries filled this need: only the sultan had direct control over them. The Janissary corps was financed through the state treasury and given the most modern weapons. The sultan posted them to newly conquered areas to serve as a police force. They also formed an important part of the imperial armies.

The great dependency of the sultans on the Janissary corps forced these Sunni leaders to tolerate the Shiite Baktashi, on whom the Janissaries relied for spiritual leadership. Of course, there were some sultans who felt that by supporting the mystic orders, including the Bektashi, they could better control the Turkoman tribes among which these mystic orders had great influence. In any case, the Bektashi, who were hostile to Sunni beliefs, felt free to expand their sect relatively safe from persecution.

However, the basic structural contradiction within the Ottoman political system, namely the inability of the Ottoman rulers to create an administrative system that did not operate to undermine their own power, was not resolved by the creation of the Janissary corps. The Janissary force increased to such a large size by the end of the sixteenth century that the Ottoman state was forced to give the Janissaries *timar* grants as a means of economic support. These policies, however, had long-term composite effects that operated to undermine state control over the Janissaries. Very soon the Janissaries came to constitute a wealthy class independent of the sultan's control. In some provinces they consolidated enough political power to appropriate state revenues for themselves. Although the Janissaries undermined the Ottoman hegemony over many of its territories, the Ottoman did not move against them because the Janissaries controlled modern weaponry, on which the military power of the Ottoman empire depended.

The Janissaries created even more political instability by entering into court intrigues. They supported the contenders who best served their economic interests. Being an armed force, they could eliminate sultans or *vezirs* who opposed their interests, placing a new contender who was more to their liking on the throne. Fearing their power, sultans acceded to the Janissaries' economic demands. Thus, political contradictions within the Ottoman state led to a conflict between the interests of the Janissaries and those of the Ottoman sultans.

However, later crises in the political economy of the Ottoman empire undermined the political power of the Janissaries, eventually leading to their destruction and to attacks by Ottoman rulers on the Bektashi as well.

Efforts by the Ottoman state to maintain economic stability by imperial expansion eventually created the circumstances that generated a profound economic crisis. Ottoman expansion ceased by the sixteenth century. During the seventeenth, eighteenth, and early nineteenth centuries the Ottoman imperial domain began to shrink. As a consequence of these developments the Ottoman state suffered a decline in its traditional sources of revenue.

The economic crisis faced by the Ottomans in the late sixteenth century was the result of a combination of interrelated factors, including the growth in military expenditures, a population increase in Anatolia, price inflation, and shifts in the international trade routes. Expansion of opportunities for merchant capital activities stimulated petty-commodity production on individual farms and feudalized cash-crop farms, which became independent of government control.

To meet the economic crisis, the Ottoman government undertook a series of reforms that did not resolve the structural contradictions but, instead, created more political instability. The Ottomans extended tax-farms to include the collection of agricultural taxes, taxes on *vakil* estates and on *timar* lands. New extraordinary taxes were imposed on peasants while the special taxes on non-Muslim populations were increased.

This new system of surplus extraction increased the exploitation of the peasantry. Usury accelerated the destruction of the free status of the peasantry through debt bondage. Peasants became enserfed or functioned as sharecroppers on the *ciftliki*, the commercial farming estates. Others turned to banditry and brigand gangs ravaged the countryside. Along with peasants, ex-*sipahi*, unemployed *softas*, displaced army irregulars, and army deserters joined these bands. Deserting army officers sometimes provided the leadership that wielded these groups into large armies threatening Ottoman control over certain areas of Anatolia.

Changes in the Ottoman society's infrastructure ultimately undermined the Janissary power base. The larger Janissary corps no longer provided the government with suitable military force to repress banditry and rebellion. The Ottoman policy of supporting this large force with *timars* and tax-farms gave rise to a military class ill trained for war. Janissary interests became more allied with the new local aristocracy, the *ayan* class, whose goal was to amass wealth.

The European powers presented both economic and military challenges to Ottoman hegemony. To preserve Ottoman power, reform-minded sultans wanted to modernize Ottoman institutions including the military. To do so they had to make some basic institutional changes such as in the old military structure. However, the Janissaries, still powerful because of their control of modern weapons, resisted these reforms. The sultans now felt that the Janissaries were expendable, for they did not help the Ottomans in their attempt to reestablish state power but actually undermined it, and their military contribution had become minimal. The Janissary ties with the Bektashi dervishes gave the government a religious justification to eliminate both groups, since the orthodox *ulema* priesthood found Sufist sects, such as the dervishes, dangerous to state interests. Since the Janissaries were expendable, so were the Bektashi. Mahmud II eliminated the Janissaries in one massive bloodbath with the help of his newly formed regular army force and, with the help of the *ulema*, tried to suppress the Baktashi as well. The Bektashi survived these attacks and maintained their power until the formation of the Turkish Republic because they elaborated the art of secrecy so successfully that they continued to operate in the face of Ottoman opposition. The leaders' control over certain mystical knowledge held forth the opportunity to novitiates to achieve great sanctity and with it great power. This was enough incentive for most members of the lower orders to adhere to the secrecy norms and the tests of loyalty required of them. The power of the *tekkeh shaykh* was absolute, and the members bowed to his will.

To avoid total destruction the Bektashi leaders not only employed threats against possible disloyal disciples within their ranks, but also concealed the true nature of their religious beliefs except from the most faithful. The *shaykhs* reinforced initiates' commitment to the order with a thorough indoctrination. Outsiders were carefully excluded from religious rituals, which took place in guarded buildings that gave no evidence that they were religious structures. Thus, the Bektashi reacted to government coercive force with varied power resources sufficient to prevent the Ottoman rulers from completely destroying the order.

Thus, the destruction of the Janissaries eliminated a political buffer that had kept the Bektashi safe from hostile government actions. As a result of government repression, the Bektashi order was forced to make structural changes in order to survive. In effect, the Bektashi sect became a secret society that instituted information-control strategies to avoid complete destruction. Intense internal discipline, along with secrecy and deception, enabled the Bektashi to prevail in spite of government efforts to eliminate the sect completely. Under these conditions government power over them was limited. By resisting government efforts to destroy them, Bektashi demonstrated their own power.

The Bektashi provide us with a case study of a secret order whose power relations with the state were rearranged and readjusted as the emerging structural contradictions within the Ottoman empire placed the sultans and the Bektashi, together with their Janissary allies, on different sides of the structural fault lines. This conflict of interest led to attempts by the Ottoman rulers to eradicate both the Bektashi and the Janissaries. To survive, the Bektashi had to draw upon existing political resources as well as create new ones. They evolved a structure of defense (or conjunctive moments) that depended on information control, which seems to have been their prime strategy. And it worked! They survived the Ottoman assault on their sect.

4

White Lotus Secret Society Activity during the Ch'ing Dynasty

THE MING COLLAPSE

Only through the use of a dialectical model can we develop an adequate theoretical perspective by which to understand secret society dynamics within the context of the wider sociopolitical and economic changes that took place within Ch'ing China. A dialectical analysis of White Lotus sect activity requires that we ask the following questions: What were the structural contradictions in Ch'ing society and what crises did they provoke? What contribution did these crises make to an increase in the incapacity of the Ch'ing state to function normally and/or inspire sufficient loyalty and support? What was the relation between White Lotus sect activity and the crises produced by the basic contradictions? Why did the White Lotus sectarianism, with or without political dimensions, constitute a threat to the stability of the Ch'ing dynasty? In what ways did White Lotus activity contribute to the intensification of the structural contradictions? And, why, in spite of government repression, did White Lotus sectarianism survive in one form or another until, at least, the end of the Ch'ing dynasty?

The successful Manchu conquest of Ming China[1] led to the establishment of the Ch'ing dynasty at Peking in 1644. Later the Manchu armies captured Nanking in 1645 and adjoining areas of south China shortly thereafter. By 1681 the Manchus had conquered all of China (Eberhard 1966:266–71).

The crises that weakened Ming rule sufficiently to enable the Manchus to conquer China were the result of structural contradictions similar to the ones that, in turn, made Ch'ing rule difficult. These problems were ones inherent in the Chinese agrarian society under both dynasties. Therefore, to demonstrate the continuity in structural features between the Ming and the Ch'ing which precipitated structural contradictions of a similar nature, I will briefly outline some of the problems faced by the Ming government that led to its fall, but which persisted during the Ch'ing dynasty.

Within Ming China the political and military superstructures had an over-determinant impact on the economic base such that efforts by the government to reproduce these superstructures led to an erosion of revenues. To reproduce the political superstructure the Ming were dependent on the peasantry and segments of the gentry for tax revenues. However, the peasantry and the tax-liable factions of the gentry class constituted a hostile environment for the state, resistant to the efforts of the government to increase their taxes. This was the basic contradiction that created the fault lines along which the Ming dynasty came into conflict with the subordinate classes. These conflicts were reflected throughout the political, economic, and ideological subsystems. The conjunctive moments initiated by the government to deal with these crises merely exacerbated the problems and resulted in increased unrest, declining production, and loss of further state tax revenues. These changes in the economic base had an overdeterminant effect on the political structure, making it more difficult for the Ming to maintain internal order and defend the state from the Manchu attacks.

In the later period of Ming rule the financial burdens on the Ming dynasty were heavy. Government treasuries were emptied because of court extravagance as well as the large pension demands made by royal descendants (Chan 1982:263, 30). Ethnic succession wars, aboriginal revolts, pirate activity, border wars, as well as sect-inspired uprisings kept the Ming armies involved in expensive military activities (Chan 1982:330, 340, 153; Rossabi 1979:186; Zurndorfer 1983:310–11; Parsons 1970:xiv; Wakeman 1985 vol. 1:30).[2]

Ming attempts to finance the increased demands of their large military forces created new economic problems. The government minted copper coins to finance their war with Japan, but the aftermath of this practice led directly or indirectly to increased inflationary pressures (Chan 1982:285). The Ming leaders also organized the *wei-so* system, which enabled military garrisons to support themselves in part by farming and in part by selling salt to merchants in return for grain supplies (Chiang 1983:20; Chan 1982:41–42). This system broke down when the corruption of military leaders led to abuses and when the government failed to pay the soldiers their full salaries (Chan 1982:189). The government was forced to hire mercenaries to bring the garrisons up to strength because many soldiers, especially on the northern borders, deserted to the Manchu armies or rebel groups (Eberhard 1966:268); Goldstone 1988:113).

Government efforts to increase revenues with new taxes merely intensified monetary problems for the Ming.[3] In A.D. 1381 the Ming initiated the Yellow Registers system, which combined the functions of the household register and a taxation ledger. A territorial unit of 110 households was set up, called a *li*. The ten richest households were chosen to be the *li*-captain households, with the other remaining hundred households to be the *jia*-head households, with a *jia* chosen to administer every ten households. One *li*-captain and ten *jia*-heads served turns in decennial rotation (Yukio 1984:283). Both the *li*-captains and the *jia*-heads were not only responsible for tax collection but also for maintaining the productive activities of the community, necessary if taxes were to be collected (Naohiro 1984:263). The leader's duties also included the provision of adequate local defense forces to defend the community against bandits and rebels.

The *li*-captains were, however, usually members of the wealthy gentry. It was in the interest of these gentry families to avoid taxes and transfer these tax burdens to the less powerful peasantry (Naohiro 1984; Beattie 1979:298).

The gentry families put land in the name of tax exempt lineages who had "official" status or acquired land outside the jurisdiction of registration (Yukio 1984:299). The gentry also avoided labor service by paying proxies to work for them (Yukio 1984:26). The poor peasant was at a great disadvantage compared to the gentry. To pay taxes they often borrowed money from the gentry at usurious rates. Many lost their land when they failed to pay off the loan. In this way the gentry increased their land holdings (Masatoshi 1984:209).

The gentry was not the only class that found ways to avoid excessive taxes. Descendants of farmers of small- and middle-sized holdings abandoned farms for commercial enterprises (Masatoshi 1984:182). Fearing increased taxes, poor peasants deserted their land to join rebel or bandit bands (Chan 1982:229, 330, 313). Unworked land led to a decline in production.

In south and central China, from the late Ming period onward, there was a dual ownership system of land tenure. Surface (or soil) and field (or subsoil) rights could be owned by two people. To avoid taxes peasant families turned over topsoil rights to the gentry who, because of their official status, were exempt from paying taxes. The peasants continued to work the land but paid rent to the gentry landlord (Yukio 1984:30; Atwell 1988:627). In cases where the gentry or merchants secured these topsoil rights as security for a loan, the peasant's rent was applied against his debt (Masatoshi 1984:209–10).

These internal financial pressures were made more severe by economic problems resulting from both natural disasters and decline in exports. In the late sixteenth century and early seventeenth century, floods and droughts destroyed harvests and created food shortages in some provinces. These poor harvests drove up the price of rice so that people lacked sufficient funds to pay for food (Atwell 1988:589).

By the late eleventh century, China's exports of silk, cotton, and porcelain to Japan and the Philippines brought increased silver to China. However, during the reign of T'ien Chi, there was a sharp drop in bullion exports from the New World which reduced the level of Sino-Spanish trade. The decline in silver also had an inflationary effect on food prices (Atwell 1988:603–4).

The Ming emperors' increased reliance on eunuchs as tax collectors tended to decrease revenues rather than improve collection. Eunuchs treated their powers to levy taxes as a personal privilege to use as they saw fit. Eunuchs profited so immensely from tax stations along the highways and waterways that trade in many areas halted, silk production declined, and the price of goods soared (Masatoshi 1984:170–72). The eunuchs kept about three times as much tax as they turned over to the government (Chan 1982:1820).

Ming revenue-generating policies led to widespread unrest, revolt, and insurrection. Banditry, White Lotus–inspired rebellions, miners' revolts, urban riots, and large-scale rebel movements were the varied consequences of these new economic demands on the population (Wakeman 1985, vol. 1:226–27, 429–30; Chan 1982:315–16, 325, 340; Zurndorfer 1983:307–10; Yuan 1979:280; Masatoshi 1984:203; Parsons 1970; Atwell 1988:609–10, 623–26).[4] The military cost of repressing such disturbances added new financial pressures on government resources (Masatoshi 1984:170), and usually the military was ineffective in suppressing interregional rebellions, since many military commanders were concerned with unrest that occurred within their specific region and that region alone (Chan 1982:344).

In the late Ming rule there emerged a political faction called the Donglin party, members of which were from diverse backgrounds although many were from small- and medium-size peasant families whose fortunes had declined as a result of increased government taxation. The Donglin faction wanted the government to initiate programs which would support such peasant families, but Donglin enemies (the eunuch faction) at the imperial court soon succeeded in destroying their influence and power (Masatoshi 1984:181–89).

Thus, the structural contradictions within the Ming social formation and within the larger social system of which it was a part (interstate relationships) created the crises for which the Ming rulers sought solutions. The conjunctive moments initiated by the rulers to solve these problems merely pushed the empire into deeper crises.

The nature of the structural contradictions that characterized the Ming state at the time of the Manchu conquest give a preview of the internal problems that the Ch'ing were to face when they established imperial control in China. The essential problem faced by the Ming state was the fact that overall revenue was basically fixed, while expenses, especially military ones, continued to rise. Military expenses were later increased by military campaigns against bandits and sectarian rebels. These military expenses added to the already excessive cost of maintaining the court, the bureaucracy, and the noble class. Ming attempts to increase state revenues created inflation and also led to covert as well as overt resistance on the part of the gentry and peasantry. By avoiding taxes the gentry shifted the tax burdens to the peasantry and commercial sectors. The powerless segments of the population either abandoned their land or turned to various forms of revolt and rebellion. These reactions not only reduced productive capacity and Ming ability to collect taxes, but also increased the military costs that stemmed from campaigns to suppress such social unrest (Goldstone 1988:144). Underpaid armies seized crops from peasants in areas in which they operated, thereby fomenting more unrest and rebellion (Wakeman 1985, vol. 1:234). Insufficient funds to pay armies motivated some commanders to joint either the Manchu or the rebel forces (Eberhard 1966:768).

RISE OF THE MANCHU

Before the Manchu conquest of China, the center of Manchu power was in the Tungus state of Ju-Chen, located on the east border of the Chinese basin in Chiang-pai. The Manchu Khans extended Manchu power over Manchuria and then invaded northern China, in 1629 and 1630, eventually capturing Beijing (Peking) in 1644 (Michael 1965:37; Eberhard 1966:266).

To administer the newly conquered areas the Manchu created military organizations called "banners" distinguished by their different colored emblems. The banners were divided into "battalions" which were subdivided into components of 300 warrior households. Initially there were four Manchu banners, but by 1614 there were eight. Eight Mongol banners were added in 1634 and eight Chinese banners in 1642 (Feuerwerker 1976:5; Wakeman 1985, vol. 1:53–54; Gernet 1972:464). Later remnants of the Ming forces, which surrendered during the Manchu siege of Beijing (Peking), were incorporated into a special military banner called the "Green Standard" (Wakeman 1985, vol. 1:480).

Each Manchu banner was given to a prince of the imperial clan (*beile*);

beiles were in effect feudal lords. The banners under their control were civil as well as military organizations controlling land on which the warriors, their families, clerks, artisans, and serfs lived (Michael 1965:60–66; Feuerwerker 1976:5).

The *beiles* maintained their power by rewarding their clan followers with booty from raids into Chinese territory. Prisoners of war became serfs who worked the banner lands or served as artisans and house servants (Wakeman 1985, vol. 1:301–4). The Manchu found it necessary, however, as expanding states always do, to limit the powers of the local leaders and to establish an administrative hierarchy loyal to the centralized authority. By means of this political bureaucracy the Manchu were able to mobilize resources and labor, institute legal controls, and communicate their wishes to the regional populations.

Chinese officials who deserted to the Manchu cause were usually rewarded with land and serfs and became influential members of the Manchu state (Michael 1965). Under their influence, the Manchu *khans* began to restrict the powers of the *beiles* by demanding more war booty be placed in the *khans'* own treasury, diminishing the *beiles'* personal authority over their own banners (Wakeman 1985, vol. 1:201) and by excluding the princes from any administrative office of great responsibility (Michael 1965:43–44).

The Chinese advisors worked to further bureaucratic development at the expense of feudal structures (Michael 1965:75), and they copied the Ming governing organization (Roth 1979:21). Responding to Chinese advice, the *khans* organized state administration into ministries (*pu*). Ministerial heads came from the imperial clan with Manchu, Mongol, and Chinese officials acting as directors and advisors (Michael 1965:76–77).

Chinese collaborators provided the administrative expertise that enabled the Manchu to set up effective Ch'ing governmental control as their armies brought more provinces of China under Manchu rule. The Chinese provided the core of experienced officials to supervise the higher- and middle-level bureaucracy (Wakeman 1985, vol. 1:446–47).[5]

Thus, as many newly forming states have done, the Manchu found it expedient to fuse the loyal ruling-class elements from the conquered Ming state with the emerging ruling class of the Manchu empire, thereby separating the disloyal class factions from the newly established bureaucracy.

CH'ING IMPERIAL POLITICAL STRUCTURE

At the center of Ch'ing governmental power was the emperor, surrounded by relatives and other trusted councilors who had been granted noble titles. Royal clansmen were given land, residences, silver, and rice allowances. Tens of thousands of acres in northern China were reserved for the imperial benefices (Kuhn 1970:8). Most of the fertile land around Beijing (the capital) was distributed to Manchu princes and banner troops. In cities outside Beijing (Peking) the military garrisons expropriated land from Chinese residents (Wakeman 1985, vol. 1:279). Chinese farmers were relocated on poorer land and after a one year's grace period were expected to contribute corvee, taxes, and rent (Wakeman 1985, vol. 1:472).

Below the emperor were the scholar-officials who, excluding Manchu bureaucrats and Chinese collaborators, had achieved higher degrees in state civil service exams. Their ranks extended down to the level of the district magistrates. At the higher levels of the Ch'ing bureaucracy the Manchu expanded their earlier synarchical structure, a dual government system with Manchus alongside Chinese in every office, the Manchu always being in a superior position (Wakeman 1975b:19; Eberhard 1966:270; Lui 1979:26).

The Ch'ing divided the empire into eighteen provinces, which were subdivided in turn into circuits (two or more prefectures), prefectures, and districts (*hsien*). The government appointed no officials for any local governmental area smaller than the *hsien* (Ch'u 1962:3; Kuhn 1970:24; Van Der Sprenkel 1967:52).

By the middle of the eighteenth century the Manchus had incorporated the Ming *li-chia* system into a decimal system of organization called the *pao-chia*. Under this system there was a registration of households in groups of ten, fifty, and so forth. The able-bodied men of a *pao* (about 1,000 households) formed a local militia (Kuhn 1970:50; Davis 1971:24). It was through this system that the local gentry carried out tax collection, organized local defense forces, and administered public works projects (Lapidus 1975:29).

CH'ING'S HEGEMONIC EFFORTS AND THEIR CONTRADICTIONS

As in all state systems, the Ch'ing emperors could not rely on force alone to maintain order or to assure the loyalty of the political office holders within their empire. They had to indoctrinate the administrative officers with political values that would assure their loyalty. To achieve this end the Ch'ing rulers required that the government officials master the Confucian classics and demonstrate their knowledge on state-administered exams.

Since leisure time was necessary for the many years of study for exams, candidates for higher degrees largely came from the gentry class of wealthy landholders (Van Der Sprenkel 1967:56; Fairbank 1967:47–48). The gentry lineages devoted considerable wealth to providing a classical education for their children in order that the children might pass the various exams and thus perpetuate the privileged position of clan members from generation to generation (Lui 1979:11). These candidates also were given financial support by friends, as well as at academies at which they studied. Once the successful candidates were appointed to official posts within the government they used their ties with high officials to seek favors for families, relatives, friends, and academies (Ch'u 1962:171).

However, in spite of Ch'ing anticipations, the examination system did not create a class of gentry officials who were totally loyal to the state. Academies at which the gentry scholars studied the classics often were poorly run, giving their students only superficial exposure to the Confucian literature. In some cases rather unorthodox versions of Confucianism were taught (Hsiao 1960:250–52); Woodside 1990:770). Through graft and bribery mediocre scholars passed exams with high honors and thereby were able to gain important government positions while highly competent scholars might not have achieved such recognition (Hsiao 1960:248). Many gentry scholars became frustrated when, due to a surplus of successful candidates for governmental offices, they were unable to join the privileged circle of gentry officials.

Due to such frustrations, some disenchanted scholars were motivated to join rebel movements or help organize tax revolts. To counter these threats the Ch'ing government enacted regulations that prevented small groups of scholars from organizing public meetings (Hsiao 1960:243–44). As Hsiao has observed, "the situation hardly favored the production of scholars who had a genuine faith in Confucianism or a true respect for the imperial government" (1960:248).

A basic contradiction in a social formation exists when the central state authority depends on the services of a class which, by nature of its structural position, must find ways to resist the authority of the state over it. The relationship between the gentry and the Ch'ing state was one of much mutual dependency and antagonism. The gentry needed the imperial state, for it was through the state's examination system and bureaucratic structure that the gentry obtained their degrees, titles, and the privileges on which their local status was based. Gentry with degrees and/or titles were exempted from labor service and their lands were kept off the property tax rolls (Wakeman 1975b:43). The state needed the gentry officials to maintain order and collect taxes at the local levels (Feuerwerker 1976:79). In fact, the initial success that the Manchu had in establishing control over conquered areas was due to the local elite who secured order and organized public projects (e.g., reclamation, irrigation, repair of public buildings) even before Ch'ing magistrates arrived (Zurndorfer 1983:313–14).[6] However, the gentry was in opposition to the imperial government when its policies threatened their clan, family, or factional interests (Lapidus 1975:27). Heavy governmental financial demands on gentry officials forced them to make illegal levies on the peasantry in order to supplement their incomes. These excessive "customary fees" levied by the gentry and other government agents on the peasantry created peasant mistrust of the government and diminished potential government revenues.

The moderate tax policies, initiated by the Manchu rulers when they conquered China, could not be maintained (Gernet 1972:481). Public and private burdens forced tax increases. Such new tax levies were made necessary by the increased cost of maintaining the imperial class and the court and by the military costs of wars, revolts, and secret society–led rebellions. The Manchus fought the attempt by the Malmuk Mongols to set up an independent state in Manchuria (Eberhard 1966:284.)[7] They also fought Tibetan rebels in western Szechuan, Moslem rebels in Kansu, and aboriginal rebels in Taiwan (Gernet 1972:490). While conducting costly campaigns against the southern Ming, the Ch'ing armies had to fight the rebel armies of Li Tzu-Cheng and Chang Hsien-Chung, which continued to create political instability in the north even after the Ming were driven southward (Rossabi 1979).[8]

The Ch'ing also expended scarce government funds on the suppression of the White Lotus and Triad inspired revolts. The White Lotus societies of China prophesied a future millennium, predictions that helped trigger many rebellions against the state. This was the main religious group involved in the Chinese peasant movements from the fourteenth through the nineteenth centuries (Chu 1967). During the Ch'ing dynasty, the White Lotus sect led rebellions in Honan and Shantung (1774), Honan (1776) and (1788), Hupei, Honan, Shenhsi, Kansu, and Szechuan (1796), Chili, and Shantung (1813). Later, in the nineteenth and early twentieth centuries, members of White Lotus sects were associated with the Nien Rebellion (1851–98) and the Boxer Uprising (1900) (Chu 1967). The anti-Manchu Triad secret societies led rebellions in Kuanghsi (1814), Formosa (1787), Canton (1817), and Hunan (1832) (Davis 1971:61). The nine years of fighting rebel forces in five provinces (1796–1804) cost the government 120 million *taels* of silver (Feuerwerker 1975:7).

However, the Ch'ing state employed methods other than direct coercion to maintain control at the local levels within the empire. The government required community attendance at local lectures at which Confucian scholars were supposed to stress key Confucian values that helped reinforce imperial authority (e.g., respect for elders and superiors, condemnation of unlawful, antisocial conduct). In many cases, however, lecturers took the role of policemen and tax collectors, giving only superficial consideration of the Confucian texts if they did so at all (Hsiao 1960:202–3).

The imperial government also sponsored state rituals, which aimed at giving a symbolic reinforcement to the legitimacy of Ch'ing authority. Through such local sacred ceremonies the Ch'ing state hoped to buttress its power by convincing the peasants and townspeople to submit to state authority, but most worshipers viewed the rites as a means to gain personal advantages for themselves and their families. They paid little attention to the political themes dramatized in the rituals (Hsiao 1960:226).

The inability of the Ch'ing state to successfully indoctrinate the Chinese populace with political doctrines that reinforced the legitimacy of its rule placed limits on its infrastructural power, thus restricting the state's ability to penetrate the social formation and effectively implement its decisions (Mann 1986:169–70).

Increased taxation came at a time when the productive capacity of the Ch'ing state was not keeping pace with the increased demands of the population. The new taxes also were added onto the already heavy customary levies made by the gentry and the officialdom. There were heavy financial demands on gentry families, which included payment of student fees, degree-holder subsidies, and examination expenses along with poor relief, support for the disabled and ill clan members, and the military costs of suppressing local rebellions (Wakeman 1966:34). Having been given the responsibility to collect local taxes, it is not surprising that many gentry tax collectors collected higher taxes from the peasants than the legal tax quotas they were supposed to pass on to the government (Lui 1979:151; Ch'u 1962:186; Lapidus 1975:29).

Once in office the successful gentry candidate who had obtained his higher degrees through the help of clansmen and friends wanted to pay off his debts to them. Such officials used every opportunity to amass wealth to repay their obligations (Gernet 1972:493). It was customary for provincial officials to levy customary fees and/or surcharges which were added to official tax quotas. Capital officials also received gifts from lower-level officials (Lui 1979:2–3). Some of this extra income also went to cover official expenses that the low government salaries were totally inadequate to finance (Lui 1979:2–3).[9]

Being on temporary appointment to districts, magistrates depended on clerks and runners (underlings) to carry out official business.[10] Since magistrates had to remit taxes in full to the central government, these local government agents were poorly paid. Such underlings obtained most of their income from "customary" levies such as fees, fines, gifts, bribes (Ch'u 1962:45–46; Feuerwerker 1976:19). Thus there was "built-in" corruption at all levels of the Ch'ing state (Lui 1979).

Not only did the customary fees cut into potential government revenues, but peasant and gentry strategies to avoid the regular tax burdens also undermined the government revenue collection. Peasants avoided both labor service and land taxes by turning their land over to a wealthy landowner and thereby becoming a tenant or serf. In turn the landowner put the land under registration of an "official" household, avoiding taxes in this way (Atsushi 1984:360).

Government fiscal resources were also threatened by outlaw bands in some local areas. Many bandit bands, organized as secret societies, demanded protection money from the peasants who were not members and even levied taxes in areas under their control. Whole peasant villages joined the secret societies to avoid some of the bandits' levies, as did local officials (Wakeman 1966:119–22). By obtaining tax revenues for themselves, the secret societies eroded the rural tax base of the Ch'ing state.

Thus, new military demands along with government corruption, extravagance, and inefficiency wasted government resources, necessitating further tax burdens. This created new structural fault lines along which covert and overt forms of resistance to state authority by the peasants and other disenchanted class factions took place. Such crises revealed one basic contradiction between the political superstructure and the economic base: the overall revenue of the state was basically fixed while its expenses, especially military ones, continued to rise.

These contradictions were accentuated by Ch'ing demographic policies, which had composite effects on the economic base. Between 1600 and 1850, China's population tripled, from 150 million to 430 million (Wakeman 1975a:17). The government encouraged population increase in order to improve production and increase the tax base by forcing the movement of peasants to unoccupied frontier areas. Settlement of these frontiers also served as a buffer against enemy raids (Nakamura and Matao 1982:259). As peasant farms reached their optimum size, the peasants increased the size of their families to enlarge the labor force and thereby intensify production. Gentry lineages also encouraged families to grow in order to increase the size and thus the influence and power of the lineage and clan (Nakamura and Matao 1982:255). But this increase in population ultimately reduced the pool of farm land available and created hardship for peasant families (Kuhn 1970:9–10; Wakeman 1975b:9, 48). Increased farm production could not keep pace with the population growth. These circumstances again illustrate the dialectical relation between structures and social practices such that conjunctive moments (e.g., demographic practices) resulted in circumstances not intended by state leaders.

The Ch'ing armies proved to be ineffective in maintaining order. Control of the armies was in the hands of the board of war. This board could delegate to the provincial governors or governor generals the right to assemble provincial battalions into larger armies. But this system was cumbersome and inefficient in dealing with local disorder (Wakeman 1975b:52). The smaller, dispersed garrisons lacked the mobility to snuff out the frequent local revolts (Kuhn 1970). Moreover, the army was not sufficiently financed. Thus, local garrisons dispatched to quell local disturbances created local resentment because the army forced the local population to provision them (Wakeman 1966; Feuerwerker 1975, 1976).

To organize defense the local elite organized militia. To finance these local militia the gentry set up centralized bureaus to collect rents from the clans and to coordinate local militia activities. These bureaus levied tolls, called *likin*, on articles of commerce coming into district capitals or market towns (Wakeman 1966; Feuerwerker 1975, 1976).

However a protracted crisis usually required employment of mercenaries and this necessitated substantial expenditures by the local elite (Kuhn 1970:87). Levies for militia expenses on the clans gave the gentry more incentive to avoid paying taxes and to skim tax money from the peasants. Of course increased taxes on the peasants and merchants created even more social unrest.

Commercial activity was thriving during the Ch'ing rule. However, the government's attempts to impose taxes on commercial enterprises led to the development of an alternative economy, which subverted the state's tax efforts. Merchants, for example, paid a tax to obtain a certificate entitling them to bring a specific amount of salt to be distributed in a defined market zone. The cost of this tax was passed on to the user. But the illegal trade, probably as large as the legal trade, undercut the legal salt merchant and, in turn, a source of government revenue (Feuerwerker 1976:93; Lapidus 1975:29; Chiang 1983). Salt and opium smugglers utilized secret societies to further their economic objectives (Unger 1975:911).

Thus, the interrelated contradictions within the Ch'ing social formation and the wider social system of which it was a part (the interstate system) produced the crises that were manifest as conflicts at various structural fault lines present in Ch'ing society. To deal with these crises the Ch'ing dynasty initiated conjunctive moments that brought about structural changes in the political, religious, and ideological subsystems (structural moments). The combination of changes in these subsystems had an overdeterminant impact both on the superstructure and the economic base. As a result of these changes new contradictions arose, probably unanticipated by the Ch'ing, which produced more conflict between the state and the peasantry as well as other alienated class factions. How these classes or class factions reacted to the new crises depended on the nature of the power resources available to them. However, the conflicts between the state and opposition classes or class factions were reflected throughout the economic, political, and ideological subsystems.

Thus, Ch'ing efforts to resolve the basic contradictions in the social formation produced secondary contradictions that negated the original solutions. Ultimately these composite effects made it more difficult for the Ch'ing dynasty to maintain control over the empire because decentralized power centers began to develop (e.g., secret religious sects, bandit gangs, ethnic revolts). The White Lotus sect represented one focus at which these emerging conflicts were manifested. The White Lotus constituted one form of collective effort by some peasants as well as members of other class factions to seek a better life. In their efforts to create a new society, the White Lotus sects either challenged state authority by organizing rebellions or by spreading an alternative worldview that delegitimized the Ch'ing authority or both. In any case White Lotus sect members were guided in their objectives more often by subjective evaluations of reality than by objective ones.

The dynamics of the power relations between the state and the White Lotus were conditioned by the power resources mobilized by each of the antagonists. Through the dialectical interplay between state actions and White Lotus resistance, both parties had an overdeterminant impact on each other at different times and places.

SIGNIFICANCE OF WHITE LOTUS SECT REBELLIONS: AN OVERVIEW

The nature of opposition to Ch'ing rule varied in its forms, objectives, and tactics. Rent and tax resistance struggles, rebellions caused by natural disasters, urban riots, separatist rebellions, and ethnic disturbances did not aim at the overthrow of the Ch'ing dynasty nor to change the basic gentry-tenant relations (Crowell 1983). The people involved in these protests attacked arbitrary exactions of magistrates, inflated customary levies, corruption of clerks, inequities in tax collection, etc. (Kazumi 1984). However, many White Lotus sect and other secret societies organized rebellions aimed at changing the existing dynastic order, thereby bringing a fundamental change in government. Thus there were basic differences in the aims of rent and tax resistance struggles and those social and economic struggles organized by some secret society organizations.[11]

During the Ch'ing dynasty there were two types of rebel movements: the northern or White Lotus system, whose members were strongly imbued with religious concepts, and the southern or Triad system, which placed its stress on the revival of the golden age of the Ming dynasty (Unger 1975:92; Chesneaux 1972:5). The southern secret organizations (or lodges) had a more elaborate authority structure with several grades of officers (Davis 1971:57). This chapter will focus on the White Lotus movement.

White Lotus sects were involved in dissident protest movements from the fourteenth to the nineteenth centuries (Chu 1967:6). The most intense period of White Lotus–led rebellions against the Ch'ing was during the Chia-Ching reign (1796–1820), within which period about one-half of the government's military campaigns were directed against the White Lotus rebels (Chu 1967:124). Such sectarian (syncretic) sects as the White Lotus constituted a type of secret society that transmitted secret or esoteric *mantras* only to their own members. Secrecy was also necessary to conceal their activities because of a history of government suspicion regarding their political ends if not outright suppression of the sects themselves (Harrell and Perry 1982:287–88; Yang 1961:223; Faure 1979:20–21). The White Lotus sects began as an orthodox Buddhist association which gradually absorbed influences from Taoism and popular religion. Later these sects incorporated a Maitreya eschotology and a variety of Taoist medical and ritual practices.

The White Lotus Society (*Pai-lien*) was founded in the early eras of the southern Sung dynasty (A.D. 1127–79). This independent association of clergy and laymen was a branch of T'ien-Tai Buddhism. The sect was founded by a Buddhist monk, Mao Tzu-Yuan, who, as a result of his sectarian activities, was accused of heresy and exiled. But his ideas were perpetuated by his followers (Overmyer 1972; Chu 1967; Muramatsu 1960:247; Chan 1969:212).

The White Lotus sects syncretized many religious beliefs: Buddhism, Taoism, Manichaeanism, folk religion, and Confucianism. Popular Taoism, which had become established in eastern and western China by the end of the second century, was subject to Buddhist influence between the third and eleventh centuries A.D. Central to Buddhist belief was the worship of a deity called the Eternal and Venerable Mother, who sent Buddhas to earth to rule over the people. The Buddhist theory of three *kalpas* (eras) predicted the transition from one cycle to the next would be heralded by calamities. The Eternal Mother would give birth to Maitreya, the Buddha in the next *kalpa* (Harrell and Perry 1982:290–91; Chu 1967:67). Orthodox Buddhism stressed that Maitreya Buddha had not yet appeared but heterodox Buddhist sects stressed the imminent arrival of Maitreya and/or that the sect leaders might be incarnations of Maitreya (Chu 1967:781; Muramatsu 1960:245; Yang 1961:234). The White Lotus sects incorporated the more heterodox Buddhist beliefs into their religious doctrine. Such heterodox influences also included the Amitabha Buddhist promise of rebirth after death in a paradise of a compassionate deity. Sects influenced by Amitabha Buddhism made claims for the effectiveness of chanting the Buddha's name along with vegetarianism (Muramatsu 1960:247). Vegetarianism and restrictions on wine and killing also reflected the influence of Mahayana and Manichaean beliefs (Muramatsu 1960:247; Overmyer 1972:49).

Manichaeanism entered China no later than A.D. 644. The Manichaean doctrine taught that the cosmos was a place in which forces of light and darkness would be at war with each other until light would triumph (Chan 1969:214; Muramatsu 1960:250; Chu 1967:25). In White Lotus doctrine the Maitreya Buddha represented light, and was the Prince of Radiance. The arrival of the new *kalpa* would be initiated by a cataclysm that would destroy the nonbelievers but leave believers untouched (Yang 1961; Chan 1969:217).

However, a substratum of indigenous beliefs remained in White Lotus ideology. Both orthodox Confucianism and rebel heterodoxy shared a belief in the spirit rule of the world and the mystic effectiveness of qualified human intermediaries. Thus, the followers of the White Lotus were impressed by the abilities of some leaders to appear to work miracles and perform effective divination (Yang 1961:231; Muramatsu 1960:248–51). Both Confucianists and Taoists used mystical spells and magical practices, elements found in White Lotus practices (Chu 1967:36). The Taoist belief in the potency of the spirit is reflected in the Confucian idea that the emperor rules because of a mandate of heaven. The mandate of heaven idea, which involved the notion of a cyclical rise and fall of dynasties, merely reinforced the heterodox religious idea about the coming of Maitreya after a period of cosmic disintegration (Muramatsu 1960:252; Overmyer 1972:678).

Thus, the White Lotus sects offered disenchanted and alienated classes or class factions a cognitive system by which they could justify their opposition to the state and challenge the ideology on which the Ch'ing dynasty justified its rule. The White Lotus religion, as we have seen, incorporated elements of orthodox Confucianism (e.g., the mandate of heaven idea) that gave its members a justification for overthrowing the Ch'ing. Under these circumstances the state efforts to indoctrinate the population in those Confucian political values that provided ideological support for Ch'ing authority often had the opposite effect. Here again we find an example of a ruling-class religious ideology containing the kind of ambiguities that give opposition groups moral justification to resist or attack state power.

In part the power of the White Lotus sects rested on their appeal to the aspirations of the peasantry and to a lesser extent other alienated class segments. It was these groups that found that compliance with state demands brought few if any benefits. Under these conditions social actors begin to assess the rationality of the ruling-class ideology and begin to seek alternatives that would satisfy their aspirations and needs.

To the extent that the White Lotus sects gave concrete articulation to the values of egalitarian peasant counterculture, they gained substantial peasant support by challenging the moral framework of the elite ideology that justified the system of inequality and exploitation. The peasant counterculture values stressed a more equal distribution of resources and more equal opportunities to produce an adequate subsistence, and uprooted peasants living in the cities found comfort in a religion that offered the possibility of personal salvation (Harrell and Perry 1982:300).[12] For various reasons the White Lotus doctrine also appealed to dissatisfied craftsmen, petty merchants, magicians, fortune tellers, folk-physicians, soldiers, sailors, lower-ranking bannermen, lower-ranking literati, military and civilian officials, and court eunuchs (Chu 1967:173).

The Buddhist belief predicting the coming of a new *kalpa*, a fundamental element in the heterodox religious eschatology, brought help and solace to White Lotus members because according to White Lotus doctrine the existing calamities supposedly heralded the transition to the next, more benevolent age (Wakeman 1966:124; Overmyer 1981:162).

The sects also offered a range of opportunities for support as well as prestige not available to the average peasant. Women were included on an equal basis with men as members of the White Lotus sects. And the hierarchy of status positions in the sects provided a ladder of success available to everyone (Overmyer 1981:156–62). Through membership in the White Lotus Society the very meaning of the peasants' lives were caught up in an alternate system of symbols and rewards.

While some heretic sects were content to practice healing through magic, reading holy books, or chanting scriptural passages, the potential for rebellion was implicit in the eschatological beliefs of the White Lotus groups (Faure 1979:194; Shek 1982). In its insistence on salvation and its contempt for temporal authority, the White Lotus doctrine contradicted the essential beliefs of Confucianism, which gave support to Ch'ing dynastic rule (Chan

1969). White Lotus doctrine was preoccupied with the future age in which the ethics and institutions of the existing order would no longer be valid (Harrell and Perry 1982:292–93). The sects propagated a spiritual vision of an ideal world which it was possible for sect members to implement in the here and now (Overmyer 1972:45). The belief in a future Buddha who would bring an end to misrule seemed to reinforce the mandate of heaven concept, which required the replacement of the emperor when he lost divine approval (Weller 1982:478). Thus, the sectarian ideology provided an alternative worldview that was in conflict with the official doctrine (Harrell and Perry 1982:276; Weller 1982:464).

White Lotus sect leaders, then, maintained control over their core of followers less through direct coercion than by the processes of conversion, and shaping the beliefs, attitudes, and wants of their members (which I have identified as strategies of persuasion). Sect leaders made clear what the potential economic and political rewards for the loyal members would be once the new era arrived with the destruction of the Ch'ing dynasty. Of course the White Lotus doctrine contained an implicit threat to nonbelievers, which predicted that they would be destroyed with the arrival of the new *kalpa*. But loyalty to the sect was based less on members' fear of punishment than on the actual rewards of membership for both men and women. Participation in the sect enabled them to actualize certain egalitarian norms they were unable to realize in the wider community.

The Ch'ing government feared and persecuted the White Lotus sects precisely because the White Lotus ideology delegitimized the Ch'ing dynasty and its normative functions. There was the constant danger that the radical doctrines of the sect might be put into political practice (Shek 1982:529–30).[13] Dynastic hostility to the sect continued down to the end of the Ch'ing rule. The one central theme in the government's repression of heterodoxy is clear: its fear of the rise of organized forces driven by religious fanaticism, integrated by a system of leadership, supported by a mass following, and strengthened by contributions that would ultimately compete with legitimate centers of power. It is certainly true that otherwise quiescent sects could be provoked into insurgency by official repression (Harrell and Perry 1982:296; DeGroot 1963, vol. 1:252–53). But there were also forces internal to the sects that could propel the White Lotus to rebellion. Revolts may have been an alternative to frustrated institutionalization. The White Lotus leaders desired a territory, a space in which to realize the full benefits for their sects. The evangelical emotion of some of the sects, coupled with the inspired teaching about the coming of a new age, could have led sect members to want to extend the potential utopia to all, with themselves in a desired place of authority (Overmyer 1981:182). In part, the compulsion to seek a political route to a better life may have also been provoked by the "salvation anxiety" of people bent on finding ways to avert their own destruction when the predicted cataclysm erupted (Wakeman 1977:210).

WHITE LOTUS REBELLIONS OF 1774 AND 1813

To illustrate the general observations I have made about White Lotus activities during the Ch'ing, I will discuss two specific rebellions organized by White Lotus sects. Susan Naquin has made detailed studies of secret society rebellions in 1774 and 1813 (*Millenarian Rebellion in China*, 1976, and *Shantung Rebellion: The Wang Lun Rebellion of 1774*, 1981). I will use these two revolts to illustrate the role of such secret religious sects in Chinese rebel movements during the late eighteenth and early nineteenth centuries. These rebellions set into motion a series of events internal and external to the secret order, which in a dialectical fashion determined the power dynamics of secret society growth and decline.

In October 1774 a thousand followers of a White Lotus leader named Wang Lun attacked three county seats in the northern China plains and western Shantung province, rallied several thousand other people, and occupied the great canal city of Lin-Ch'ing. They held Lin-Ch'ing for three weeks before being crushed by the Ch'ing military force. In the autumn of 1813 the White Lotus Eight Trigrams, led by Lin Ch'ing and associated sect leaders, planned a rebellion that involved a simultaneous uprising in several cities of northern China, including Peking (Chili province). The attempt to seize the Forbidden City in Peking was thwarted, but it took the government troops three months to restore complete order in the province.

The sect members who formed the core of the rebellious groups were illiterates or semiliterates from both urban and rural backgrounds. A few were minor elites such as traders, monks, and shopkeepers. Membership in the White Lotus sects provided the peasants with a means of avoiding increased dependency on the landlords and opened up the possibility of their carving out their own autonomous niches. Disprivileged groups of this sort seem to have felt a special need for spiritual solace of sectarian beliefs. Converts developed new forms of discipline and self-sufficiency to avoid illness, achieve health, and seek alternatives for social mobility not available to them in the local community. Women found an equal status to men in the White Lotus, a position superior to their normal role. In the Eight Trigrams revolt there was a special women's battalion, "The Red Clothed Women Braves," which fought with other rebel divisions (Chu 1967:171).

Leaders and their disciples taught boxing, therapeutic yoga, meditation, and physical self-discipline. Wang Lun, leader of the 1774 rebellion, taught his followers the art of going without food for a considerable period of time by consuming small amounts of purified water. He also healed the sick by making them suppress their respiration and taught the art of boxing (De-Groot 1863, vol. 1:297).

The Eight Trigrams taught the benefits of an eight-character chant. Such knowledge was unavailable to outsiders. By making converts privy to such restricted information, the sects created stronger ties of devotion and dependency, thus increasing White Lotus power over members.

Meditational White Lotus sects set up by Wang Lun, Lin Ch'ing, and their disciples lived in scattered communities. The sect consisted of several scattered groups of believers organized into a loose chain of teachers and disciples. Members along the chain did not necessarily know one another, though their leaders might have known them. In this way certain families served as a source of religious leadership for disciples over many generations. Hereditary sect leadership in one family prevented fission (Naquin 1982).

These sects spread their influence in unique ways. Members who were boxers or healers traveled about the countryside either treating their patients or competing at market fairs with other boxers. In the course of these activities they made contact with potential converts. In this way the White Lotus sect gave disciples an opportunity to establish their own following, thereby spreading the society's influence.

The White Lotus doctrine predicted a coming *kalpa* in which the appearance of the Maitreya Buddha would bring an end of the old order thereby initiating a new millennium. Such doctrines put pressures on the sect leaders to actualize their predictions. Predictions that never occurred would produce a loss of faith and some members might defect. These millennial expectations often drove the White Lotus into uprisings, even when there was not always a large base of support among the peasants.

Such pressures were present in the sects led by Wang Lun and Lin Ch'ing. This is suggested by the fact that Wang claimed to be the reincarnation of Maitreya Buddha destined to save his followers from catastrophe initiated by the third *kalpa*. Three years before the 1774 uprising Wang had talked openly of a possible new era, predicting a forty-five-day *kalpa*. Lin Ch'ing and the other Eight Trigrams leaders claimed similar leadership roles and made similar predictions. After consulting the stars, Lin Ch'ing learned that he was chosen as the "Whitest Being," hence the "Heavenly Emperor," while his two associate sect leaders were to become "Earthly Emperor" and "Manly Emperor," respectively (Chu 1967:180). Lin Ch'ing also read in the stars the date on which the rebellion should occur (DeGroot 1863, vol. 2:421).

There is also evidence to suggest that the government had arrested the leaders of White Lotus sects a few years previous to the 1774 and 1813 White Lotus led rebellions (DeGroot 1863, vol. 1:295–96, vol. 2:409–10). Wang Lun, Lin Ch'ing, and their disciples may have feared the government would sooner or later move against their sects. By conquering provinces, they may have thought that they could establish a territorial base for their movement, thus making their sect free from government suppression. And when the broader White Lotus membership realized that their freedom to find comfort in sect activities was threatened by state interference, they would have been particularly prone to respond rebelliously.

During the actual rebellions there was a greater danger that the hardships of battle might cause disaffections. To reinforce the loyalty of sect members sect leaders stressed that only sect members would escape the destruction that the third *kalpa* would bring. Only sect members would find salvation by being physically and spiritually unified with the Eternal Mother. New recruits were pressured to demonstrate their loyalty to sect leaders by committing crimes. By so doing these members would then be more deeply involved in the rebel cause.

Sect leaders proclaimed that a successful rebellion would result in the formation of a new society in which White Lotus members would occupy important positions. The Eight Trigrams planned to set up future political orders with a triumvirate leadership under which eight "kings" ruled over eight divisions which, in turn, were divided into eight lordships (sixty-four in all). The Eight Trigrams promised to reward members who gave money or grain to the White Lotus rebels. They would be given land and official positions, the size of the contribution determining the importance of the gift-givers' future positions. Wang Lun and his disciplines made similar, though vaguer, promises of future political and economic rewards. Wang Lun promised ranks and titles such as "king" and "palace lady" to his relatives as well as his close associates.

The nature of White Lotus military power during the actual rebellion was in part determined by the size of the rebel group. The size, in turn, depended on the number of sects brought into the rebellion and the number of people drawn to it once the violence began. Wang Lun failed to unite a wide network of sects. Once the rebellion began the White Lotus was unable to gain support from many peasants. The rebellion took place in an area of west Shantung where the Great Canal system had brought a general prosperity due to the commercial activities connected with canal transport. There was no general unrest. The total rebel force consisted of only about two to four thousand individuals.

The initial government efforts to suppress the revolt were made difficult by the fact that the army was dispersed and the local gentry leadership, which might have given local resistance, was weak and ineffective. However, once the government army was mobilized, the rebellion was quickly put down.

By contrast the Eight Trigrams pulled together a number of small, independent sects from Honan, Chili, and Shantung into a unified group (Chu 1967:169–70). The rebel force was divided into eight divisions, each referred to by one of the Eight Trigrams characters. Thus, support for the 1813 revolt was better organized than that of 1774. More peasants joined the sect's military forces. The areas in which the revolt emerged were in economic distress (Honan and nearby provinces). High grain prices had resulted in food shortages. These conditions, along with droughts, floods, and the appearance of a comet in 1811, were considered calamities so severe that they signaled the coming of the predicted apocalypse. The total force eventually put into the field by the Eight Trigrams was about one hundred thousand, considerably larger than Wang Lun's army.

Whatever the size of the rebel force or the nature of its leadership, inherent organizational problems facing rebel leadership made a successful long-term challenge to government power highly unlikely, even at the provincial level. The extensive organizational structure which was necessary for the preparation of a rebel effort made total secrecy impossible. Community members, living in close proximity to the sectarians, soon learned something about the sect's plans and often reported this information to the gentry. Once the government learned of the White Lotus plans, they could arrest key leaders and thereby disrupt the timing and coordination of the rebellion. Those who joined the rebel movement in the final stages of rebellion did not have the strong ideological or social commitment to the rebel cause that most sect members did. The recent joiner's faith in the movement was usually quickly dissipated when the rebel forces suffered defeats or setbacks.

Widespread peasant support for these particular White Lotus rebellions was short-lived. One reason for this was the fact that the sect leaders did not clearly formulate a program for a new society which provided for the reallocation of land resources, reduction of taxes, and similar economic measures. Moreover, rebel demand for food and other resources put demands on the peasantry that they resented, further undermining support.

Thus, during sect-led rebellions, the White Lotus leaders had less effective control over the rebel forces than over the more permanent sect membership.

The immediate rewards for joining the rebellion were less apparent to recent recruits than to the regular sect members, especially after a few military defeats. Promise of future rewards was not sufficient to assure the loyalty of followers who had only recently joined the rebel armies. Therefore, rebellion organizers put less reliance on ideological controls and more on coercive ones. Information-control strategies also were less effective during these insurrections in protecting the sect from the government's acquisition of intelligence about sect activities.

Defeat of the rebellion did not lead to the disappearance of the local White Lotus sects. Some reorganized under new leadership and later again attempted to translate the subversive eschatology into a political force. Others de-emphasized the millennial message and became politically inactive. Yet, such quiescent sects might become politically active again due to official repression.

The White Lotus religious beliefs, then, had a recoverability despite the destruction of specific sects. Therefore the White Lotus doctrine continued as a political threat to the Ch'ing dynasty in spite of all its efforts to destroy this religion.

In the long run, of course, the recurrent White Lotus rebellions undermined state control by creating new economic problems. These insurrections forced the government to divert resources to the armies that were assigned the job of suppression. For example, the three-month Eight Trigrams insurrection cost the government 4 million *taels*. Such military cost depleted the government reserves, forcing increased taxes, with further unrest being the consequence (Feuerwerker 1975:7).

SUMMARY

In this chapter my analysis of Ch'ing society activity is based on a dialectical model. The interplay of structural and conjunctive moments must reflect underlying structural processes, which it is the job of theory to conceptualize. These structural processes, while they may limit or restrain certain actions, do not specify the exact options social agents will choose to solve commonly perceived problems.

To understand the historic context in which White Lotus sect activity occurs (along with other forms of anti-Manchu movements) we must conceptualize the Ch'ing social formation as a dynamic whole, formed of subsystems or structural moments working toward opposite goals, thereby creating the structural contradictions that placed the secret sects and state authorities on opposite sides of the structural fault lines which emerged as a result of such contradictions. Because of the mutual constitutedness of the subsystems, movement and change in one subsystem brings change in the others. Structural moments or subsystems that react back on the first bring further change within the total social formation.

The subsystems established by the Ch'ing dynasty to govern the vast Chinese empire and to extract surplus wealth from the producing classes came into contradiction with one another. In attempting to control the conflicts resulting from these contradictions, the Ch'ing dynasty used more than military means. The government set up structures through which they tried to spread the type of Confucian political values that reinforced their own political authority. But the ideological/symbolic subsystem established by the government to spread such orthodox political values among the gentry and the peasantry often produced the opposite effect because of ambiguities in the Confucian doctrines and the failures in the enculturation mechanisms. This misconstrued political indoctrination had a negative impact on the political subsystem, since gentry officials, lacking sufficient loyalty to the state, utilized their political positions to bring economic advantages to themselves, their clans, and their friends, contrary to the long-term interests of the state.

Thus contradictions among the ideological, political, and economic subsystems produced new crises necessitating state action. But the conjunctive moments initiated by the Ch'ing rulers to deal with these crises merely intensified the ideological, political, and economic conflicts between the state and opposition groups.

Understanding White Lotus activities under the Ch'ing dynasty requires that these secret sects be viewed as one type of reaction (or conjunctive moment) to the crises produced by contradictions inherent in the Ch'ing state. White Lotus activities, including the rebellions organized by some sects, must be analyzed as instances of a dialectical process in which White Lotus behavior and ideology was one of several responses to the government efforts to deal with the crises generated by these structural contradictions. Members of the same social class who were subject to the same crisis situation might go through different types of recursive analysis that would lead to different patterns of reaction, though some of their basic objectives might be similar. The range of options available to the White Lotus leaders depended in part on the reactions of the Ch'ing government to the sects as well as the internal dynamics of cult development. The dialectic of interaction between cult leaders and their followers and between the cults and the Ch'ing state determined the different trajectories of development particular sects followed.

The basic structural contradictions apparent in Ming society and the ones that weakened Ming control to the degree that the Manchu conquest of China was possible continued as a fundamental feature of the Ch'ing state. To maintain stability in the empire (i.e., to maintain existing structural moments) the Ch'ing pursued policies that both actualized and perpetuated the structural contradictions. These contradictions produced crises that resulted in conflicts between the state and segments of the population (e.g., rebellion, banditry, succession movements). Some of these opposition activities were transitory while others were not. The White Lotus religion perpetuated itself throughout the period of Ch'ing rule, thus becoming a structural moment that was, in part, responsible for the appearance of conjunctive moments at certain points during this rule.

The long-term composite effects of Ch'ing economic and political policies led to the crises which provoked rebellion and resistance. Ch'ing attempts to perpetuate certain state structures produced counteractions that undermined the ability of the Ch'ing to maintain stability. Benefices were given the Manchu princes and the banners in northern China. This government policy was vital if the loyalty of the Manchu royalty and the military were to be assured. But these benefices forced Chinese farmers onto marginal land, thereby creating resentment and opposition. The creation of a bureaucracy of scholar-officials, who were paid very low salaries, to administer the empire gave birth to the system of in-built corruption. The immense drains on government finances made by the court and the military made this salary system necessary. But the special fees and bribes required by government officials to carry out duties or to dispense favors to subordinate officials, especially when they were more excessive than customary norms dictated, led to various forms of popular social protest and resistance to new taxes.

Some officials also stole money from the funds allocated for irrigation improvements and flood control projects. Such ravaged treasuries were too depleted to carry out successful public works projects. Therefore natural disasters, such as floods and droughts, were more devastating than they should have been had adequate hydraulic projects been carried out.

Successful degree candidates, usually members of the gentry, who obtained official positions were exempt from most land and labor taxes. This exemption served as a way in which the Ch'ing could both attract members of the gentry into government and ensure their loyalty. But as a result the tax burdens were shifted to the less powerful and influential peasant families who, in turn, developed strategies to avoid taxes. These discontented peasants were also a potential recruiting ground for bandit gangs and sect rebels.

As there were many financial demands on the gentry families and clans, including duties of a military and political nature, these local elite were forced to find ways to avoid paying even the legal taxes they owed the government. Still the Ch'ing leaders increasingly relied on the gentry to maintain local order, manage public works, collect taxes, and organize and finance militia. In order to support these operations the gentry imposed new taxes on poorer members of their own clans and peasants. Since these new levies were far beyond the rates that customary norms defined as fair, social protest increased.

Ch'ing attempts to increase finances by taxing merchants trading in salt and opium, for example, were subverted by the development of an "alternative" economy by smugglers in these products, which undercut the legal commerce and deprived the government of tax income. Ch'ing attempts to increase food production in underpopulated, marginal areas of the empire by encouraging population growth eventually led to an insufficiency of food in certain provinces, resulting in further social unrest.

These structural contradictions within the Ch'ing state produced the fault lines at which conflict occurred. White Lotus sectarian activity was one reaction to such crises. Along with Triad secret society activity in southern China, it was the most persistent point of opposition to Ch'ing rule. Even quiescent White Lotus sects propagated a religious doctrine that questioned the legitimacy of Ch'ing rule by foretelling the possibility of a cataclysm which would bring a new order. But neither the suppression of potentially rebellious sects nor the destruction of the sects that had led rebellions stopped the spread of the White Lotus sectarianism. White Lotus doctrine had a recoverability in spite of the Ch'ing government's success at destroying sect organizations.

In the dialectical interplay between the state and the White Lotus sects the power relations between them were defined by the nature and extent of the government's efforts to destroy the sects, and the degree of success which the sects had in preventing the Ch'ing from doing so. The power relation between the state and the White Lotus sects was a contingent one. Through various information-control strategies the secret sects were able to avoid government destruction. But such power resources as secrecy, persuasion, and espionage did not provide the secret orders with sufficient protection once these sects led open revolts against the state. Under these circumstances the normally intense power that sect leaders had over their followers gave way to more extensive power because the leaders lost their ability to command a high level of mobilization and commitment from the total rebel army. As a result, the Ch'ing military forces were able to eventually crush the White Lotus–led insurrections.

White Lotus sects perfected various secrecy strategies in order to avoid government detection. Discovery of the sects and their leadership by the government was difficult because the leaders moved or changed their names, changed the name of the sect, and maintained covert contact with relatives and pupils who were banished or in prison. If male leaders of the sect were imprisoned the women from the leadership family might take over administration of the sect's religious activities. Recruitment of new members could be done quite secretly because many leaders were traveling boxers, yoga teachers, or healers who could attract new members in the course of their other activities. Thus, secret society recruitment took place in "structural spaces" free from government detection or supervision.

The pattern of sect development was one of diffusion and fragmentation. After a teacher's death his pupils became leaders of new sects. But this regular fission was a source of protection for the White Lotus sectarians because the sect size was not large enough to normally attract the government's attention.

Barriers to government detection of the sects occurred when lower level semi-official elites were themselves initiated into the sect. These officers were the very ones that the government relied on to detect these sectarian troublemakers. Thus, by initiating such individuals, the sects subverted the normal process of government surveillance and created a screen to hide their activities.

However, the White Lotus rebellions were never successful. Most sectarian leaders were unable to coordinate a large-scale military force loyal enough to defeat the government forces. Moreover, secrecy broke down when the sect leaders began to plan such large endeavors. The local gentry soon learned of these activities and reported them to the government. Leaders then could be arrested and revolts might be crushed.

Even when a particular sect was destroyed the fact that the power within White Lotus sects tended to gravitate to and remain in the hands of hereditary leaders and their families assured that the sect could be perpetuated in some form by family members not arrested and imprisoned.

The successful implementation of power by White Lotus sect leaders over their followers throughout the period of Manchu rule seems to have depended less on coercive tactics than on intensive sectarian indoctrination. By such indoctrination sect leaders assured themselves that they had a core of members who aspired to the same goals as themselves.

The continued presence of White Lotus sectarianism accentuated the crises faced by the Ch'ing dynasty. White Lotus ideology provided a justification for sect members to find ways to avoid government levies and taxes, thereby undermining the state's efforts to increase revenue. In turn,

White Lotus–led rebellions, even though unsuccessful, caused considerable expense to the government, which had to finance the armies that suppressed the rebel forces. These expenditures, of course, were in addition to outlays such as those for military campaigns against bandits and ethnic and tribal succession movements. Depletion of government treasuries for these and other ventures necessitated new taxes, which in turn created more resistance on the part of peasantry, craftsmen, and merchants. These were the composite effects of prevailing government policies.

Thus, in attempting to repress secret society activities, the Ch'ing state merely accentuated the existing structural contradictions rather than resolving them. The study of the White Lotus sect suggests that a secret society may not always develop enough power resources to overthrow a state government or even carve out an autonomous territorial niche. Nonetheless, the successful implementation of state power over a secret society at any historic instance does not resolve the structural contradictions that generate conflict between secret societies and the state. For the ruling class to survive it must reproduce the prevailing relations of production. But in so doing the existing structural contradictions are also reproduced, leading to state conflicts with secret societies and other groups. Attempts by the state to repress the secret societies produce conjunctive changes in these secret orders (e.g., new information-control strategies) which enhance their power resources and thus their ability to resist state control. Unlike the Ch'ing state, the White Lotus sects were able to maintain a foci of *intensive* power by their ability to command a high level of mobilization and commitment from members. Thus, the state could suppress secret society organized rebellions but not totally eliminate the White Lotus as an anti-Manchu political force.

5

Chinese Secret Societies in Malaysia

The evolution of Triad secret societies in Malaysia cannot be understood unless we conceptualize these secret orders as sites at which various overdeterminant conjunctive moments (subsystems) operated to structure the dynamics of Triad-state relationships. Such conjunctive moments were overt manifestations of economic and political contradictions within colonial and postcolonial Malaysian society. Emerging within the social formation and the larger social system within which the Malaysian social formation was a part, these contradictions produced the fault lines at which conflicts between the state and secret societies appeared within the ideological, political, and economic subsystems.

Within immigrant communities secret societies can play a political role if the state lacks the resources to establish direct control over the immigrant minority, and local leaders come to rely on the secret societies to maintain order. Under these circumstances the nature of the evolving state–secret society relationship will depend on whether the secret societies help or hinder the state in the reproduction of the social formation. The study of the Triad secret societies in Malaysia serves to illustrate a historic instance in which a colonial state found it expedient to outlaw secret societies in order to protect its economic interests. The study of the Malaysian Triads also demonstrates how outlawed secret orders are able to develop new power resources that enable them to survive albeit with changed structure and functions. Thus in Malaysia the power relations between the Triads and the state have been and continue to be a dynamic, contingent relation, rear-ranged and readjusted over time.

Chinese immigrants to Malaysia, many of whom were already members of secret societies in China, organized similar secret associations in Malaysia. But these secret societies performed different functions in Malaysia than they did in China. The role of Chinese secret society organization and the nature of its structure changed throughout Malaysian history. Such changes reflect the changing position of the Malaysian Chinese within Malaysian society and their role in the conflicts generated by the contradictions within the Malaysian political economy.

Before European contact the Malay peninsula had been populated by Malays who were immigrants from Melanesia.[1] From the sixteenth century onward Portuguese, Dutch, and British traders made contacts with Malaya, establishing coastal settlements.[2] These Straits Settlements (Penang, Malacca, Singapore Province, Wellesley, and Dindings) eventually fell under British control. By governing the ports of the Straits the British were able to control maritime trade to eastern Southeast Asia and the Orient. These key ports also gave the British control over regional as well as local trade (Jomo 1988:138).

By the middle of the nineteenth century, tin mining had become a lucrative enterprise within the Malay states. Malay chiefs and sultans encouraged Chinese immigration as a source of labor to work the mines. Other mines were owned by Chinese capitalists in the Straits Settlements (Butcher 1979:5).

Soon rivalries between coalitions of Malay and Chinese led to civil war, often fought between secret societies representing these various factions. As a result of this conflict tin production fell. Chinese capitalists and European merchants in the Straits Settlements requested that the colonial government intervene in the tin-rich western Malay states of Perak, Selangor, and Negri Sembilan to end the strife (Butcher 1979:6). By 1896 these states, together with Pahang, were brought under a centralized British administration in the form of the Federated Malay States (FMS). The expectation was that such intervention would give British business interests unchallenged dominance over tin mining, industry, and commerce in these regions. These ambitions of British capital were disappointed due to unexpected challenges by Chinese entrepreneurs (Jomo 1988:143). By World War II the British had gained control of the four padi-growing[3] northern Malay states (Unfeder-ated Malay States) of Kedah, Perlis, Kelatan, Johore, and Trengganu (Jomo 1988:143–45).

The British made treaties with the Malay sultans, which gave the British considerable control over Malaya's affairs (Clutterbuck 1973:33).[4] There were nine Malay states ruled by Malay sultans with British advisers, two Straits Settlements (Penang and Malacca) governed by British officials, and Singapore, which was headed by a British governor (Clutterbuck 1973:32).

After overcoming the resistance of certain factions within the precolonial ruling class, the British set out to co-opt the Malay aristocrats by recruiting the Malay ruling class into the middle echelon of the colonial bureaucracy. These Malay "administocrats" occupied a position immediately subordinate to the British administrators. The Chinese and the Indians were excluded from government offices and the civil service (Jomo 1988:245; Ting 1982:112). Being comfortably salaried, the Malay administocrats took little interest in capitalist enterprise (Jomo 1988:207).

The Japanese invaded Malaya in 1941 and their occupation of Malaya, Singapore, and the British Borneo lasted three years and eight months. The Japanese executed thousands of Chinese in the name of "anti-communism." The Japanese occupation brought into prominence the Malayan Communist Party through its guerrilla army, the Malayan Peoples Anti-Japanese Army (MPAJA) (Miller 1965).[5] Because of Japanese brutality many young Chinese joined the MPAJA.

The Kuomintang also organized a band of guerrillas called the Malayan Overseas Chinese Self-Defense Army (MOCSDA), which was always at odds with the MPAJA (Blythe 1950).

Refused a role in the postwar government, the Communists returned to the jungle and took up arms with the aim of disrupting the national economy and inflicting casualties on security forces. They hoped to eventually establish a republic in Malaysia. Heading these communist insurgents was Chin Peng, the head of the Malayan Communist Party. The government declared a state of emergency in 1948, which was not to end till 1960 when the communist force no longer posed a threat. In the course of the emergency the government resettled hundreds of thousands of Chinese in new villages away from jungle areas in order to deprive the communist army sources of food and new recruits (Strauch 1981:60–62).

In 1957, toward the end of the emergency period, Malaya gained independence from British rule. Penang, Malacca, and the nine Malayan states formed the independent "Federation of Malaya" (Malay Union). Singapore and the two British territories in Borneo (Sarawak and Sabah) joined the Federation in 1963, forming the Federation of Malaysia. But in 1965 Singapore separated from Malaysia and became a republic (Ting 1982; Means 1976).

The first independent government was formed by the intercommunal Alliance Party, each component of the party drawing membership from one of the three major ethnic groups: Chinese (Malaysian Chinese Association [MCA]), Malays (United Malay National Organization [UMNO]), and Indians (Malaysian Indian Congress [MIC]).[6] Between 1952 and 1969 the governing Alliance Party stressed national issues and dealt with ethnic rivalries ambiguously to avoid divisions among Malays, Chinese, and Indians within the Alliance Party (Rabushka 1973:48). However, continuing challenges to Malay control by non-Malay parties encouraged the leaders of the UMNO to form the Barisan Nasional (National Front) to replace the Alliance.[7] The Front enabled the UMNO to provide a multiracial facade around a Malay core provided by the UMNO. The Malaysian Chinese Association and Malaysian Indian Congress were acceptable to the Front only so long as they cooperated with the Malay core (UMNO and other Malayan organizations associated with it).

Under this new set up the MCA and MIC had reduced influence (Miller 1965). The aim of the Malaysian rulers was to give only lip service to a multiracial society and to firmly maintain Malayan rule at the expense of the political rights of the non-Malayan populations. The UMNO leadership could do this because the non-Malayan population had no power within a government dominated by Malays. Non-Malay support for the National Front was no longer indispensable (Vasil 1980:224–25).

The Malay-dominated government instituted policies and laws favorable to the Malay ethnic group rather than to the non-Malay minorities because Malay leaders claimed that the Malay are the rightful owners, since they were the original inhabitants of the area. The Malay viewed the Chinese and Indians as merely permanent guests brought to Malaysia by tin and plantation interests. Therefore, the state constitution gave Malays special privileges in regard to civil service appointments, the granting of university scholarships, acquisition of business licenses, and new land titles. For opposition parties to even raise questions publicly about such Malay privileges was made unlawful (Rabushka 1973:19, 30–32; Hui 1988). Malay was designated the official state language and was required in all government-supported schools (Nagata 1979:220).[8]

CHINESE IMMIGRATION

While the Chinese frequented the Malay peninsula as early as the fourteenth century, mass Chinese immigration into Malaya only took place late in Malay history. Penang was practically an uninhabited island in 1786. The same was true of Singapore in 1819. By 1641 there were only three to four hundred Chinese in Malacca (Blythe 1950:14; Mak 1975:51).

The period of large-scale Chinese immigration into Singapore and Malaya was largely the result of European expansion into Southeast Asia, particularly British intrusion (1786–1914). British encouragement of Chinese immigration reflected their adherence to a laissez-faire policy supporting the free movement of both labor and capital (Rabushka 1973:17). Chinese capitalists followed the colonial flag to the Straits because the British colonialists imposed stable political conditions and opened up new economic opportunities (Jomo 1988:150). Large groups of Chinese artisans, farmers, and laborers came to Malaya following the British occupation of the Straits Settlements (Penang 1786, Singapore 1819, Malacca 1829) and the subsequent British expansion into the Malay states (Ting 1982; Means 1976; Alexander 1983; Freedman 1960:26). The British economic policies enabled Chinese to start business enterprises and gave them opportunities to accumulate wealth. As the Malay states came under British protection (1886–1914), tin mining expanded in Perak and Selanger, developments that led to a great demand for Chinese labor in those states. These mines were financed by Chinese merchants living in Penang, Malacca, and Singapore (Ting 1982; Purcell 1948).

The Chinese capitalists dominated the tin mining sector despite efforts by British capital to get control of tin production in Malaya.[9] The labor-intensive exploitation of shallow tin deposits were more appropriate to the small-scale capitalized operation of the Chinese than to the heavily capitalized operations of the European companies (Jomo 1988:161). The Straits' Chinese merchants invested in the tin enterprises through middlemen, called "mine advancers," who used the Chinese merchants' capital to secure control of the ore produced and provided the tin-miner-cum-employer with sufficient funds to carry out production (Jomo 1988:161). Having access to cheap Chinese immigrant labor enabled the Chinese-owned mines to produce at a low cost (Jomo 1988:163).

Western capital only took over tin production once the surface deposits of ore were exhausted and there was a need for heavy capitalized production of the deeper ore deposits, which labor intensive methods of the past were unable to accomplish (Jomo 1988:168).[10]

With the erosion of opportunities for employment in mining,[11] most Chinese, except for the wealthy families, turned to self-employment in small enterprises since they had limited access to land. The Chinese also had restricted wage-employment opportunities, and therefore became self-employed small-scale producers, traders, and fishermen. Others established businesses based on prostitution or gambling (Jomo 1988:174). Some

Chinese merchants established gambier and spice plantations in and around Penang and Singapore (Jomo 1988:151).

European capitalists invested in sugar cane, pepper, coffee, and tea.[12] As a result of the rubber boom, which commenced in the early part of the twentieth century, the colonial government helped British capital to gain control of rubber production (Jomo 1988:151).[13] For these enterprises European capital mainly hired immigrant Indian labor (Jomo 1988:560).

These various industries, both Chinese and European, created a large demand for Chinese labor (Ting 1982:105). By 1901 the Chinese accounted for 46 percent of the population of Perak and 65 percent of the population of Selangor (Ting 1982:105). By the 1940s the Chinese constituted about one-third of the population of the Federated States and three-fourths of the population of Singapore (Clutterbuck 1973:33; Freedman 1960:25).

There were two patterns of Chinese immigration, one based on kinship ties and the other based on the credit ticket system. Some Malay Chinese businessmen returned to China to recruit staff from among relatives (Yen 1986:4). Most Chinese came to Malaya under a credit ticket system and the subsequent private recruiting system. Under the credit system labor brokers (captains of junks or labor agents) in China worked in conjunction with brokers in Malaya to recruit Chinese coolies and pay for their passage. When these laborers arrived in Malaya, the brokers sold them to employers for a profit. Many coolie brokers were secret society leaders (Yen 1986:113–14).

Some Chinese came willingly to Malaya to escape the famine and strife in China. Others were forced or tricked into emigration (Alexander 1983:9–10). Some brokers kidnapped women in China, bringing them to Singapore for sale to brothel keepers (Yoong 1961:101–2). To avoid British control of this trade, brokers shipped the women via Shanghai and Saigon because the British officials had no authority to search ships from these ports (Yoong 1961:101–3).

The Chinese laborers worked for the employer for a fixed wage until their debt was paid. To repay himself for the money paid the broker the employer usually forced the coolie to work for food and clothing for the first year. But even after the second and third year the laborer might still owe the employer his shipping costs (Alexander 1983:13).

Some employers reduced their wage bill by binding workers to their job under the "truck system." By advancing items to the coolies for personal consumption (including opium) at higher than usual prices, the employer put the laborer in debt. Thereby, the employer as the merchant-creditor created a more permanent work force bound in debt to him and recovered a considerable portion of the wages as payment of the debt (Jomo 1988:163–67).

Coolies who were not sold immediately were confined to coolie depots (or *barracoons*). Secret society members guarded these warehouses to prevent coolies from escaping or from being poached by other brokers from other warehouses (Yen 1986:113–14).

After the abolition of the credit ticket system in 1914 a private recruitment system evolved to replace it. Contractors (*kepala*) were sent by Chinese employers to recruit workers in the businessmen's native villages or districts in China. The recruiters paid the transport costs of the workers (*sinkheh*) and the workers were obliged to work for the employers until their debt was paid (Ting 1982:106–7; Means 1976).[14]

The secret society protected the personal welfare of the immigrants, arranged employment, and provided job protection. It also assured employers that the laborers would not run away and that there would be no strikes or other disturbances. Initially, the colonial government found secret societies useful to them since these societies assured a steady supply of labor for mining and plantation enterprises on which the economy of the Straits and Malay States depended. In Perak and Selangor, for example, about four-fifths of the colonial government's revenue came from duty on tin exports and the sale of state monopolies to Chinese capitalists (Butcher 1979:9). The secret society also provided an institutionalized means for maintaining labor discipline, settling disputes, maintaining law and order within the Chinese labor camps, and offering welfare services, which the British were unable to do (Mak 1981; Andaya and Andaya 1982; Douglas and Pedersen 1973).

British tolerance of Triad activities also reflected the colonial policy of noninterference in the affairs of indigenous communities. The colonial administrators were content to let the Malays, Chinese, and Indians retain their separate cultural and linguistic heritage as long as their communal interests did not challenge those of the British (Koon 1988:6–7).

Early attempts by some colonial officials to restrict Chinese immigration were opposed by ship owners, merchants, mine owners, and plantation owners, whose economic fortunes were tied to their ability to acquire a steady supply of cheap labor (Blythe 1969:167).[15] Thus, an unrestricted immigration of Chinese, Indians, and Indonesians into Malaya was allowed by the British until 1929. The 1930 Immigration Restriction Ordinance and the Aliens Ordinance of 1933 restricted the free flow of Chinese immigrants as well as Indians and Indonesians. By this period the cost of recruiting from China had become prohibitive, so it was cheaper for employers to recruit local labor. These ordinances therefore crippled the broker recruiting system (Ting 1982:107–8).

CHINESE COMMUNITY ORGANIZATION

The communities of Chinese in Singapore were organized on the basis of surname and dialect ties.[16] Surname associations linked men who came from widely separated communities in China. The common surname gave an indication of either traceable or putative descent from a male ancestor, thus establishing common clan membership (Freedman 1960:46). Such clan-based or lineage-based organizations provided an important source of support for Chinese immigrants. Associations (*kongsi*) based on surname identity fostered traditional values such as ancestor worship and offered members various kinds of social and economic support (Yen 1986:74–85).[17]

Dialect groups were formed by Chinese immigrants who shared similar regional outlooks and customs, based on the areas from which they had emigrated. The British, like the Portuguese and the Dutch before them, dealt with the Chinese through *kapitans*.[18] In many cases the *kapitan*, though an important official in one dialect association (*kongsi*), administered an area in which several dialect groups (*pangs*) resided. Since the *kapitan* tended to safeguard the interests of his own dialect group, other *pangs* within the *kapitan*'s jurisdiction formed their own associations to protect their own interests (Yen 1986:42–43). The *pang* members worshipped together in association clubhouses, paying homage to their preferred gods and goddesses (Yen 1986:45–55).

The dialect groups gave free assistance to their members in job searches, health care, and burials. Before being appointed as a *kapitan*, a dialect leader was usually the head of his dialect association. Once he became a *kapitan*, his dialect group expected him to use his newly acquired influence to enable his group's members to get jobs and acquire more rights and privileges from the government. In turn his dialect association gave the *kapitan* power to resolve disputes within the dialect group and to provide leadership for numerous projects. The economic demands on the *kapitan* necessitated that such leaders come from wealthy families, usually members of the Chinese merchant class (Yen 1986).

Chinese dominance in supplying labor for mining and cash-crop plantations was maintained by *pang* organizations, which bought shares in cooperative ventures in mining and plantation agriculture (Mak 1981; Blythe 1969).[19] The colonial government also rented out tax-farms to such dialect groups, which thereby obtained a monopoly on the collection of duty in exchange for a fixed sum per year (Blythe 1969).

The tax or excise-farming system was first begun in Penang in the late eighteenth century and spread to Malacca and Singapore in the early nineteenth century. Successful syndicate bidders were given a monopoly to collect duty and revenue from the sale of arrack, pork, or opium. Taxation on gambling was also a lucrative element in the excise-farming system (Mak 1988b:234).

Each dialect group monopolized certain occupations and/or businesses. Hokkiens were active in commercial pursuits, the Cantonese were mainly artisans, the Teochews controlled gambier and pepper trade, and the Hakkas concentrated on farming, while the Hainennese served as shop assistants and servants (Mak 1980:466; Yen 1986:117). Dialect groups also tried to maintain and expand their control over certain profit-making activities such as prostitution, opium trade, alcohol sales, and gambling. The British gave the farmers exclusive rights to sell commodities and services in return for rent paid to the government. There was fierce competition among dialect associations over these economic concessions. Some *pangs* tried to break the monopoly of other dialect groups over such businesses (Yen 1986:197).

Between 1931–17 the Chinese secret societies were also involved in the *kangchu* system. The *kangchu* was a master of a certain section of the waterfront in Johore who collected taxes, controlled cultivation rights, set up businesses, and performed government functions. For the powers granted the *kangchu* by a local Malay ruler, he had to pay an annual royalty to the Malay sultan. The secret societies helped the *kangchu* carry out his administrative functions.

ROLE OF THE CHINESE SECRET SOCIETIES

Most *kapitans* were powerful officials within the secret societies.[20] If they were the heads of secret associations that enrolled members from various dialect groups within their community, the *kapitans* relied on the secret societies to enforce their decisions and keep order (Mak 1985:157). In most circumstances each secret society served the interests of a particular *pang*, since their membership was largely if not entirely from that dialect group (Mak 1975a:55, 1980:78–79, 1983; Blythe 1969; Yen 1986). In these circumstances conflicts among secret societies merely reflect the antagonistic interests between *pangs*.

Secret societies provided each *pang* with sufficient power to maintain and consolidate control over its "excise farm." The secret society kept smuggling in check and protected the *pang* from attack by rivals (Yen 1986:116, 117, 122).

The secret societies also controlled the trade in women from China. Since most early Chinese immigrants were single men, the lack of women among the overseas Malay Chinese communities led to the development of brothels. Each secret society provided its respective dialect group with women to run its brothel and provided the brothel with protection against competitors. For these services the dialect association paid the secret society a regular monthly fee (Yen 1986:123).

As we will soon learn, the British reliance on dialect groups and their allied Triad societies for the management of tin production and the administration of tax farms as well as concessionary businesses was to have unanticipated consequences for British colonial interests. These Chinese economic monopolies soon put their interests in conflict with those of European capital. Such emerging conflicts were "composition effects," not consciously planned by the colonial government but the results of short-term decisions made by the British colonial officials who wanted to expand their economic interests in Malaysia. These decisions had unexpected, long-term negative consequences for European capital.

THE TRIAD SOCIETIES IN MALAYSIA

Chinese immigrants came from areas of China in which the Triad secret society, also called *Hung* or the Heaven and Earth Society (*Tien Ti Hu*) was powerful, largely in the provinces of Fukien, Kwangtung, and Kwangsi.[21] All Chinese societies in Malaysia stemmed from the Triad society of southern China. The Triad societies in Malaysia were not organizationally linked, though there were a few occasions when several branches might bond together temporarily (Freedman 1960:331).[22] The Triads in Malaysia came to be known by various names, including *Ghee Hin*, *Ghee Hock*, *Hai San*, and *Gom Seng* (Comber 1962:10). In recent years these main groups have splintered, giving rise to secret societies that have few Triad connections (Seah and Ag ASP 1978).

There is some evidence to suggest that secret societies were active in Penang as early as 1798 and in Malacca as early as 1818. But the most complete description of a Triad initiation ceremony was reported in 1824 (Mak 1988b:231).

By the 1840s secret societies may have initiated as many as 10,000 members in Singapore out of a Chinese population of 20,000 (Freedman 1960:30). In 1879 the official register of "dangerous societies" showed a total membership of nearly 24,000. By 1881 the total male Chinese population of settled areas was 72,571. Of these, 33,103 were secret society members (Freedman 1960:32).

The Triad secret order of southern China represents a society that advocated national independence of China from the alien Manchu rule.[23] These Triad societies played an important role in organizing revolts against the Ch'ing rulers, but in Malaya the Triads were not normally opposed to the colonial administration (Freedman and Topley 1961:12–13).

The Triads maintained power over their members and protected themselves from any outside interference by a combination of punishments and information-control strategies (secrecy, espionage, and indoctrination). These power resources enabled the secret societies to minimize membership disloyalty, deny outsiders accurate information about the Triads, as well as learn beforehand of any attempts by the government to move against their organizations so evasive measures might be instituted.

To help minimize the possibility that recruits would prove disloyal, secret societies engaged in a rigorous screening of candidates recommended by trusted members.[24] In addition, various ritualistic methods, as well as threatened sanctions against members violating societal codes, were used to assure member loyalty (Mak 1988b:10).

Once initiated into the Triad lodge, a member owed complete commitment to the organization. The Triads took over responsibility for many aspects of a member's life. The Triads forbade sexual relations between members and fellow members' spouses or daughters. Homosexual acts were also forbidden. The society prohibited exploitation of fellow members. Triad leaders ordered those members killed who became untrustworthy.

The Triad laws spelled out specific punishments for rule violations including blows, loss of ears, and death by decapitation. Probably these punishments were carried out just frequently enough to impress on all Triad members the danger of disobedience (Mak 1981:707; Comber 1962:63–69). Since so many violations carried the death penalty, such punishments could not have been carried out very frequently as the number of members in any one lodge would have been drastically reduced if they had been. Of course, death was the punishment for the betrayal of fellow members to the government, as was the punishment for the sale of Triad secrets to outsiders. There were rules against murder, robbery, cheating of fellow members as well as against embezzling society funds and against the abuse of power by leaders.

The early Triad societies had a fairly elaborate organizational structure. In Singapore one secret society was organized along the following lines: general headman, two secretaries or masters, some district headmen, two treasurers and four fighters. Two larger secret societies in Penang had a similar structure: one general headman, two deputy headmen, three assistant headmen, one secretary or master, five district headmen, one judge, four senior councillors or treasurers, twelve junior councillors or fighters, and some other minor positions (Mak 1988b:232–33).

The general headman had administrative responsibilities in a district of a major secret society. He had control over several lodges. A district headman issued orders to local lodge members and enjoyed the right to promote members within his own lodge. He also had the obligation to resolve internal disputes. The master, being versed in passwords and rituals as well as societal legends, managed the society's initiation ceremonies. Judges helped headmen maintain order and settle disputes. These officials were responsible for conducting surveillance against suspected members whose activities were thought to endanger the society's interests. Masters and judges did not belong to any particular lodge. The master held an initiation ceremony by invitation of a particular lodge. In a like fashion judges were invited to mediate and settle disputes between particular lodges. The treasurer was in charge of societal funds while the tiger generals and fighters were obligated to defend the society against rivals and collect subscription fees from members (Mak 1981:63–70).

The Triads developed an intricate initiation ceremony with an oath of secrecy penalty, the violation of which was death (Pickering 1879).[25] Initiations were held at night in secluded places. The ceremonial lodge was arranged to represent a walled city. "New horses" (recruits) were brought by "horse leaders" (recruiters) to the gate of the lodge. They were challenged by a vanguard. Passwords were exchanged and the initiation began. The stages of initiation corresponded to incidences in the traditional history of the society (see Tai 1977 for an alternate explanation of the ritual symbolism). The candidates passed through three "doors," each represented by wooden or bamboo posts with lengths of red paper or cloth stretched between them. The first door was called the Hung Door; the second door led into the Hall of Loyalty and Righteousness. Recruits were interrogated by the guards before passing through these first two portals. The third door was the door of the City of Willows, leading to the Red Flower Pavilion. The Hung Door refers to the name of the secret society. The Hall of Loyalty and Righteousness refers to the Shrine of the God of War in the Chinese pantheon and the tutelary deity of the Chinese Triads. The door of the City of Willows was the Triad symbol for the lodge itself. The Red Flower Pavilion altar contained images representing various persons mentioned in traditional history of the Triads (Comber 1957). Also on the altar were a censor inscribed with the phrase "'Overthrow the Ch'ing and Restore the Ming,' a foot ruler to measure the conduct of the brethren, a pair of scales to symbolize righteousness and justice, a magic mirror to reveal good and bad, and a number of altar candles" (Purcell 1948:9).

After a long catechism within the Red Flower Pavilion, a white cock was decapitated as a symbol of the fate which would fall upon a traitorous member. The initiate's middle finger was pricked with a needle, then his blood was mixed with wine and the chicken blood and the initiate made a solemn oath of fidelity and secrecy by drinking the mixture.

At the end of the ceremony the candidate handed over his entrance fee wrapped in red paper. Candidates then were given a certification or diploma bearing the legend of the lodge and other secret inscriptions along with copies of the secret rules, regulations, oaths, and punishments (Purcell 1948:8–11; Comber 1961:30–54; Topley 1961:300–1).

Secret societies collected useful intelligence information through espionage. Dialect group *kapitans* served the interests of the secret society by becoming a "double role players," establishing the sort of relationship with the police, public officials, and other influentials, which served secret society political interests (Mak 1988b:5).

RELATIONSHIPS BETWEEN THE TRIADS AND THE STATE

By the end of the nineteenth century the large increase in Chinese immigration had created more job seekers than job opportunities (Andaya and Andaya 1982). The power of each secret society to attract members and to expand its influence rested largely on its ability to get jobs for the new immigrants within its *pang*. Pressure built up on each secret order to expand its monopoly over other job areas previously controlled by other secret societies. Conflicts broke out among Triad secret societies over control of revenue farms, mining fields, gambling operations, opium dens, and prostitution (Wynne 1941; Purcell 1948).

There was serious secret society factional fighting in Singapore in 1829, 1846, 1851, and 1854. The 1854 conflict involved fighting between the Cantonese and Hokkiens secret societies, which lasted ten days and resulted in 1,200 killed or wounded (Cheng 1950:10). The Penang riots of 1867 and the Larut wars of 1862 and 1872 were triggered by economic rivalries between dialect societies and the secret societies that represented them (Comber 1957:24–25; Wynne 1941). There was a great deal of secret society conflict which took place in the tin and mining areas of Perak, Malacca, and Selangor where dialect associations through their secret society allies fought for possession of tin mines and the control of the opium trade to the miners. In some of these fights the Chinese secret societies were supported by their Malaccan secret society allies, the White and Red Flag associations (Wynne 1941).[26]

The increased conflict among Chinese secret societies, manifested in street riots and battles, threatened the economic interests of the European and Chinese businessmen (Andaya and Andaya 1982). *Kapitans*, who were prominent heads of the secret organizations, began to fear that such secret society wars were bound to spread and that such disturbances would bring financial ruin to them if they were expelled from Malaya, once their affiliations to the secret societies became known to the authorities. Thus, *kapitans* and other prominent Chinese businessmen preferred to pose outwardly as being unassociated with the secret societies, letting any blame fall on a few dummy headmen who were considered the "official" secret society leaders (Wynne 1941).

The colonial government was motivated to take action against the Triads, not only by the economic disruption caused by secret society conflict but also as a means of breaking Triad control over the labor supply. Western capitalists in Malaysia had great difficulty in recruiting an adequate labor force owing to the control that the secret societies had over Chinese labor supply for the *pangs* (Jomo 1988:163). The colonial government began to take decisive action.[27] The Dangerous Societies Ordinance was enacted in 1869. This ordinance required that societies classified as "dangerous" be required to register along with all their office bearers and members. These measures proved to be ineffective in controlling the secret associations. So in 1889 a new ordinance was adopted. "Dangerous" societies were declared unlawful and all other societies were required to register (Cheng 1950:10).[28] As a consequence of this official suppression secret societies went underground, working through front organizations (Mak 1981; Douglas and Pedersen 1973:31). Society discipline was loosened, giving minor leaders an opportunity to free-lance as heads of gangs of blackmailers or bullies (Wynne 1941).

This government action against the secret societies encouraged some of the prominent Chinese members of these organizations to cut free of the secret orders. To do so some of them converted to Christianity or sought British citizenship (Wynne 1941). Since Chinese leadership in Malaysia is measured by the capacity of the Chinese leaders to secure benefits for the Chinese community from powerful non-Chinese patrons, continued or overt association with illegal secret organizations would undermine the leaders' ability to carry out this role and thus retain their power (Koon 1988:15).

The crack-down by the British on the Triads did not eliminate these secret societies in Malaysia. The power relations between the state and the secret orders was subject to maneuver and strategic bargaining by the power agents on both sides. The evolving relationship between the state and the Triads was dependent on both external and internal historic dynamics affecting this power connection.

The Japanese occupation of Malaysia during World War II created new problems for the Chinese secret societies. The Japanese made concerted efforts to eliminate the secret societies by exterminating their members. Some secret society leaders collaborated with the Japanese but most joined the anti-Japanese resistance movements. Japanese agents infiltrated the Triad orders and betrayed secret society leaders. To protect themselves the secret society officials set up duplicate societies or dummy organizations with the same names, secret hand signals, and codes as the genuine groups (Alexander 1973:24).

Once the British returned to Malaysia in September 1946, they suspended the Societies Ordinance and Banishment Ordinance as a result of a secret agreement with the Malayan Communist Party, which wanted to encourage the formation of political parties. The enforcement of these ordinances would have constituted a direct challenge to communist groups in postwar Malay and Singapore (Douglas and Pedersen 1973:35).

Relaxation of restrictions on secret societies was also related to the Federation (Malayan Union) government's fight against the communist rebels. The government wanted the anti-communist secret societies to help carry out this fight against secret societies supporting the communists. The Hua Chi and Hung Min societies, together with their front organizations, supported the Kuomintang. Hua Chi had a strong representation among the tin miners in Selangor but later formed branches in other provinces, with its major strength in Kuala Lumpur. Among its ranks were members of the police and home guard. Hua Chi formed close ties with Hung Min after the Japanese surrender in 1943. Hung Min was involved in murder, robbery, and kidnapping as well as protection rackets. Rich Chinese merchants joined both the Kuomintang and Hung Min (Comber 1957:24–37).

The Chi Kung supported Dr. Sun Yat-Sen but later a wing of the Chi Kung gave their support to the Malayan Communist Party at the end of World War II.[29] They backed the communist rebels and joined the communists in combating the political activities of the Hua Chi and Hung Min (Means 1946:29).

With the formation of the Peoples Republic of China in 1949 many Triad societies in Malaysia became supporters of the new government. But the communist government's campaign against secret societies in China diminished their enthusiasm for the Malaysian communists (Comber 1957:38).

This "freedom of association" policy allowed Triad secret societies to reestablish themselves. Following the formation of the Malayan Union the growth in secret society activity was also stimulated by a fear within the Chinese community that once the British left, such secret organizations would be the only sources of protection for the Chinese against a Malay-dominated government (Douglas and Pedersen 1973:36).

Once the communist guerrillas were defeated, the government enacted new ordinances, the Criminal Justice (Temporary) Provision Act of 1955 and the Criminal Law (Temporary) Provision Act of 1958, which imposed heavy penalties on secret society members found guilty of criminal offenses and allowed the police to detain active secret society members for extended periods without charge (Mak 1981:63; Au-Yong 1972:100–1). These new measures reduced secret society violence to a considerable extent (Seah and Ag ASP 1978:88).

Changes in the political economy of Malaysia, begun before World War II, accelerated after the defeat of the Japanese. Both government and private business began to recruit from local populations on the basis of universalistic criteria rather than particularistic criteria (speech, ethnic, racial identity). The government civil service opened up job opportunities for the Chinese as well as Muslims, with training and skill being the chief criteria for employment (Mak 1981; Alexander 1973:40). Dialect groups became less important as sources of support for economic opportunity. In turn the need for secret society protection of the *pangs'* monopolization of occupations and businesses evaporated.

Secret societies saw many of their other traditional functions taken over by competing organizations. Wealthy Chinese businessmen turned to the more reliable security firms for industrial protection. Chinese leaders at the national and grass roots levels came to depend on their ties with the MCA and its influence within the Alliance Party and later the National Front to pursue their political and economic objectives (Heng 1983). Trade unions began to provide job protection to Chinese workers, and Christian churches converted many potential secret society members to a religion hostile to Triad beliefs (Mak 1981).[30]

The response of the Triads to their eroding membership base and hostile government actions serves to again illustrate that power relations constitute a dialectical interplay between induction and resistance. As a result of this interplay the power relations between the state and the Triads was changed. The societies that survived simplified their internal organization, disguised the true nature of their activities, found ways to serve the interests of postcolonial political parties, and established protectionist rackets in gambling, brothels, bars and, more recently, the construction industry (Seah and Ag ASP 1978; Mak 1975a). In such illegal pursuits secret societies have been protected from police crackdowns by "double-players"—police officers who have been bribed by the societies to take care of their interests (Mak 1975a:13).

The breakup of the ethnic group monopoly over certain areas of economic opportunity have forced the secret societies to recruit members from more diverse backgrounds. The societies have sought young members from primary and secondary schools (Mak 1981). For example, in Ipoh Town (Perak) the Hsiao Pa Hung Kongsi had 10,000 members in 1952 but 90 percent of these were schoolboys from the ages of twelve to eighteen (Mak 1975a:3). Youth from the ages of fourteen to twenty-five are most susceptible to secret society influence. They have little or no education and are unskilled for most trades (Seah and Ag ASP 1978:91). These new youth gangs were initially backed by older secret societies as a means to disguise their activities from the police and to preserve their territorial control over rackets. But now the gangs operate independently of the older Triad associations (Mak 1975a:7). Malaya-Eurasian and Indian youth gangs now dominate the protectionist and extortion rackets, at least in Singapore. They have adopted appellations such as Billy the Kid, Sombrero Boys, Yankee Boys, B–22, Little Wanderer, and so forth (Comber 1957:56; Adkins 1962:23; Seah and Ag ASP 1978). Members in these gangs come from the same neighborhood but from diverse ethnic, dialectic and clan backgrounds (Top 1961; Mak 1985:155).[31] The breakup of the Triad societies into smaller units has often been dictated by tactical considerations. Tactical fragmentation and regrouping is necessary to avoid police suppression. Large societies have broken up into smaller groups with new names and identities. Later gangs may re-group into larger and more efficient secret associations if a large size proves to be beneficial (Seah and Ag ASP 1978).

Despite their illegal status secret societies still have enough wealth and organizational power within the Chinese community to make it rewarding for certain political groups as well as Chinese businessmen to, covertly at least, seek secret society support. The Malaysia Chinese Association, at the local levels at least, has recruited members of the secret societies (Koon 1988:80). The secret societies have been employed by opposing political parties to disrupt their opponents' rallies and meetings, intimidate voters, distribute literature, etc. (Means 1976:29; Koon 1988:80). For these services the secret societies received money and/or protection from politicians (Mak 1975a:10).

Wealthy businessmen also have provided the secret societies with protection. If the success of former bookmakers, gambling-den operators, brothel operators, and illegal lottery operators was due to secret society protection, these businessmen repay this debt to a secret society by providing bail, hiring lawyers, or contributing money to help a secret society member avoid arrest by fleeing town (Mak 1975a:13–14). Some secret societies have collected funds for annual community festivals and celebrations organized by ethnic associations (Mak 1981). Their members have also participated in them. In Ipoh Town (Perak), for example, the Ling Pa Kongsi have participated in the annual Chiu Huang Ye (Nine Mighty Deities) religious festival, which lasts a month (Mak 1975a:10).

The basic source of modern secret society power comes from its protectionist activities. Operators of some of the illegal and socially undesirable businesses cannot always get police protection. Secret societies fill this need. Internal migrant workers that have flocked to the towns and cities lack kinship support groups. Secret societies take over the function of kinsmen for such migrants (Mak 1985:156–57). But even legitimate businesses threatened by criminal gangs seek secret society protection. Secret societies have penetrated public housing construction by requiring contractors to pay the secret society protection money in order to prevent damage to their equipment that would delay construction work (Seah and Ag ASP 1978:91). In a similar fashion secret societies have extracted protection money from hawkers, hotel keepers, taxi drivers, dance hostesses, boatmen, shipping contractors, and others (Comber 1957:41).

Each secret society has a monopoly over the collection of protection money in a particular territory. All businesses that are conducted within the boundary of an operational territory of a society are protected if they pay regular fees (Mak 1975a, 1981). Secret society control over protectionist territories is challenged by two groups: the corrupt police officers and rival societies. Illegal business operators (prostitution, drugs, etc.) may prefer to pay police for protection rather than the secret society (Mak 1981). Rival societies seeking to establish a base of power may encroach on the territory of other societies. This attempt precipitates open conflict between groups, bringing about police crackdowns. To avoid this, secret society officials of rival organizations may attempt a peaceful resolution in conferences called "tea-table talks" (Mak 1981). However, such negotiated compromises may be undermined by the society "fighters," called tiger-generals, who provoke fights with rival organizations in order to build their reputations, the only means by which they achieve mobility within the secret society itself (Mak 1981).

Thus, the overdeterminant impact of the legal superstructure on secret society organizations has produced counterdeterminant conjunctive moments by the secret orders. Through structural changes and the formation of new ties with legitimate political organizations, the secret societies have extended power over segments of the Chinese community.

SUMMARY

The study of Triad-state relations in Malaysia gives us further illustrations of secret society activity as a historic dynamic and of how the evolution of relations between secret societies and the state is conditioned by the structural contradictions developing within the social formation and how in turn these contradictions are perpetuated or resolved by secret society praxis.

During the nineteenth century, basic contradictions emerged between the British colonial state and Triad organizations. The British administrators were dependent on dialect groups for various economic and political functions and thus, indirectly, on the Triad organizations that helped the Chinese dialect groups to carry out these activities. The willingness of the British to give the Chinese considerable economic and political freedom reflected the British laissez-faire ideology. Eventually efforts by the secret societies to expand the economic monopoly of their dialect groups led to open conflict among Triad societies and, thus, political instability.

The power of the Triads not only undermined colonial authority in Malaysia but also made it difficult for British colonial officials to serve the interests of European capital in the area. With Europeans gaining control of mining and other economic enterprises of Malaysia, secret society control over the labor supply hindered the growth of the capitalist sector. To resolve the crisis produced by this basic structural contradiction, the colonial government attempted to destroy Triad power. Thus, the growth of Chinese secret society power had an overdeterminant impact on the colonial superstructure with a counterdeterminant response within the legal and ideological subsystems. The British abandoned their laissez-faire ideology, insofar as it applied to the Chinese community, by enacting laws that were designed to crush Triad power.

Following World War II the independent government of Malaysia, now dominated by the Malays, continued this process of secret society repression. These efforts were consistent with the Malay ideology which viewed the Chinese (and the Indians as well) as not truly legitimate members of Malaysian society.

Until the end of the nineteenth century the colonial government in Malaysia tolerated secret society activities because these societies served as agencies for the management of Chinese immigration and for control and protection of the Chinese labor force. Eventually, however, the economic and political role of the secret societies began to clash with the economic interests of the colonial government.

This structural contradiction resulted from the fact that the Triad societies, for the most part, served the interests of the dialect groups with which they were associated. The *pangs* depended on the secret society to protect their monopoly of certain businesses and occupations and, when necessary, to take over control of businesses from other dialect groups. These inter-*pang* rivalries manifested themselves in secret society riots and fights. Moreover, since the Chinese had no representation in the colonial government, riots were also the only way dialect groups could express their opposition to changes in government policy that affected their interests adversely. Later these structural fault lines were accentuated by a depressed world economy which brought a decline in plantation and mining production, resulting in a large labor force without jobs. To maintain power, each secret society had to expand its monopoly over job areas controlled by other societies. The resulting violence between the Triad societies produced political instability on a magnitude sufficient to discourage foreign capital from investing in the Malaysian economy.

In addition, the Triad societies helped maintain a Chinese monopoly over the tin-mining enterprises that the British desired to break. The secret societies also channeled Chinese laborers to Chinese capitalist enterprises, denying Western capital in Malaysia access to this labor force. The original government tolerance for secret society activity had not anticipated this longer-term composite effect.

Thus, in pursuing their own self-interests, the secret societies came into conflict with the economic and political interests of the British colonial government. For these reasons the British acted to suppress all the Triad societies.

Even though some secret society leaders may have anticipated these severe state sanctions, the structural position of the secret society within the Chinese community necessitated that its leaders use violence as a means to achieve its ends. The secret society served the interests of the dialect group to which its members belonged. And to maintain and/or increase its power the dialect association assumed a combative stance against other dialect groups. The secret society members from each dialect group engaged in these confrontations.

Power relations between the state and the Triads were not stable relations but were subject to strategic interaction and rearrangement up until Malaya's independence (1957). Triad power waxed and waned, depending on whether a particular government in Malaysia viewed the Triads as supporting or subverting existing governmental policies.

During their period of occupation the Japanese forced most Triad societies to cease their activities. After the Japanese defeat the British and later Federation governments relaxed enforcement of the anti-secret society ordinances in part to give the anti-communist secret societies free reign against the communist rebels. This policy led to a general resurgence of secret society activity. Secret societies allied with the Kuomintang, and the CPM engaged in bitter rivalry. But the defeat of the communist rebels ended the government's tolerance of Triad disruption, and the postcolonial government employed harsher measures against the Triad groups.

Secret society power was not only weakened by government crackdowns, but by other developments within the Malaysian political economy. Changing economic conditions led to the replacement of Chinese entrepreneurs by European capital, the official abolishment of tax-farms, increased opportunities for employment freed from ethnic and speech criteria, and the loss of support of secret societies by the Chinese elite. The older structures, which had given support to Triad activities, evaporated. The traditional Triad system came into contradiction with the interests of the independent government and the newly emerging economic institutions.

To survive within the new political climate secret societies were forced to simplify their rituals and develop organizational strategies that stressed decentralization and recentralization, depending on their immediate circumstances. Front organizations were formed to disguise the continued existence of the older Triad groups.

Such conjunctive strategies were defensive, but each secret society also had to seek a new power base within a specific territory. The secret societies began to recruit young men with limited schooling and limited skills; these younger recruits ran the protection operations. The new recruits in a particular Triad group now came from *different* dialect and surname groups.

These reactive strategies seem reasonable in light of the government crackdowns, the erosion of the support by dialect groups, and the desertion by the wealthy Chinese class. But for the traditional Triad societies the long-term consequences were less than beneficial. The "tactical fragmentation" of the larger Triad societies into smaller groups eventually undermined Triad control over these groups, which began to operate independently of their parent societies, preserving neither the older rituals nor the administrative structures.

Legitimate Chinese political parties have secretly relied on the secret societies as a local power bases for their parties. But the political groups have tried to conceal the nature of these alliances with the secret organizations from the general public to avoid negative reactions which could erode their political support. Such alliances, including those with certain wealthy Chinese businessmen, have enabled the secret societies to maintain their power base within the Chinese community.

The government success at destroying, for the most part, the older Triad system created new problems for the Federation of Malaysia state as well as for Singapore. The proliferation of small, criminal secret societies perpetuated the criminal structures within the Chinese communities. New fighting between secret societies over "protection" territories increased.

By destroying the older Triad system, the Malaysian state had created a new secret society system that came into contradiction with state interests. New fault lines have emerged at which the state and secret societies come into conflict. These conflicts do not pose a serious threat to the reproduction of the modern Malaysian political economy, but they do undermine government control over significant segments of the Malaysian Chinese community.

Triad-state relations in Malaya support the observation that state tolerance or hostility for secret society activity reflects the extent to which secret societies undermine state efforts to reproduce the relations of production or facilitate them. The ebb and flow of secret society–state relations may be dictated by this consideration for the most part.

The long-term dangers of secret society activity may not be readily apparent to state agents until efforts are made by state officials to implement economic and political plans that place the state in direct conflict with secret society interests. Once these conflicts at the structural fault lines emerge, the government is never reluctant to enact laws that make secret societies illegal. But as our study of the Triads reveals, secret societies are resilient organizations. They have developed strategies by which they utilize various information-control processes to their advantage, denying information to the police but gaining vital information through espionage within the government itself. By developing these defensive power resources and finding new functional niches within the political and economic structures where their services are desired, they find ways to survive.

6

The Broederbond of South Africa

THE GROWTH OF AFRIKANER POWER

The Broederbond (the Bond) of South Africa is a secret organization whose goal is to protect and advance the welfare of Afrikaners. To achieve this goal the secret order makes sure that their members achieve prominent policy-making roles in government and also helps them gain influential positions in industry and the professions. Through such means the Broederbond strives to perpetuate a separate Afrikaner nation with its own language and culture. To promote Afrikaner nationalism the Broederbond requires that members speak Afrikans at home, at work, and in the community at large (Wilkins and Strydon 1979; Pirie et al. 1980).

The Broederbond represents a secret society that has evolved from a position in which it was subject to state repression (because it opposed the government's political and economic policies) to its position today as a dominant force within the ruling National Party. To protect itself from its enemies the Bond threw a rigid veil of secrecy over its membership and activities. As a secret society it was also able to subvert a wide range of other organizations by placing its members in influential positions within them. Using secrecy as a power resource, the Broederbond eventually was able to place the National Party in power. The racial policies formulated by the Bond and implemented by the National Party have enabled Afrikaners to obtain positions of economic and political power in Africa, positions they once did not enjoy.

Yet the racial policies have now come into contradiction with the economic and political realities of modern South African society. Attempts by the

Bond leadership to moderate its original racist programs have brought division and disaffection by conservative members. Conflicts within the Bond and between the Bond and various Afrikaner class segments are a direct manifestation of the contradictions within South African society that have generated the crises which threaten white hegemony. The nature of Afrikaner response to these crises is, in part, influenced by their class position. The Bond has formulated reformist policies more favorable to its middle-class and business-sector members. These policies are opposed by white labor and poor rural farmers; the Bond has lost support of these segments of the Afrikaner population. Thus, threats to current Bond power do not stem from the failure of its secrecy structure, but from the erosion of its support within the Afrikaner community.

To understand the role that the Broederbond has played in the politics of South Africa, we must study the emerging contradictions within the South African society as they have affected the Afrikaners and their relations with the black population and other segments of the white elite. Therefore, I will give a brief review of South African history first, concentrating on the contradictions within the South African political economy preceding and during the rise of the Broederbond.

EARLY AFRIKANER HISTORY

The Cape Colony in South Africa originated when the Dutch East Indian Company established a way station for Dutch ships at Cape Town in 1652. Five years later the Cape became a colony. By 1657 a small group of Dutch-Germany settlers (Free Burghers) had established independent farming settlements which soon expanded beyond the colony's effective boundaries, taking over land seized from the indigenous African population (Ume 1981:176). To do heavy work the Dutch settlers (along with Germans and French Huguenots) brought in slaves from Madagascar, Mozambique, and the Dutch East Indies. By the mid-1800s there were 20,000 Europeans in the colony (Carter 1982:95, 1986:345; Simson 1980:47).

Some of these early settlers were large-scale ranchers who gained land easily and, as easily, moved onto new land once their pastures were overgrazed. After several generations of unhindered movement with little government interference, these *trekboers* came to regard all government as an interference with their personal liberty (Lemon 1987:19).

The English occupied the Cape in 1795 and annexed it in 1815, in order to deny the strategic site to France's Indian trade. The British and Afrikaner (Boer) came to have conflicting economic interests. These structural oppositions were accentuated by divergent political and ideological frameworks.

The different racial policies of the British and Afrikaner served to identify the nature of the contradictory interests between the two groups at the ideological level. The conflicts that emerged at the fault lines between the two populations eventually led to armed struggle. But the military defeat of the Afrikaners did not lead, as the British had anticipated, to the Afrikaners' integration into British-dominated South Africa. In such circumstances the overdeterminant political subsystem can lead to counterdeterminant changes in other subsystems of the social formation. This was the case in South Africa, Afrikaners resisted integration at the political and ideological levels. To seek a resolution of these conflicts the British granted self-government to South Africa as a dominion within the British Commonwealth.

Shortly after establishing their control in the Cape, the British adopted policies that the Boers (Dutch settlers) found objectionable. The British abolished slavery in 1833 and passed laws protecting the Coloured class. (Coloureds are of mixed racial descent). In 1822 the Cape government made English the only legitimate language of the courts and the schools (Harrison 1981:48). As a result of these policies the Boers lost their slaves and suffered a shortage of land, labor, and capital. They also felt that their way of life was under attack (Muller 1981:153).

Between 1834–36 the Boers began their Great Boer Trek to escape the oppression of the British (Simson 1980:57; Carter 1986:345). The trek was organized by Boer farmers who sought new land to the north and northwest of the Cape borders. During the course of the decade following 1836, from twelve to fourteen thousand *trekboers* moved out of the Cape Colony (Lemon 1987:26).

The first attempts by the Boer trekkers to establish a new state in Natal failed when the British annexed the area in 1845. But shortly thereafter the Boers were able to establish two republics: the Orange Free State and the South African Republic (Transvaal) (Carter 1982:96; Muller 1981:180). The British recognized the independence of these republics in 1855 and 1852, respectively. By 1870 there were 45,000 Afrikaners living in the republics with three-fourths of them in the Transvaal (Bundy 1979). The all-white male electorates in the republics stood for the principle of no equality between black and white in church and state. By contrast the British government provided the Cape Colony, through the Constitutional Act of 1853, with a nonracial franchise for the Cape's representative assembly. This provision was continued when the Cape received internal self-government in 1872 (Carter 1986:246).

The discovery of diamond fields at Kimberly in 1867 and gold at Witwatersrand (Transvaal) in 1886 led to industrial developments that had a profound impact on the economic and social life of the Boer subsistence farmer and herder (Carter 1982:96; Du Plessis 1981:283). Coal resources were soon developed to supply power to the mines and emerging railway systems (Houghton 1971:13). Mining also created a large market for agricultural products (O'Meara 1983; Houghton 1971). The commercialization of agriculture forced small-scale and inefficient farmers off the land. Such farmers were compelled to sell farms to absentee landlords or mining companies (Nattrass 1981:61; O'Meara 1983; Welsh 1975:250). Some Boer farmers turned to gold mining. Others entered the transport business carrying supplies to and from the mines (Van Schore 1981:240).

British interest in gaining control over the Boer Republics was a natural outgrowth of the dominance of British capital investment within the South African mining industry (Simson 1980:47; Atmore and Marks 1974). The Cape government feared that the republics would become so strong that they could dominate all South Africa (Van Zyl 1981:304; Houghton 1971:14). These fears were accentuated when the Afrikaner government in the Transvaal refused political rights to foreigners (*uitlanders*) who came there largely to exploit the mineral resources owned by the republics (Carter 1982:97; Cape 1967:91).

Such tensions between the republics and the British gave way to more direct conflict. The British annexed Transvaal in 1877 but returned it to Afrikaner control when the Afrikaners defeated the British army in 1881 (Carter 1986:96). Cecil Rhodes, prime minister of the Cape, and the British government also had a hand in a coup attempt known as the Jameson Raid, which failed, thus preventing the British from getting control of the Transvaal (Bunting 1964:14; Van Zyl 1981:310). These confrontations led inevitably to the Anglo-Boer War of 1889–1902. Thus, the British went to war with the Boers in order to establish in South Africa the necessary infrastructure by which they could maintain and develop their economic interests.

AFTERMATH OF THE ANGLO-BOER WAR

The British won the war but at a terrible price. The British military devised a search-and-destroy policy designed to eradicate the resistance of the Boer commandos that were fighting them. The British razed Boer villages to the ground, slaughtered or carried away the bulk of the Boer livestock, and destroyed about 30,000 Boer farms in the process (De Kock 1968:20; Davenport 1977:146; Meredith 1988:10). Dispossessed Boer women and children, numbering some 120,000, were placed in concentration camps by the British. About 26,000 of these died in the camps (Bunting 1964:17).

The war also forced the removal of black Africans from their lands in the war zone and resulted in the destruction of their homes and crops. About 80,000 black Africans were placed in camps. Other African refugees were allowed to grow subsistence crops along the railway lines on land vacated by the whites (Bundy 1979:201).

The Peace of Vereeniging in 1902 marked the demise of the Boer republics. The British government first tried to anglicize the Boers (hereafter called Afrikaners) by making English the major medium of instruction and encouraging English immigration into South Africa. But later the liberal government, under Sir Henry Campbell-Bannerman, granted self-government to South Africa. By the South African Act of Union in 1910, South Africa became an independent dominion within the British Commonwealth as the four colonies merged into the Union of South Africa. The two defeated Boer republics united with the Cape and Natal.

Newly established centralized state authority become the foci at which older contradictions manifest themselves. The new South African government became such a foci. Contradictions not only between the political and economic interests of the Afrikaners and the British government but also between the Afrikaners and the South African British-speakers and the blacks (and other nonwhite groups) created the crises with which the new South African government had to contend. However, government efforts to resolve these problems led to new fissions among the Afrikaners and the other racial groups.

The first election took place in 1910. While Cape liberals fought for an extension of the Cape's nonracial franchise throughout all of South Africa, the all-white national convention that drew up the terms of the union eliminated the African vote from the general electoral process (Carter 1986:347). The nonracial franchise applied only to the Cape (eliminated as well in 1936).

The South African Party won the 1910 election. Louis Botha, a former Afrikaner general, became the prime minister and his cabinet contained two other Afrikaner generals, Jan Smuts and J. M. B. Hertzog. There were a number of English-speaking South Africans in Botha's cabinet as well (Meredith 1988:11–12).

For the next forty years there were three major themes that dominated South African politics: South Africa's relationship with Britain, the relationship between Afrikaners and the English-speakers, and the policies to be pursued toward blacks and other nonwhites (Lemon 1987:45).

Questions related to the future of English-Afrikaner relations in South Africa divided the Botha-Smuts government. There was friction between the Botha-Smuts faction and the faction led by General J. M. B. Hertzog. The

Botha-Smuts policy aimed at eliminating racialism between the English and the Dutch by reconciliation of the two populations into "one stream." Hertzog advocated a "two-stream" approach, whereby the British and the Afrikaner were to develop separately, side-by-side, with neither subordinate to the other (De Kock 1968:25; Bunting 1964:22–23).

The new South African state was required to secure supplies of cheap labor for the capitalist enterprises. Through state actions the racial division of land was legitimized. The government also administered an array of new controls and coercive measures over the labor force. The fact that under the migrant labor system the African workers retained some base in the peasant economy of the labor reserve areas made it possible for the Afrikaner government to present the tribal political organization as an alternative to black representation in the central state.

Even before the Anglo-Boer War the mines and large-scale white farmers found it difficult to obtain cheap black labor. Imported indentured Indians (on sugarcane plantations) and Chinese (in mines) served as inadequate substitutes (Magubane 1978:263–64). After the war this shortage of African labor continued (Magubane 1978:264–65). Black peasants were able to avoid wage labor by renting land from whites or buying back land with money from the sale of farm surpluses (Bundy 1979:198). Some Africans also leased Crown land (Bundy 1979:207).

For Afrikaners and other whites the replication of the economic base on which their livelihood depended was made difficult by the existing political superstructure. It was in white interests to force changes in the legal subsystem. But such changes were to have an overdeterminant impact on the blacks' political and economic systems.

Black labor shortages caused mine owners and some white farmers to put pressure on the government to establish a law that would undercut the independent economic base of the African peasant by limiting their access to farmland. The Natives Land Act of 1913 did just that by placing restrictions on tenancy (leases of land for cash, share of crops, or part-time labor) as well as on squatting (Liebenberg 1981:395; Carter 1982:98; Simson 1980:51; Magubane 1978:266; Harrison 1981:69; Lemon 1987:36; Wolpe 1980). The 1913 Act eliminated the richer African peasantry that had begun to emerge with the expansion of the local market for agricultural commodities following the development of the mining industry (Davies, O'Meara, and Dlamini 1988, vol. 1:169–70). The introduction of taxes also forced black peasants to enter the labor market (Lemon 1987:36).

In 1936 the Native Land and Trust Act expanded native reserves from 7.3 percent of total land base to 13 percent. This left 87 percent of land in South

Africa for whites (Bundy 1979:231). The 1936 Act prohibited Cape Africans from acquiring land outside these designated reserves as well as limited the number of labor tenants residing on white-owned farms (Harrison 1981:69; Davies, O'Meara, and Dlamini 1988, vol. 1:169–70).

Black businessmen were hindered by legal restrictions on their right to own or lease businesses and property and by a licensing system that kept their opportunities for such economic enterprises at a minimum even in the reserves or black urban townships (Lipton 1985:18).

By limiting the development of the African subsistence and business sectors, the government forced the Africans into wage labor. The mines could pay Africans a wage considerably below subsistence needs, since the women and children of black miners were expected to farm lands on the reserves (Magubane 1978:255, 262; Simson 1980:55). Lipton points to the effect of the 1913 Land Act when he observes that it "destroyed a class of African tenant farmers in the 'white areas' and led to increased population pressure in the homelands which, combined with taxes, converted many African farmers into labour migrants to white areas to work" (1985:104).

To reinforce the reserve system, the Afrikaner government established a tribally based but state-installed political structure for the Africans and also instituted a system of influx control. The "pass laws" legislated by the government aimed at the maintenance of a cheap labor system by restricting the freedom of movement of blacks so as to channel workers where the employers needed cheap labor, enforcing employment contracts by making workers stay where needed as long as required, and by barricading the surplus black population in rural reserves until their labor was required (Lipton 1985:18; Davies, O'Meara, and Dlamini 1988, vol. 1:171). The Pass Law Act of 1932 enabled the government to control the flow of African labor into "white areas," particularly towns, and to allocate labor between sectors and regions (Lipton 1985:18). The Pass Law required the Africans to carry reference books indicating their right to be in an urban area (Ume 1981:170).[1]

These policies favored the mining industry's system of housing migrant workers in all-male compounds and also hindered the free movement of Africans wishing to leave white farms and reserves. To further insure that black workers would remain on the white farms, the government enacted the 1932 Native Service Contract Act, which required that government departments not recruit labor from white rural farm areas. It also legally tied all members of black families to their white farm employers (Lipton 1985:91). Without these various laws white farmers would not have been able to control their black labor supply because farm wages were about 64 percent of the cash wages in mining and 27 percent of the black wages in manufacturing (Lipton 1985:98).

Black populations that had access to representative institutions constituted a threat to white control. Therefore the government opened an attack against the nonwhite franchise in the Cape Province. The 1936 Native Representation Act removed the African voters from the common roll and introduced a segregated system in which four whites represented all African interests in Parliament. The 1936 Act also set up a Native Representative Council for Africans. This body had only advisory powers. Coloureds remained on the common roll (James and du Pisanie 1987:43; Lipton 1985:17; Magubane 1978:27–28).[2]

However by the 1970s all Africans, Coloureds, and Asians were excluded from representative institutions of the Afrikaner state. Africans were supposed to exercise political rights through tribal structures while Coloureds were represented by the Coloured Representative Council and the Asians by the South African Indian Council (Davies, O'Meara, and Dlamini 1988, vol. 1:135).

After the Anglo-Boer War, impoverished Afrikaners left the rural areas in vast numbers, migrating to the urban areas. In 1890, only 36 percent of all the Afrikaners lived in towns, but by 1921, 56 percent of the Afrikaners lived there (Nattrass 1981:131). The exodus of farmers from the rural communities also drove the petty bourgeoisie from the rural towns as well (O'Meara 1983:26).

The economic decline of the Afrikaner farmers was due, in part, to Britain's policy during the Anglo-Boer War of laying waste to vast areas of the Transvaal and the Orange Free State. But white poverty in rural areas was also the result of the Afrikaner's poor farming methods, droughts and disease affecting the livestock, inheritance laws that led to the subdivision of land into small, uneconomic holdings, and the spread of commercial agriculture (Meredith 1988:16; Horwitz 1967:140–65).

By 1920 poor whites constituted 60 percent of the Afrikaans-speaking population (Carter 1982:98). Those migrating to towns and cities were poorly educated, ill-equipped for industrial jobs, and had a traditional aversion to industrial manual work (Walsh 1974:251); their prospects were grim. The Carnegie Commission report estimated that in 1930, 17.3 percent of the white families, nine out of ten of them Afrikaans-speakers, were in dire poverty with another 31 percent so poor they could not adequately feed and clothe their children (Meredith 1988:18).

Living in the urban townships next to Africans and working side by side with them at work places, Afrikaners grew to fear African competition and the challenges that these contacts imposed on their beliefs in their own racial superiority (Carter 1959:237).

The economic prospects of the small Afrikaans-speaking middle class were also limited. The English-speaking South Africans dominated the civil service as well as management positions in private industry and commerce (Serfontein 1978:11; O'Meara 1983; Harrison 1981:651). Mining, manufacturing, and commerce were controlled by British capital (Houghton 1971; O'Meara 1983). Afrikaner traders were being undermined by competition from Indian traders (O'Meara 1983:168).

In his address to the 1968 *Bondsraad* (the annual congress of the Bond) during the jubilee celebrations, Dr. Piet Meyer vividly described this period in Afrikaner history as he perceived it. He said that the Afrikaner *volk* had not only been humiliated in schools and shops but that

> it was more oppressive in our daily existence as members of an all-embracing socio-economic whole, of an impoverished platteland and British-Jewish-dominated growing urban complexes. We were the poor and the Poor Whites, the Boers without markets and without capital: the lowly-paid skilled workers in the mines and the factories; we were the civil servants in the inferior jobs, on the railways, in the post office, in the police.
>
> When the great drought came, we were the first who had to toil merely to live; and when the Great Depression came, we were the first unemployed. Brotherhood did not escape this all; it was in it and struggled with it. (Cited in Serfontein 1978:37.)

The large, poor white class and the growing group of impoverished Africans resorted to strikes. As a result the government sponsored legislation that would regulate management-worker relations and increase the opportunities for whites to obtain jobs in government and private industry.

White mine labor found their economic position very insecure. In the 1920s the black dock workers and later the black miners secured some wage increases through strikes organized by the Industrial and Commercial Union. Mine owners attempted to cut costs by shifting jobs from unskilled whites to blacks. In 1922 this action led to strikes by the white unions, which turned into a general strike. The government used force to put down the ensuing violence (Carter 1986:348; Simson 1980:67; Harrison 1981:78; Mac-Shane, Plant, and Ward 1984:26).[3]

This strike led to the passage of the Industrial Conciliation Act in 1924, which was devised by the Smuts government as a device to prevent strikes by setting up a complex conciliation machinery.

Ultimately support for the state rests on the ability of its leaders to provide the basic requirements of the population, which constitutes its base of political support. To retain its power, the new South African government had to find ways to open up new economic opportunities for the Afrikaners. To do so the government erected a legal structure that favored white labor over that of blacks and other nonwhite workers and that counteracted British discrimination against Afrikaners within the government and business corporations.

The job bar was entrenched in the Mine and Works Act of 1926, which amended the 1911 Act. Blacks were barred from skilled mining jobs. Such laws reinforced the "civilized labor" policy, which protected state workers from being undercut by blacks and provided whites preferential employment in unskilled jobs at higher rates of pay than blacks (Bunting 1964:47; Lipton 1985:19). The earlier Wage Act of 1923 had already fixed the pay scale for whites far above that of black Africans (Carter 1980:19), who were also excluded from registered unions (Simson 1980:129–35). White trade unionists could participate along with employers on industrial councils and boards. This participation gave white workers more power than black labor to set their wages and more access to jobs (Lipton 1985:19).

As I have indicated, General Hertzog opposed the conciliatory policies of the South African Party (SAP) toward British interests in South Africa. In 1912, Hertzog left the SAP and he and his followers formed the National Party (NP) in 1914, which, in alliance with the Labour Party, won power in 1924 (Cape 1967:96). The National Party favored strict separation of whites and nonwhites to preserve the purity of the Afrikaner population, channeling of black labor to white farms and mines, protecting white labor from black competition, and reducing British dominance within South Africa (Bunting 1964:25).

Hertzog first moved to achieve more independence for South Africa and to counteract British dominance. At the Imperial Ministers Conference of 1926 he called for greater independence for the dominions within the framework of the empire. The resulting Balfour Declaration gave the dominions equal status as members of the British Commonwealth though united by common allegiance to the Crown. By 1927 the National Party gave up its stated aim to achieve independence from Britain and accepted the declaration of the Imperial Conference (Bunting 1964:39). Hertzog's abandonment of efforts to establish an independent republic for South African whites incensed many white nationalists, who considered his abandonment of republicanism a betrayal of Afrikaner interests (Meredith 1988:15).

Afrikaners also feared that their language and culture would be submerged by the British. The Treaty of Vereeniging (1902), which ended the Anglo-Boer War, provided that both English and Dutch languages would be taught in the public schools of the Transvaal and the Orange River Colony if the parents of the children demanded it. In reality this meant that English became the dominant language of instruction (Bunting 1964:19; O'Meara 1983; Serfontein 1978).

The Dutch Reformed Church resisted these language policies, and set up private schools to further Christian-National Education. Dutch was the major medium of instruction, Calvinist theology was stressed, and Afrikaner consciousness was promoted (Spies 1981:365; Meredith 1988:12). However, English-speakers continued to hold contempt for Afrikaans. Thus, the Afrikaners were at a disadvantage in seeking jobs in government, industry, and the schools dominated by the English.

The discrimination by the British against Afrikaners within the government was counteracted by new legal measures. The Hertzog government passed the Language Act of 1925, which facilitated the rapid promotion of Afrikaans-speakers in state bureaucracy (O'Meara 1983:39).

While the National Party's labor policies under Hertzog were generally favorable to mining, its nonracial plans were much more costly to the mining interests. Protection of local industry and state-sponsored companies such as ISCOR (Iron and Steel Corporation), which set high prices for products needed by the mining industry, did not serve the economic interests of the mining industry (Lipton 1985:264–65; Milkman 1979:269). Even so, between 1900 and 1937, mining expanded at the expense of agriculture with minerals constituting about 60 percent of all exports (Milkman 1979:265).

The depression years of the early 1930s created mass unemployment within South Africa. The economic hardships of the 1930s were made worse by Hertzog's gold policies, which undermined the competitive positions of the mines and farmers on the world market. Even the nationalized industries such as ISCOR had to lay off white workers (Lipton 1985:267).

The unpopularity of Hertzog's economic policy forced him to seek a political alliance with Smuts in order to retain power. So in 1934, Hertzog and Smuts, together with their followers, formed the United South African National Party (United Party, or UP). The UP continued to pursue policies favorable to agriculture and labor (Lipton 1985:267).

The outbreak of World War II in Europe forced South Africa to make a choice between neutrality (favored by Hertzog) or support for Britain and the Commonwealth (advocated by Smuts). Smuts's view prevailed, and Hertzog resigned as prime minister (Bunting 1964:74–75).

After World War II, manufacturing income grew while mining income fell (O'Meara 1983:226–27; Houghton 1971; Simson 1980:75). The economic crises of the 1930s gave way to the economic prosperity brought by World War II. This economic stimulus pulled most of the poor whites out of poverty (Horwitz 1967:201). There was an increase of the black labor force in manufacturing with many blacks taking over more semi-skilled and skilled jobs (Houghton 1971:43; MacShane, Plant, and Ward 1984:28; Bunting 1964:43–44).

The economic stimulus that the war provided the South African economy resulted in economic growth and, in turn, labor shortages. The apartheid policies came into conflict with the new economic realities. Thus, during the period of 1939–48 there was some erosion of apartheid restrictions.

Government commissions observed that the effects of industrialization and poverty on the crowded black African reserves would inevitably bring about a larger and permanent black African urbanization. Industrialization required that African workers should be stabilized in towns and provided with improved education and pay, and prospects for promotion. Only in this way could the type of workforce be developed in South Africa that was required by modern industry and a modern economy (Lipton 1985:21). The job color bar, the pass laws, and migrant labor were criticized as unjust and inefficient.

Responding to the commission's recommendations, the government eased the color bar and created new training facilities for blacks in order to expand the supply of skilled labor. Black-white wage ratios narrowed, though still far in favor of the whites (Lipton 1985:21). The 1945 National Education Finance Act gave support to black children's education out of the general revenue budget rather than from African taxes as in the past. The Unemployment Insurance Act of 1946 entitled African workers (other than those in agriculture and mining) to state unemployment benefits (Simson 1980:133). There was also some easing of the restriction on black business.

THE BROEDERBOND AND ITS POLITICAL ROLE IN SOUTH AFRICA

The economic and political policies of the South African government put its leadership in conflict with the Afrikaner nationalists. The nationalists opposed the government's accommodation to British capital, its acceptance of dominion status for South Africa rather than total independence from Britain, its inability to challenge the monopoly power of the British-speakers in finance, banking, and industry and, with the end of World War II, its efforts to weaken apartheid restrictions on the black population. The

Broederbond emerged at this fault line dividing the Afrikaner nationalists from the government leadership to champion the nationalist cause. To achieve nationalist objectives, the Bond worked to overcome the class divisions within the Afrikaner community by using the Christian-Nationalist ideology as a cementing force.

The contradictions within the South African political economy, which I have briefly sketched, insofar as they affected the Afrikaner population in a negative way, served as the sociopolitical catalyst for Broederbond formation. As the Bond gained more power among the Afrikaner population, its own policies began to accentuate the cleavages within South African society, not resolving the contradictions but fueling the conflicts that were precipitated by them.

The Bond grew out of a group called the *Johg Suid Africa* (Young South Africa), which was formed early in 1918.[4] Starting with fourteen individuals in 1918, its membership grew to around eight thousand in the 1980s (Bloomberg 1989:33). Later this organization changed its name to the Afrikaner Broederbond (Afrikaner Brotherhood) and turned itself into a secret organization in 1921, to protect its members from economic reprisals. Later, attacks by the government on members of the organization as well as frequent attempts by unfriendly newspapers to expose the organization accentuated the Bond's desire to protect itself through secrecy (O'Meara 1977:159; Serfontein 1978). Secrecy, aside from operating as a form of self-defense, has given the Bond a greater freedom to penetrate other organizations useful to its cause (Bloomberg 1989:73).

The Bond's major center of strength was in the Transvaal and the Orange Free State but in recent years its influence has become more widespread throughout South Africa (O'Meara 1977:158).

The Broederbond's major goals seem to have been very clear:

> "1. Removal of everything in conflict with South Africa's full international independence.
> 2. The ending of the inferiority of the Afrikaans-speaking and of their language in the organization of the state.
> 3. Separation of all non-white races in South Africa, leaving them free to independent development under the guardianship of the Whites.
> 4. Putting a stop to the exploitation of the resources and population of South Africa by strangers.
> 5. The rehabilitation of the farming community and the assurance of civilized self-support through work for all White citizens.
> 6. The nationalization of the money market and the systematic coordination of economic policies.

7. The Afrikanerization of public life and teaching and education in a Christian-National spirit while leaving free the internal development of all sections in so far as it is not dangerous to the state." (Cited in Bunting 1964:49–50.)

Since its inception, the general aim of the Bond has been to protect the Afrikaner by means of a widespread and effective secret organization against vilification, humiliation, and oppression. However, in reality, throughout most of its history the Bond has promoted the interests of the Boer middle class. Yet to expand middle-class political power the Bond has had to seek support from other class segments (O'Meara 1983; Pirie, Rogerson, and Beavon 1980).

Until the early 1930s there was considerable political turmoil within the Bond over its political objectives. But the Bond began to build a basis for political support for petite-bourgeoisie-class interests (O'Meara 1977). The Bond opposed the South African Party (SAP), whose leaders favored the wealthy farmers and mining interests (O'Meara 1983; Serfontein 1978; Davenport 1977). The Bond gained support for its policies of compulsory bilingualism in schools and the opening of occupational opportunities for Afrikaners in civil service and in the senior- and middle-management positions in manufacturing, mining, and commercial enterprises (Cape 1967; O'Meara 1983). The Bond's support for apartheid policies won them farming and working-class support because influx control assured farmers that there would be sufficient African labor in rural areas and labor reservation codes protected white workers from African competition (O'Meara 1977; Serfontein 1978). In this way the Bond sought allies by appealing to the agricultural interests and to Afrikaner workers. The Bond's search for support from various class segments is explained by its obsession with the dangers of class division and conflict and its stress on the interest of all Afrikaner folk in common political, economic, and cultural goals (O'Meara 1977; Walsh 1974:249). Such an emphasis is not surprising since the petite bourgeoisie could not sustain state power on its own. Threats to these alliances would isolate the Afrikaner bourgeoisie (O'Meara 1977:162). There was also widespread Afrikaner support for the Bond's goal of forming an independent Afrikaner-ruled republic free of political ties to Britain (achieved in 1961).

The National Party came into power under Hertzog in 1924. Strong opposition within the Bond developed against the National Party's fusion with the South African Party in 1934. The Bond also opposed Hertzog's two-stream policy aimed at the eventual merger of Boer and English-speaking South Africans into one nation and his acceptance of South African sovereign status within the British commonwealth rather than total independence (O'Meara 1983; Villiers 1971; Davenport 1977; Cape 1967). Such compromises, the Bond felt, stood in the way of their goal to wrest British capital's control of the South African economy. To do so the Bond needed to create a financial network enabling the Afrikaner bourgeoisie to gain a foothold in industry and commerce (O'Meara 1983).

The Bond aimed to promote unity within the deeply divided Afrikaner population. To help unify the diverse class segments within Afrikanerdom, the Broederbond developed a coherent ideology based on Christian-Nationalism. This Christian-Nationalistic doctrine was based on a selective interpretation of the early-twentieth-century Calvinist theology of Abraham Kuyper (Bloomberg 1989:4–13). It consisted of a body of closely integrated ideas that incorporated the view of the Afrikaners as the "chosen-people-with-a-mission," stressed authority, hierarchy, and discipline, and expressed a desire for a privileged and elitist leadership and the glorification of God and nation. The Broederbond justified the Afrikaners' monopoly of political power by the belief that the Afrikaners had the divinely bestowed responsibility to act as guardians of the backward people in South Africa (i.e., all nonwhites). The Afrikaners' mission was to help the nonwhite races to become self-supporting. One basic tenet of Christian-Nationalism was the supposition that the world was divided into races, nations, and cultures that were divinely fixed and immutable units. Between such groups and the white race there were unequal distributions of talents, virtues, and intelligence.

According to such beliefs the state has an organic status and character. To serve the nation is a sacred duty. The interests of the *volk* transcend the interests of its members. As true believers the Afrikaners must be active in all areas of the community and must spread the gospel into every area of human association.

In endorsing the Christian-Nationalist doctrines the Broederbond also defined their ideological enemies, namely liberalism, modernism, humanism, Marxism, individualism, and rationalism. Such forces, the Bond believed, divided the Afrikaners into classes or unified sections of the Afrikaner population either with the English or with the Africans and other nonwhite groups, thus attacking the concept of Afrikaners as an organic unit. Such dangerous doctrines spread beliefs that questioned the Bond ideology, which pictured the Afrikaners as a divinely chosen people with a unique language, culture, and history and thus constituting an organic unity from which foreign elements, such as the English and blacks were excluded (Meredith 1988:23).

The Bond recognized that class divisions within the Afrikaner population created the potential for conflicts that might weaken Afrikaner unity and undermine the Bond's ability to acquire state power for the Afrikaners. By spreading a Christian-Nationalist ideology throughout the Afrikaner population, the Bond was able to stress themes that unified the Afrikaners rather than divided them and thereby defined the agenda of issues in a manner which brought the classes together for a common mission.

To dramatize the heroic character of the Afrikaner people in their epic struggle against the British and the blacks, the Broederbond organized a centenary Great Trek celebration. Beginning in 1923 these celebrations sent Afrikaner celebrants on a commemorative route from Cape Town to Pretoria. The participants gave speeches at the towns through which the trek passed, exhorting Afrikaners to remember their heroic past and their chosen destiny. Afrikaners perceived their historic trek to escape British control as evidence that "God had summoned the Boers for the same mission as the Israelites of the Old Testament who had trekked from Egypt to escape the Pharaoh's yoke and to establish the promised land" (Meredith 1988:26).

To expand its political base, the Bond began to penetrate all major institutions of the Republic of South Africa. A network of 810 cells (with five to fifty members each) has enabled the Broederbond to infiltrate members into town and city councils, school boards, universities, agricultural unions, state-controlled radio and television networks, industry, commerce, banks, building societies, professional organizations, various provincial administrations, and national government departments including the civil service, army, police, parliament, and the executive offices (Wilkins and Strydon 1979:366–71; Bloomberg 1989:51–54). Thus the Broederbond has been actively involved in secret penetration of every sector of African society. It has laid the foundations of its organization and created the many front organizations that have enabled it to get an octopuslike grip, first on African nationalism and later on the government structure itself. Thus, to gain power the Bond has tried to penetrate other organizations with the aim of using their resources, facilities, and machinery to achieve Bond goals (Bloomberg 1989:44).

The highest authority of the Bond is the thirteen-member *Uitvoerende Raad*, elected by the annual congress of the Bond, the *Bondsraad*. This executive committee delegates authority for day-to-day operations to a management committee called *Dagbestuur*. Regional councils send delegates to the annual congress to represent the interest of the cells (*afdelings*) in their area (Serfontein 1978:127; Wilkins and Strydon 1979:357–62).

The Bond also has fourteen expert study commissions dominated by intellectuals and clergymen. These commissions draft policy statements on racial and political issues, which have a strong influence on the formulation of the government's legislative programs (Bloomberg 1989:34).

Since 1929, the major policy-implementing body of the Bond has been the *Federasie Van Afrikaaner Kultur Verumigings* (Federation of Afrikaan Cultural Associations [FAK]). The FAK consists of a federation of some 2,000 Afrikaner cultural organizations including church councils, youth and student associations, and scientific and educational organizations (Serfontein 1978; Villiers 1971; Carter 1959:256–58; O'Meara 1983:63, 73). Thus the FAK consists of a federation of autonomous groups, each with its own mass base and unique sphere of operations. It is through the FAK that the Bond works to preserve Afrikaner culture and to promote communal cohesion. At the local levels FAK policies are carried out by local FAK committees, which supervise and coordinate Afrikaner cultural efforts in the area. The Broederbond, then, uses the FAK as its "mouthpiece, a cloak for its public activities and a machine for transmitting Broederbond ideas into every Afrikaner organization, local community and home" (Bloomberg 1989:55).

The FAK has also been influential in promoting the business interests of Afrikaner members through the establishment of an Afrikaner bank that provides financial backing to Afrikaners' business undertakings, and an institute to encourage and promote Afrikaner business enterprises. As O'Meara suggests, "it is clear therefore that the Bond played a major role in the mobilization of Afrikaner capital and enterprise, and in initiating the establishment of Afrikaans' enterprises in spheres which until then had been closed to the Afrikaner" (1983:147).

To combat the power of what Afrikaners' considered "Anglo-Jewish" capitalist power in South Africa, the Bond proposed *volkskapitalisme* (people's capitalism). In promoting *volkskapitalisme* the FAK mobilized the profits of Afrikaner farmers, the savings of Afrikaner workers, and the surplus wealth of the Afrikaner petite bourgeoisie (Davis, O'Meara, and Dlamini 1988, vol. 2:271; Meredith 1988:25). The FAK organized a National Economic Conference in 1939, which brought together Afrikaner financiers, industrialists, businessmen, labor leaders, and other interested parties to develop and implement a strategy to improve Afrikaners' economic status. The conference established the *Reddingsdaadbond* (RDB) under the control of the Economic Institute (EI), also organized by the conference. The aim of the RDB was to promote consumer cooperatives, technical training, economic resources, and to encourage Afrikaners to organize commercial and industrial enterprises (Carter 1959:261). By 1946, the RDB had 65,000 members and it was providing small-scale Afrikaner businessmen with loans (Uys 1989:222).

Thus, the RDB constituted an economic movement aimed at welding all Afrikaners, regardless of class, into a single economic unit and thereby increasing Afrikaner wealth. The RDB attempted to become a supraclass organization embracing industrial workers, small-scale shopkeepers, farm cooperatives, and rich capitalists. RDB leaders argued that British capitalism was based on selfish motivations while Afrikaner business should aim at promoting the interests of the Afrikaner *volk* as a whole. But in spite of the RDB's attempt to distinguish Afrikaner capitalism, or "people's capitalism," from British forms, Afrikaner capitalists, as we will see, once they had developed their economic power, came to define their class interests more narrowly than the economic well-being of the Afrikaner *volk* (Bloomberg 1989:129).

The RDB was responsible for the organization of the *Afrikaanse Handelsinstuut* (AHI) in 1942, which was formed to coordinate and advise small-scale Afrikaner traders. It attempted to displace the alien Indian traders and gave support to the government cheap labor policies and apartheid (Davies, O'Meara, and Dlamini 1988, vol. 1:79–80). Through such groups as the *Volkas Group* and *Federale Volksbeleggings Korporasie Beperk* (People's Federal Investment Corporation Limited or FVB), controlled by the Broederbond, Afrikaner businessmen were able to establish a foothold in gold mining and other industries (O'Meara 1977; Davies, O'Meara, and Dlamini 1988, vol. 1:70–75, 79–80). To combat non-Afrikaner capitalism, the EI encouraged state capitalism. As a result a number of parastatal industrial enterprises were organized under government control (Uys 1989:223).

These Bond economic strategies, once translated into economic policies by the Nationalist administration, led to increases in the size and scope of the Afrikaner enterprises and the growth of the Afrikaner business class. Before World War II the Afrikaners controlled less than 10 percent of trade and commerce, 5 percent of finance, 3 percent of industry, and less than 1 percent of mining. The mid-1960s saw the Afrikaner share of commerce increase to more than 25 percent, of finance to 21 percent, of industry to 10 percent, and of mining to 10 percent (Meredith 1988:109). By 1975, Afrikaners controlled 21 percent of private industry compared to 10 percent in 1948. Between 1948 and 1975 Afrikaner control of industrial output rose by 43 percent. With this industrial development there was a corresponding increase in the number of Afrikaners in white-collar jobs from 28 percent in 1948 to 65 percent in 1978 (Charney 1987:8). Between 1942 and 1952 the number of Afrikaner corporate directors rose by 295 percent, and business managers by 208 percent, while the number of Afrikaner merchants increased by 203 percent (Bloomberg 1989:213).

The Broederbond made efforts to penetrate the white labor unions in order to win the Afrikaner workers away from existing trade unions. In 1934 the RDB helped set up a railway union, the *Spoorbond*. Also, through the efforts of the RDB, the Broederbond took control of the Mine Workers' Union in 1948. The RDB also helped to organize the White Workers' Protection Society (WWPS) in 1944, which was able to recruit white workers in various industries. The WWPS supported racial job barriers and opposed mixed unions (Davies, O'Meara, and Dlamini 1988, vol. 2:247–48; Bunting 1964:256; O'Meara 1977:183–85; Villiers 1971:400). The National Council of Trustees (NCT), also organized by the FAK, provided financial backing to these Afrikaner trade unions (O'Meara 1977:180).

The Broederbond has established a strong foothold within the Dutch Reformed Churches. The Dutch Reformed Churches (DRCs) refer to the three major African Calvinist churches in South Africa: *Nederduitse Gereformeerde Kerk* (NGK—the Dutch Reformed Church), and two smaller groups, *Gereformeerde Kerk* (GK—Reformed Church) and *Nederduitsche Hervormde Kerk* (NHK—Dutch Reconstituted Church). In the early 1930s the GK theologians were a dominant force in shaping the Broederbond's Christian-Nationalist ideology. The GK religious leaders were assisted by influential groups within the NGK. This Christian-Nationalist ideology stressed the doctrine of the immutable exclusiveness of all ethnic groups, the need for class harmony among the Afrikaner folk who had been elected by God to control South African economy, and gave biblical justification for apartheid laws (Davies, O'Meara, and Dlamini 1988, vol. 2:271–76).[5]

As we have seen, the Broederbond had made great efforts to strengthen this Dutch Reformed heritage. In some senses the Bond considers itself a group of Calvinists who carry out religious work in fields that the institutional church professes not to operate (Bloomberg 1989:38–39).

Both the Reformed Church and the FAK have been strong supporters of Christian-National Education. The FAK promoted Christian-National values through the Institute for Christian Education. This institute stresses the vital role of mother-tongue (Afrikaans) instruction from nursery through university, thereby making English a foreign language. This mother-tongue emphasis has resulted in the formation of separate Afrikaans-speaking and English-speaking schools (Bunting 1964:193). The Christian-National doctrine not only dominates the school ideology of the Afrikaner schools but also those of the African and English schools as well (Bunting 1964:198). Such values stress a Calvinist viewpoint, which gives total support to apartheid policies (Carter 1959:266–72).

Through the FAK the Bond has organized separate Afrikaner associations for the boy scouts, university students,[6] chambers of commerce, and other organizations. The Bond has even organized a conservative racial affairs body called the South African Bureau of Racial Affairs (SABRA), which gives total support to the separate nations ideology of the Broederbond (Cape 1967:124; Serfontein 1978:126). Of the nineteen founding members of SABRA at least eleven were Bond members (Bloomberg 1989:216). SABRA was organized in 1947 as an alternative to the liberal South African Institute of Race Relations. After internal struggles among the reform factions and those advocating "pure" apartheid (*verkramptes*), the conservative faction has come to dominate SABRA policy-making (Davies, O'Meara, and Dlamini 1988, vol. 2:276–77).

Bloomberg succinctly summarizes the general Broederbond objectives when he states:

> The Broederbond is . . . concerned with the Afrikaner nation as a totality and with advancing all its interests. Internally it enhances the spiritual and material quality of Afrikaner's domestic life. Externally, it intervenes on Afrikanerdom's behalf in society as a whole with the objective of bringing all facets of state society under Afrikaner sway. (1989:37)

Nearly from its inception the Broederbond has shrouded its activities and membership in secrecy. External threats to the organization and its membership have increased.

The dialectical struggle between the Bond and the early South African state resulted in efforts by the government to repress the secret organization. States and rulers who meet political resistance among their citizenry become insecure about their ability to govern. In these circumstances central authority turns to coercion to regulate dissent (Schatzberg 1988). Such was the case with the South African government.

During the period in which Hertzog and Smuts held power, the Broederbond became active in support of opposition to the policies of both leaders. The Bond orchestrated opposition to Hertzog's English policy, criticizing his failure to achieve a republic status for South Africa free of British association. Hertzog counterattacked. At Smithfield in November 1935, he gave a speech attacking the Broederbond, pointing to its deep inroads within Afrikaner organizations and the dangers to political stability that it posed to South Africa (Serfontein 1978:194–204). Hertzog pointed to the close connections between the Purified National Party (Gesuiwerde Nasionale Party [GNP]), his opponents, and the Broederbond. He also claimed that as about one-third of the Bond's members were teachers, the Broederbond was in a powerful position to indoctrinate school children in Bond ideology (Bloomberg 1989:109–10).

In 1944, President Smuts put a curb on the Bond by publishing a special government gazette that prohibited civil servants and teachers from belonging to the Bond. Refusal to resign from the Bond resulted in fines, reduced rank and salary, or dismissal.

As a result of this curb, the Broederbond executive committee instructed the teachers and civil servants within its membership to resign from the Broederbond as a tactical strategy. Thus, within three months after the ban, 40 percent of Bond members had resigned their membership (Bloomberg 1989:197; Serfontein 1978:74).

The Smuts government took this action because the Bond opposed Smuts's policy of one united nation of Afrikaans- and English-speakers. Moreover, many high-ranking Broederbond members had close ties with the Nazi government in Germany and some even engaged in subversive activities through a paramilitary organization called *Ossewabrandwag* (OB).[7] This opposition came at a time when the South African government was giving military support to the British in their fight against Germany (Cape 1967; Serfontein 1978:64).

To assure themselves of a membership completely devoted to their Afrikaner cause, the Bond engaged in selective recruitment, making sure that only Afrikaners strongly committed to Afrikaner values and objectives gained admittance. The Broederbond has always been a small secret society, emphasizing political effectiveness rather than size. The Bond restricts membership to the financially sound, white Afrikaner, especially Protestant males over the age of twenty-three, who have demonstrated their support for an Afrikaner nation with its own language and culture (Wilkins and Strydon 1979:377–82). Few members of the working class can afford the entrance fees and special levees. Teachers, academics, clergymen, and civil servants form the backbone of the organization (O'Meara 1977, 1983). Its membership also comprises a substantial cross-section of the Afrikaner elite, including prime ministers, state presidents, governors, generals, university presidents, provincial administrators, and civil service heads (Bloomberg 1989:34).

But even selective recruitment does not eliminate the possibility of subversion or defection. The Broederbond uses the threat of expulsion to enforce discipline. This threat can be a powerful one. Total excommunication will lead to ostracism by members as well as economic sanctions that can ruin careers and businesses (Wilkins and Strydon 1979; Serfontein

1978:11). As I have indicated, members gain political, professional, educational, and business advantages from membership. The Bond works to place members in influential positions in all sectors of South African society. Therefore members have a strong incentive to avoid expulsion from the body.[8]

Everything about the organization is secret: membership, officers, activities, meeting places, and objectives. Newly initiated members must give a sacred oath to carry Broederbond secrets to their graves. A new member only gradually learns the inner secrets of the organization. Elaborate security measures are employed to keep internal communication confidential and to protect them from falling into the wrong hands. There are strict rules limiting contact between members and relatives who are not members. All meetings in a member's house must take place when his wife, children, or other relatives are absent. A father may not discuss Broederbond activities with his son even if his son belongs to the Broederbond youth organization (*Ruiterway*). Complex society devices are used to hide the place and time for the larger regional or annual national meetings. And no Broederbond member is allowed to join other secret or semi-secret orders which might compete for their loyalties (Wilkins and Strydon 1979:377–82).

The executive committee keeps a constant surveillance on the membership. Monthly attendance reports from local cell leaders enable national officers to determine which members may be showing disaffection by their frequent absence from meetings. This information may reveal to the Bond potential security risks (Wilkins and Strydon 1979:377–82).

To assure themselves that the Bond's policies are being appropriately implemented, the Bond's executive committee has established a system of watchdog committees whose members are prominent Broeders. Such watchdog committees operate in total secrecy. Their job is to make sure that Bond members perform their duties properly and carry out the Bond's policies within educational, religious, business, labor, professional, and political organizations (Wilkins and Strydon, 1979:400).

However, there have been deep internal divisions over policy that have threatened the stability of the Bond. A pact between the National Party and the English-speaker-dominated Labour Party brought General Hertzog to power. Some members of the Bond who opposed this pact were purged (O'Meara 1977:163–64). Later General Hertzog faced opposition to his policies led by a breakaway faction called the Re-united National Party (Herenigde Nasionale Party [HNP]) headed by Dr. Malan (Cape 1967:111). This split in the National Party led to internal conflict within the Bond between the *Gesuiwerde* or Purified Nationalists supporting Malan and the Smelter or Fusionists faction who supported Hertzog and his merging of the

National and South African Party into the United Party. The Fusionists were eventually purged. Most recently, Bond leaders expelled members who opposed the government's reform policies (see below) (O'Meara 1983:60). In this way the Bond leaders maintained control by eliminating internal dissension so dangerous to Bond unity (Serfontein 1978).

Thus, the expansion of the Broederbond power in South Africa has resulted from a combination of information control (secrecy) strategies, espionage, indoctrination, and coercion. By denying their enemies, inside and outside of government, information about Bond activities and membership, the Bond, in the long-run at least, has been able to protect itself from external threats. Since it is a secret organization, however, the Broederbond cannot realize its programs itself: it must place its members in influential positions within key societal institutions. Thus, the Bond has attained its political objectives through the National Party, its cultural influence through the FAK, its religious domination through the Dutch Reformed Church, and its economic reforms through the FAK's Economic Institute (Bloomberg 1989:35). By placing its members in key organizations the Bond has found varied sources for intelligence, which keeps its leadership alert to potential sources of threat to the Afrikaner cause or, more specifically, to the Broederbond itself. Internal intelligence also has given Bond leaders foreknowledge of possible defections or untrustworthy members who could betray Bond interests. Factional divisions within Bond ranks cannot be tolerated. The most powerful faction has ousted the less powerful in order to maintain unity and loyalty among the brethren. At regular Bond meetings the Christian-Nationalist beliefs are also given constant reinforcement.[9] Thus, through such power resources the Bond leadership has maintained an intense system of control over the membership.

THE NATIONAL PARTY'S APARTHEID POLICIES

The growing political power of the Broederbond was revealed with the election of the National Party, which came into power in 1948. The Party was formed by D. K. Malan and his followers when they split from the United Party in 1934, forming the Purified National Party, and, later, in 1939, the HNP. In 1951 the HNP merged with the Afrikaner Party to establish the Nationalist Party (NP), still commonly referred to as the National Party. The Broederbond has had a strong influence within the NP. Malan and other Nationalist members of Parliament (MPs) were Bond members (Meredith 1988:22). Bloomberg accurately depicted the relationship between the Bond and the National Party when he stated that the Broederbond has been "the unofficial . . . central policy-making organ, coordinating the entire mechanism of the Nationalist movement in its parliamentary and extra-parliamentary forms" (1989:36).[10]

The Nationalists reversed the modest welfare reforms of the Smuts and Hertzog governments. The National Party was also determined to redress the perceived inequalities between the English- and Afrikaans-speakers.

The National Party enlarged the legal base on which apartheid rested. Since coming into power the Nationalists have enacted about 150 laws enlarging the apartheid system (Maud 1974:300). They rejected Hertzog's policies favoring British Afrikaner unity along with his attempts to transact more friendly relations with the Coloured population. The Nationalists advocated more social separation among the races, denial of African rights in white areas, tightening of the pass-laws and the job color bars, and economic development in the homelands or Bantustans (Lipton 1985:268; Carter 1982:101–2).

First on the Nationalist agenda was the formation of a republic. The rise of the National Party foretold the end of South Africa's participation in the commonwealth. The 1960 referendum gave the Nationalists a mandate to form a republic, and the Republic of South Africa Constitution Act of 1961 turned the referendum vote into a legal reality (Bunting 1964:156).

The 1948 Nationalist victory marked the exclusion of the economically dominant English minority from political power. The Afrikaner government retired the English officials from senior posts in the civil service and the armed forces. Broederbond members replaced Smuts's appointees (Bunting 1964:136; Meredith 1988:32).[11] The state sector soon became not only an Afrikaner preserve but a Bond one as well.

By 1971–73 the public sector's share of fixed investment had doubled from 6.5 percent in 1946–50 to 11.5 percent (Meredith 1988:109). State enterprises included railways and harbors, iron and steel, electronic power generation, heavy engineering, and oil production from coal. These parastatals became training grounds for Afrikaner entrepreneurs.[12] Separate schools for English-speakers and Afrikaans-speakers were made necessary because mother-tongue education in the schools was made mandatory (Bunting 1964:136–41).

To consolidate their control over the Afrikaner population and to limit the political power of the Africans, Coloureds, and Asians, the National Party enacted the Prohibition of Mixed Marriage Act of 1949, which amended the Immorality Act of 1927. These laws prevented interracial marriages and extramarital relations, thus preventing any fraternity across racial lines. The Group Areas Act of 1950 restricted each ethnic group to defined places in or near urban areas.

The new Bantustan strategy devised by the Nationalists was based on the idea that the native Africans were not South Africans but belonged to different "ethnic nationalities" possessing different cultures. The regime eventually distinguished ten different national groupings based on traditional tribal homelands. These ten separate nations were to be given rights of self-determination. According to the Nationalist plan, each was eventually to emerge as an independent state. Crucial to the success of the plan was the creation of a tiny black bourgeoisie class in the Bantustans dependent on apartheid for their continued existence as a class (Davies, O'Meara, and Dlamini 1988, vol. 1:197–217).

To implement the new Bantustan policy, the Nationalists abrogated the Natives Representative Council in 1951. In the same year, the Bantu Authorities Act was passed by Parliament which provided for tribal, regional, and territorial Bantu authorities on the reserves. The Promotion of Bantu-Self Government Bill of 1959 restructured the Bantu Authority system by setting up eight territorial authorities (later expanded to ten). Under this Bill the Bantu authorities in the homelands were given power to levy taxes, control public works, and allocate licenses and trading rights. The South African government retained the right to choose, dispose of, or veto any homeland authority (Meredith 1988:75).

The 1970 Bantu Homeland Citizenship Act made Africans citizens of one of the Bantustans (homelands), even those who had never lived outside of white areas. Until the Bantustan achieved independent status, such Africans had a dual citizenship. But after 1976, when four Bantustans (Transkei, Bophuthatswana, Venda, and the Ciskei) became "independent," their citizens were unilaterally deprived of their South African citizenship (Davies, O'Meara, and Dlamini 1988, vol. 1:209).

After 1960 the Bantustan policy led to an acceleration of a program of mass forced removal of Africans from rural and urban areas. Between 1960 and 1970 about two million people were forcibly moved into the Bantustans (Davies, O'Meara, and Dlamini 1988, vol. 1:208).

Extensive restrictions were placed on African labor mobility. The Native Laws Amendment Act of 1949 set up a national system of labor bureaus to recruit and allocate African labor. The Act also restricted the flow of African workers available to the towns so that there would be an abundant supply of black labor available for the mines and farms (Simson 1980:155–56). Various amendments to the Urban Areas Act (1952, 1953, 1957) provided that no African could remain in an urban area for longer than seventy-two hours without a permit unless the person fell under the "Section 10" provision, which applied to Africans born and permanently residing there. Section 10 exceptions were made only in the case of those Africans who had worked in an area continuously for one employer for not less than ten years and for more than one employer for not less than fifteen years (Carter 1980:33; Lipton 1985:26). But Section 10 rights were gradually weakened, forcing families into short-term leasehold houses in the townships (Lipton 1985:26). And by 1968 African laborers without Section 10 rights were given a maximum of one-year's residence in prescribed areas, but then were forced to return to the reserves and be reassigned to an old or new job by the labor bureau (Lipton 1985:351). This regulation forced large sections of the African labor force to oscillate between rural areas (homelands) and the workplace.

Such influx controls, of course, were aimed at restricting the number of Africans entering white areas, especially the towns. These laws also limited the number of Africans that could acquire permanent residence in prescribed urban areas and rechanneled African labor toward white farms when necessary (Lipton 1985:2627).

Between 1948–76 the Nationalist government moved to eliminate "black spots" in rural areas (areas under control of African freehold farmers). New regulations also forced African labor tenants and squatters off white farms and sent them back to the reserves. They now constituted a labor surplus not needed on mechanized corporate farms (Freund 1984:51; Carter 1980: 33–34). About one million squatters were affected by the new laws (Bunting 1964:150).

Through a series of industrial, union, and education acts the Nationalists strengthened the position of white labor vis-à-vis black labor. The Industrial Conciliation Act of 1954 split the trade union movement along racial lines and allocated job reservation on a racial basis (Bunting 1964:270–71). The Bantu Education Act of 1957 restricted Africans to lower echelons of the public service (Ume 1981:178). The 1959 Extension of University Education Act excluded nonwhites from hitherto open universities and provided for the establishment of segregated colleges on ethnic lines for various nonwhite races (Ume 1981:178; Bunting 1964:154).

As apartheid restrictions became more oppressive under the Nationalist government, further resistance by blacks, Asians, and Coloureds developed. These resistance movements emerged despite the passage of the 1950 Suppression of Communism Bill, the 1953 Public Safety and Criminal Laws Amendment, and the 1960 Unlawful Organizations Act, all of which were directed against the continued passive-disobedience tactics of the African National Congress (ANC) and allied Asian, Coloured, and white political organizations (Carter 1980:25; 1986:353; Simson 1980:155). The latter groups formed a Congress of the People, which adopted a multiracial Freedom Charter in 1955. Leaders of the Congress were arrested for treason in 1956, but later all were acquitted during trials that stretched over a five-year period.

Later the ANC split into two factions, one of which supported the multiracial objectives of the Charter and the other emphasized African nationalism.[13] This latter faction later formed the Pan African Congress (PAC).[14] Later nonviolent protests organized by the PAC at Sharpeville in 1960 resulted in the police killing 67 protestors and wounding almost 200 persons, including women and children. At this point the government declared a state of emergency and outlawed the ANC and PAC. Nearly 2,000 people were arrested and detained (Carter 1982:114–18).

The failure to bring political change by peaceful protest led ANC leaders to turn to violent tactics. The ANC hoped that a campaign of sabotage would disrupt the economy and force a change in white attitudes toward apartheid. Thus, in June 1961, the ANC organized a separate military wing, which was given the name Umkhonto We Sizwe (MK), "The Spear of the Nation," which included in its ranks white, Indian, and Coloured terrorists. The MK carried out more than 200 attacks over the next eighteen months, mostly on public buildings, railway lines, and power installations in the major towns (Meredith 1988:100). These raids caused about 1.4 million dollars in damage to 90 power pylons and transformers as well as considerable damage to police stations and vehicles (Magubane 1990:344–45).

In a parallel fashion the Pan African Congress also organized a terrorist underground movement called Poqo, whose aims included murdering whites. Poqo also plotted to murder black police, black informers, and black collaborationist leaders (Meredith 1988:102).

In spite of the South African government's successful repression of these terrorist organizations within South Africa, MK continued to operate from sanctuaries outside South Africa. By 1980, Umkhonto had renewed terrorist activity, bombing strategic projects such as SASOL (an oil-from-coal facility), a Transvaal power plant, a Durban electrical plant, and a defense force main compound at Victoria (Carter 1982:121–23). To stop these attacks the government began military action against ANC strongholds in neighboring countries.

Aside from terrorist activity, the early period of Nationalist rule was marked by an increase in rent strikes, bus boycotts, and various local uprisings in the urban townships (Saul and Gelb 1986:11–12). Unrest culminated in the June 1976 Soweto protests at which 360 schoolchildren protesting use of Afrikaans as the language of instruction in their schools were slaughtered by the police. The government then banned the militant black organizations and newspapers, arresting both leaders and editors (Lipton 1985:34).

By the 1980s the ownership and control of the major means of production in mining, manufacturing, transport, trade, and finance was largely in the hands of locally based conglomerates, state corporations, and a few foreign-based multinationals. The manufacturing sector continued to contribute more output than agriculture and mining combined. Compared to the developed countries, however, the capital-goods sector (heavy machinery and equipment) was small. Most capital goods had to be imported. Manufacturing did not make a major contribution to export earnings. Gold exports were the major foreign-exchange earner. Because of these conditions the expansion and/or contraction of the South African economy depended, and still does, on foreign exchange receipts, largely from gold and foreign investment (Davies, O'Meara, and Dlamini 1988, vol. 1:51–54).

Locally based conglomerates have included the Anglo-American Corporation, which has owned 69 percent of the total capital invested in South African mining, and the South African National Life Assurance Company, a large Afrikaner insurance and financial organization. State corporations have included the South African Transport Service (SATS), which has controlled railways, harbors, and South African Airways; Iron and Steel Corporation (ISCOR), which has controlled more than 75 percent of South African iron and steel production; and Suid Afrikaanse Steenkool Olien Gaskorporasie (SASOL), which has manufactured oil from coal.

By the end of the 1980s there were some 2,000 to 2,500 foreign-controlled companies in South Africa. Foreign investment in South Africa has been vital to the South African economy because it has generated foreign exchange necessary for the import of machinery and equipment on which economic expansion depends, enabling local producers to gain access to modern technology. More recently, foreign investment has helped finance the large deficits in state budgets (Davies, O'Meara, and Dlamini 1988, vol. 1:90–94).

English-speakers have maintained a dominant position in the South African corporate economy. In the early 1980s South African companies in Afrikaner hands represented less than 20 percent of the gross domestic product (GDP). English-speakers controlled 90 percent of South African manufacturing and 85 percent of the banking industry (Carter 1980:89). Nonetheless, English-speakers have been excluded from any significant input into major government decision-making (Lipton 1985:312–13).

It is obvious, then, that the Broederbond has had an overdeterminant impact on the interrelated subsystems that constitute the South African social formation. As a result of the Bond activities the Afrikaners have gained new economic and political power. The Bond's successful efforts at spreading the Christian-Nationalist ideology throughout the Afrikaner population has, until recently at least, served to unify Afrikaners as an ethnic group.

However, the conjunctive moments (the apartheid system) proposed by the Broederbond and executed by a government under Bond domination has created new fault lines along which new conflicts have emerged. These conflicts threaten the reproduction of Afrikaner power—if not all white power—in South Africa. One composite effect of the numerous apartheid laws has been the creation of a system that acts as a barrier to new economic growth. Operating as sort of a superstructural "brake" the apartheid system has made it more difficult for the government to reproduce the modern economic system on which its power is based. This has placed monopoly capital and other business interests in opposition to Afrikaner leaders who continue to support the apartheid solution. Thus, the Nationalist government faced the political consequences of a primary contradiction within South African society. This contradiction resulted from the Afrikaners' dependency on apartheid to maintain their economic and political power—a system which, at the same time, created a hostile nonwhite population. Because of apartheid restrictions on nonwhite education, this population did not have the appropriate training and skills vital to the growth of the modern South African economy on which the well-being of the Afrikaner population depended.

With the negative impact of the apartheid system on the nonwhites, new fault lines have developed between this population and the government. These fault lines have produced such serious conflicts that the state has been forced to finance a very expensive security system to prevent the complete erosion of government authority. These new conflicts between the Afrikaners supporting apartheid and the nonwhite groups have been fought at various political, economic, and ideological levels. While specific anti-apartheid groups have been banned by the government or gone underground, the black nationalist and multiracial ideologies of the anti-apartheid opposition have continued to gain strength. Anti-apartheid ideologies have a resilience that outlasts any particular group that professes them.

NEW CONTRADICTIONS

The 1970s and 1980s have been a time of crisis for the political economy of South Africa. By the 1980s the South African economy had fallen into stagnation with high inflation, corporate bankruptcies, and a decline in retail sales, in real wages, and in the GDP. Since 1981 there has been a 4.2 percent decline in the GDP. In 1983 manufacturing output was down 9.1 percent from 1981 (MacShane, Plant, and Ward 1984:51). Even gold production has declined. In 1975 South Africa produced 75 percent of the gold mined in the free world, but only ten years later South Africa's gold production fell to 56 percent (Magubane 1990:354). Today many of the less efficient gold mines may soon face bankruptcy. Only one-half of South Africa's large gold mines were very profitable in 1989 (Dunn 1990b).

With inflation on the increase (18 percent in 1983) there has been an erosion in the standard of living. There is increased unemployment among blacks (Adelman 1985:22–23).[15] A significant number of whites are also unemployed (Legassick 1985:590; Davies and O'Meara 1988:73). Most of South Africa's economic problems are the direct or indirect result of the Nationalist apartheid policies. South Africa exports fewer goods than is necessary because it cannot compete with goods produced by its foreign competitors who use skilled labor more extensively (Kibble and Bush 1986:217). The large South African corporations have increased mechanization. With this capital intensification there has grown a need for more skilled labor. A skilled labor shortage has existed for two decades (Lipton 1985:145). By 1981 there was an 8 percent shortage of skilled craftsmen and apprentices and a 12.1 percent deficiency of needed scientists, engineers, and technicians (MacShane, Plant, and Ward 1984:51).

At the time of publication blacks could not provide a remedy for this labor shortage. There are fewer than 1,000 black lawyers and physicians and only a handful of black engineers and accountants. The dearth of skilled black artisans is even more dramatic (Rotberg 1990a).

The pool of educated blacks from which employers can draw new skilled workers has been limited by the poor educational opportunities available to blacks. In 1970 the South African government spent sixteen times as much for white education per capita than for blacks. Even under the recent reform administration of Frederick de Klerk the South African government gives white children eight times as much financial support as they give black children (Tygesen 1991). Smaller numbers of nonwhites have graduated from primary and secondary schools and universities than whites (Meredith 1988:133).

The racial job bar also has led to the creation of the skilled labor shortage. The job bar has limited industries' access to skilled black workers and raised the labor cost of manufacturing. Such constraints on growth put South African industry at a competitive disadvantage with other foreign businesses

(Lipton 1985:137). Limited access to skilled labor has forced South Africa to seek some types of modern technology at high import costs from abroad. This further fuels inflation (Kibble and Bush 1986:216; Saul and Gelb 1986). And low black wages discourage the development of a vigorous internal market (Houghton 1971:49). The job reservation system has wasted South Africa's resources by preventing blacks from rising to positions that reflect their true abilities and has made for inefficiency among both white and black labor by removing the incentive of healthy competition (Lemon 1987:165).

The seriousness of the situation was reflected in the fact that in 1976 the Associated Chambers of Commerce began calling for an end to job reservation and restrictions on black job training (Carter 1980:901).

Migrant labor policies have limited employers' freedom to choose their own African labor (Horwitz 1967:314). As the demand for skilled and unskilled black labor increases the cost of labor turnover also increases. Skilled labor requires training time and cannot be easily replaced by new migrants to urban areas (Wilson 1975:179). Not unexpectedly the Federated Chamber of Industries has called for the stabilization of a black urban middle class (Carter 1980:91).

The contradictions between Nationalist apartheid policies and the economic realities in South Africa during this period are pointed out by Lemon when he states "the rapid economic growth of the 1960s and 1970s had demanded increasing black urbanization and occupational mobility which were at odds with the perpetuation of job reservation and a rigid influx control system and which accentuated the unreality of channelling all black political expression through the homeland" (1987:325).

During the early period of Nationalist rule, black union strike activity was limited. But between 1971–75 there was increased black union militancy. This increased union activity was partly due to black dissatisfaction with the wage differentials between black and white workers. Between 1948 and 1973 white workers' wages rose 416 percent, while black workers' wages rose only 36 percent (Meredith 1988:153). An economic downturn during this period leading to increased black joblessness resulted in further worker unrest (MacShane, Plant, and Ward 1984:21).

The period between 1970 and 1984 saw an increase of African trade unions from 13 to 22 with the total number of union members increasing from 16,000 to 40,000 (Meredith 1988:141). During this period there was also an increase in the number of strikes (Davies and O'Meara 1988:67). From about 1983 to 1990 there has been a 700 percent increase in time lost in black strikes especially in the automobile, metal, chemical, food, and mining industries (Kibble and Bush 1986:273).[16]

Increased black militancy has forced the government to invest huge sums in its national security force, the government's largest nonproductive investment. Since 1961 defense expenditures have increased from 77 million dollars to 3.2 billion in 1981 (Magubane 1990:357).

Not only has apartheid required large investments in the security force, but the dual system of services for blacks and whites has resulted in the duplication of transport and educational systems, which constitutes a large financial drain on both the public and private sectors (Kaslow 1990).

South Africa's economic problems were worsened by the economic sanctions imposed by the country's major trading partners against its racial policies. The United Kingdom banned the import of oil, gold coins, iron, and steel. West Germany, Italy, France, and Japan instituted similar bans. In addition to banning imports of coal, iron, steel, uranium, oil, and gold coin, the United States placed restrictions on the import of agricultural products, including food and sugar (Battersby 1987b:4–10). However, in the spring of 1991 the twelve-nation European Community, the United States, and Japan lifted these economic sanctions (Battersby 1991g).

A number of major multinational corporations have disinvested, including such American companies as General Motors and IBM, and the UK's Barclays Bank (Battersby 1987b:4). Of course, most American corporations have only sold out to local South African managers who continue to sell their products.

These international sanctions have had an impact on the South African economy. International sanctions and disinvestment have depressed consumer spending by 15 percent and lowered the country's GDP by at least 10 percent (Kaslow 1990). It is estimated that without external sanctions the current unemployment total of 4.5 million could increase to 7.8 million by the turn of the century. With continued sanctions, the unemployment figure would be about 9.8 million by the year 2000 (Battersby 1987b:6).

Aspects of the apartheid system have been under attack for some time by the South African business community, especially by monopoly capital. In January 1985 a phalanx of business interests, representing four-fifths of the country's employers, published a manifesto that called for changes in the government's apartheid policies (Meredith 1988:199). The managements of such South African conglomerates as Anglo-American Corporation, SANLAM, the Barlow Rand Group, and the Rembrandt Group have called for reform (Davies, O'Meara, and Dlamini 1988, vol. 1:85–89).[17] These business leaders have advocated a program that would scrap job and training bars, including the erosion of horizontal barriers to labor mobility. Corporate leaders have also argued for improvement in the standard of living for blacks by giving blacks higher wages, improved education, better health services, and improved housing. Many businessmen have favored the removal of restrictions on black business and property rights. These economic leaders also argued for the legitimization of black unions in order to promote political stability. However, equal political rights, one-person-one-vote, has not been on the businessmen's political agenda (Lipton 1985:288; Adelman 1985:187–89).

It soon became clear to the Bond leadership that resolution of the contradictions that were producing the conflicts between the government and the nonwhite populations and within the Afrikaner population itself required changes in the apartheid system. However, initially at least, the Bond proposed cosmetic apartheid reforms that threatened neither the Christian-Nationalist ideology nor the political and economic interests of white labor and rural white farmers. But these reforms satisfied no one. In reality, they accentuated the existing structural contradictions and intensified the internal and external political conflicts. The minority white elite were dependent on an essentially hostile nonwhite labor force, largely black, that was insufficiently trained to provide the skills necessary to run the modern South African economy and had no political rights. This was the primary contradiction that some Bond leaders came to realize could only be resolved by the destruction of the apartheid system not by its reform.

Thus the hegemonic message of Christian-Nationalism, which formed the ideological basis for apartheid, no longer unified the white elite and certainly did not capture the loyalties of the nonwhite populations. As in all state systems there was a discrepancy between the state ideology and lived reality (Miliband 1990:347). This discrepancy has forced the South African state to create new policies more consistent with this reality in order to maintain its power. The Broederbond has played a decisive role in the formulation of these reforms.

THE TOTAL STRATEGY

Faced with both internal and external attacks on the apartheid system, and with prominent businessmen pointing to the obvious link between certain economic problems and the apartheid structure, recent Nationalist leaders have tried to "modernize" their apartheid policies, but still retain the essential principles justifying white minority rule.

Prime Minister John Vorster was the first Nationalist leader to deviate from the strict apartheid doctrine. He worked toward a policy of multinationalism under which the black and white nations of South Africa should cooperate on a basis of equality without discrimination (Lipton 1985:50).

Vorster was convinced that he could reduce international hostility toward South Africa by fostering close relations with new black African states as well as by developing more open interracial sports policies, allowing black teams to compete in South Africa and allowing interracial African teams to compete abroad.

However, Vorster was less flexible in modifying the economic barriers to black advancement. Under pressure from Vorster, white unions were encouraged to let nonwhites, including Africans, perform skilled labor in white areas when there was a shortage of such labor (Lipton 1985:59). Yet the Vorster government tried to prevent the formation of black unions by enacting legislation that set up works and liaison committees, a means by which blacks could communicate with management (MacShane, Plant, and Ward 1984:55).

Prime Minister Vorster's government was unable to deal with the series of crises that threatened South Africa's political stability. A new alliance of big business—both Afrikaner and English—and the military made new demands for reform. The demands of big business for the type of reforms already discussed coincided with the disquiet among the top officers of the South African Defense Force (SADF) over security issues. These new political forces led to a change in Nationalist leadership (O'Meara 1983:53).

P. W. Botha succeeded Vorster as prime minister in 1978. Botha's whole cabinet and more than 80 percent of the National Party members of parliament were Broederbond members. Thus, Broederbond views on apartheid reforms were reflected to a significant extent in government policy. A secret Bond policy document leaked to the press in October 1986 defined the new Bond position on apartheid reforms. The Bond argued that no race group should dominate another. Residential segregation was desirable although racially mixed areas on a voluntary basis would not necessarily threaten Afrikaner survival. Culturally linked mother-tongue education in Afrikaner schools was essential for Afrikaner survival. Statutory discrimination should be abolished and freedom of association allowed. Blacks must be included in the constitutional process to the highest level, sharing either directly or indirectly in the election of the government and participating at all levels of decision-making that affected their interests. In no circumstances should one race dominate another (Uys 1989:218).

Botha's so-called "total strategy" began to incorporate some of the Bond's cosmetic reforms as they applied to apartheid. His reforms largely promoted the interests of monopoly capital and the military. They included the legalization of black trade unions, the repeal of laws banning interracial sex and marriage, and even doing away with the pass laws. Some hotels, trains, and buses were desegregated. His policies also aimed at eroding the vertical color bar (or job bar) and providing blacks with more access to quality education. A new constitution was introduced that maintained white political supremacy while it provided separate uniracial parliamentary bodies for Coloureds and Asians but none for black Africans (Davies and O'Meara 1988:69; Magubane 1984:215).

The total strategy visualized a rigid division of the African population into blacks who had rights to residence in white cities (in segregated townships) and those unemployed populations that would remain perpetually imprisoned in the impoverished Bantustans and let out only as contract labor.

Under Botha the Nationalists tried to co-op the support of the black middle class. Section 10s were granted business and property rights. State owned houses in black areas were put up for sale to blacks at bargain prices (Lipton 1985:59–70). Blacks with permanent resident rights would have freedom to live and work in urban areas other than where they currently reside (Lemon 1987:323). Such policies were aimed at driving a wedge between settled black populations and the less permanent labor migrants (Saul and Gelb 1981:8; Carter 1980:44; Davies and O'Meara 1988:701). These new policies also helped businessmen because black urban insiders supplied skilled labor while migrant unskilled Africans served the businesses need for unstable, low-cost labor (Wilson 1975:82).

While the Botha government abolished the hated passbooks, its control of housing served as a new form of influx control. By controlling housing availability in urban areas the government regulated the distribution of the black population (Lemon 1987:323). Aside from housing control the government had other indirect means of population control: subsidized wages for employees of firms that relocated near homelands, provision of facilities in distant commuter areas, placing severe limits on land available to blacks in urban areas, use of anti-squatting laws, and maintenance of racial group areas (Greenberg 1987:68).

Job reservation laws were relaxed. The government did not oppose the business community's 1977 Code of Conduct, which advocated equal employment opportunity. To gain white acceptance for more black occupational mobility, the new laws upgraded white jobs and downgraded black skilled jobs by giving lower status and pay to the black occupations (Lipton 1985:63). The government no longer gave support to the rule that previously prevented whites from working under blacks (Lipton 1985:63). Except for managerial and administration positions, blacks' share of skilled white-collar jobs increased. However, the South African state, the largest employer in

South Africa, continued to maintain wide pay differentials between whites and blacks.

The Botha government committed itself to the creation of more equal educational opportunities for all races. In the early 1980s there was an increase in the number of African secondary schools as well as the number of blacks attending the South African universities. At the university level the racial quota system was ended in 1986 (Lemon 1987:324–25). But the teaching standards for blacks remain low. Expenditures for black education per capita is still one-seventh of that spent on whites (Meredith 1988:196). There are similar disparities in allocated funds for black and white education in the 1990/1991 budget in spite of the fact that black school enrollment is almost seven times that of whites (Engel 1990).

The continued inferiority of black educational opportunities is revealed in the results of the 1989 high school matriculation exams. While 200,000 black students took these exams, only 42 percent passed. Of the 37,000 white students who took the exams 97 percent achieved passing scores (Rotberg 1990).

Under Botha, political reform was cosmetic. Both the government and businessmen opposed the one-person-one-vote reform and still do. Declining numbers of whites and increasing numbers of Africans have convinced both governmental and corporate leaders that white rule is necessary for political stability.[18] The business leadership believes that white power will perpetuate the political conditions essential for their business operations and even their personal security (Lipton 1985:178–79; Legassick 1985:587).

In order to maintain white rule in face of a declining white population, Botha's government enacted a new constitution in 1984, which created three separate legislative chambers, one for Coloureds, one for Asians, and one for whites. Black Africans would not be included. By so doing Botha hoped to split the nonwhite population and prevent a political alliance between the liberal English, Coloureds, and Asians.

Under the tricameral system whites send their elected representatives to the House of Assembly, the Coloureds their elected representatives to the House of Representatives, and the Asians their elected representatives to the House of Delegates. Having the largest number of representatives, the white House of Assembly will dominate the Parliament (James and du Pisanie 1987:38–39).

The executive is given greater powers and is freed from obligations and accountability to representative institutions. The president can appoint the cabinet, which must consist of members from the three chambers. The president has the power to determine which issues are matters of concern to each separate chamber and which are of common concern. In matters of common concern, if joint committees cannot come to agreement, the President's Council, dominated by whites, makes the final decision (Carter 1980:73; Lipton 1985:52ff., 312–13; Saul and Gelb 1986:970; Davies and O'Meara 1988:71).

The dictatorial power the new constitution gave Botha enabled him to prevent the legislative chambers of Coloureds and Asians from promoting popular demands or thwarting his policies as well as prevented anti-reform forces in white chambers from blocking his reforms under the "Total Strategy" policies (Davies, O'Meara, and Dlamini 1988, vol. 1:137).

In order to implement his policies of "Total Strategy," Botha propelled the military into a significant role within the executive branch. The military not only helped formulate military policy but overall state strategies as well. This influence was exercised through the State Security Council (SSC) (Davies, O'Meara, and Dlamini 1988, vol. 1:126). The SSC directed a network of management centers (JMCs), Sub-JMCs (at the metropolitan level), and mini-JMCs (at local authority levels), all under the command of senior military officials or police officials who were required to alert the SSC of trouble spots or potential grievances within the black townships (Meredith 1988:216–17).

States, as we have seen, often use secret, illegal means to control groups that threaten their power. The South African state was no exception. Recent evidence suggests that the Afrikaner government funded a secret military organization called the Civil Cooperation Bureau (CCB), which directed a network of assassins who killed anti-apartheid activists. At least forty-nine anti-apartheid activists have been assassinated since 1977 and since 1978 there have been 166 attempted assassinations (Battersby 1990g, 1991e; Laurence 1990a; Meldrum 1990). How many of these operations were conducted by the CCB is not known. Since such assassinations were obviously in direct violation of the South African constitution the activities of the CCB were kept secret.

Political reforms did not significantly increase black political power. The Black Local Authority Act of 1983 gave local township councils more power to collect taxes and rents as well as to control various services. The Regional Service Council Act of 1985 set up a two-tier system of political representation which consists of lower-level Primary Local Authorities (PLAs) and Regional Service Councils (RSCs) over a whole urban region. These RSCs encompass all local authorities within particular regions. White local authorities, black African town and village councils, and Asian and Coloured management committees are responsible for basic local services (Greenberg 1987:63).

However, the system is set up to minimize the power of the Asians, Coloureds, and black Africans on the RSCs and maximizes voter support for the more conservative elements on the PLAs (Charney 1987:28). Blacks constitute a small minority on the RSCs despite the fact they represent a majority in the service areas. The reason for this is that representatives on the RSCs are allocated according to the taxes paid within the authority. This taxation rule assures that the industrialized white areas get the majority of the seats. Moreover the administrator of a region is not elected by the councils but is appointed by the central government (Lemon 1987:290–92).

Botha's policies produced further resistance on the part of the black African, Asian, and Coloured populations. Beginning in 1984, students and workers became involved in a series of protests that spread throughout South Africa. The government brutally suppressed these uprisings in 1986 and imposed a nationwide state of emergency.

Opposition to the new constitution was organized by the United Democratic Front (UDF) and the National Forum (NF). The UDF was a broad-based anti-apartheid group that was organized in August 1983. Some 600 organizations eventually became part of the Front. The UDF was sympathetic to the ANC and its nonracial objectives.[19] Competing with the UDF was the National Forum Committee. This group was organized in June 1983 by the Azanian Peoples Organization (Azapo), a black consciousness group. Unlike the UDF, Azapo barred white membership from the NF (Meredith 1988; MacShane, Plant, and Ward 1984:126). Opposition of these fronts to the new constitution seems to have been successful since few Coloureds and Asians have participated in the elections for the Tricameral Parliament (James and du Pisanie 1987:380–90).

Blacks have also showed great dissatisfaction with the new system of local government. Only 21 percent of the voters turned out for elections for the twenty-nine new councils held in 1983 (Meredith 1988:195). Blacks have viewed town councilors as "collaborators" or "sell-outs." Most town councils are no longer operating because the councilors have been assassinated or forced to resign (Greenberg 1987:54–56).[20] These forms of black resistance, along with student school boycotts and strikes, forced the government to declare a state of emergency in July 1985 (formally lifted in March 1986, but reinstated on a national basis in June 1986).

Not long before he gave up power, Botha appeared to have begun to move toward the type of political reforms advocated by the Broederbond in its 1986 secret policy document. The Botha government proclaimed the principle of South African citizenship for all Africans. Botha invited blacks to serve on the National Statutory Council to discuss a political agenda for future black political participation (James and du Pisanie 1987:44). He also proposed that blacks be included on the President's Council (Lemon 1987:322).

But the Nationalists continued to expand the power of Bantustan leaders, preparatory to giving them "independence." The 1979 Black State Constitution Act gave the governments of the Bantustan wide powers to detain people without trial and to ban meetings, individual publications, and organizations. Many of these repressive measures have been directed toward groups resistant to the movement of Bantustans to the status of independent states (Davies, O'Meara, and Dlamini 1988, vol. 1:210). In this way the South African government has thrown its political support to thoroughly discredited and unpopular collaborator chiefs in the Bantustans.

By the end of 1982 these governmental strategies had resulted in four Bantustan regimes being granted independence (Transkei, Bophuthatswana, Venda, and Ciskei).[21] A fifth, KwaNdebele, was being prepared for independence. Citizens of the "independent" states have been unilaterally deprived of their South African citizenship (Davies, O'Meara, and Dlamini 1988, vol. 1:209). The various Bantustan regimes sustain themselves only because they are backed by full repressive power of the South African state and because various Bantustan legislatures are dominated by government-paid chiefs who have supported the apartheid line.

Botha's administration, like past Nationalist administrations, tried to rework Bantustan policy to create a homeland for Africans with a strong enough economic base to reduce the numbers of Africans living in white areas by attracting them back to the homelands (Lipton 1985:67).

To increase economic development within the Bantustans (or Nations) the government tried to encourage industrial development there. It gave white corporations economic incentives to relocate on the borders of the reserves (Carter 1982:109; Lipton 1985:76).

Pretoria recast the decentralization policy in regional framework. The government established growth points in eight economic zones that cut across Bantustan borders and/or brought the economic zones closer to the metropolitan border (Lipton 1985:79). Businesses that refused to move to growth points were subject to various sanctions (Lipton 1985:77). But not enough jobs were created at growth points to halt black influx into white areas (Lipton 1985:77).

The Bantustan population increased from 7.4 million in 1970 to 10.7 million in 1980. This population increase has outstripped the ability of the development schemes to support the homeland populations (Meredith 1988:151). The Bantustan residents' main source of income is from members who migrate or commute to white areas of South Africa.[22] Only one-fourth of the income earned by homeland populations in 1973 was generated in the homelands themselves. The average GDP per capita in the Bantustans in 1973 was less than one-twentieth that of white South Africa (Meredith 1988:151). Africans in homelands import more food than they grow. Few families can support themselves through subsistence activity (Bundy 1979:221–24).

The characteristics of the homeland economies undermine government attempts to stimulate development there. The fragmentation within the homeland territory results in inadequate communication and transport networks. The homelands lack external economies that limit inter-industry linkages and prevent the development of legal, financial, and advertising services (Lemon 1987:174).

Both the increase in black union membership and in union strike activity has motivated Pretoria to try to gain more effective control over black unions and to give black workers more wage concessions (Saul and Gelb 1986:8). Until 1979 African unions, though not illegal, had been excluded from registration under the Industrial Conciliation Act of 1956. Under this law employers bargained with registered and officially recognized unions through industrial councils. Multiracial unions were forbidden. In 1979 this act was amended so that Africans could join registered trade unions (Carter 1982:24). Even so, some unions remain unregistered but employers have continued to negotiate with them (Lipton 1985:68; Kibble and Bush 1986:227).[23]

The new black union power, along with pressure from the business community, has forced the government to allow larger wage increases for black workers than for whites. From 1970–83 the real wages for Africas in manufacturing and construction rose by over 60 percent compared to 18 percent for whites. There have been similar wage increases for Africans in the gold mines and for those working on white farms. Yet Africans have a long way to go to catch up to the average white wage. Today the white share of the total personal income in South Africa is just under 60 percent, while for blacks it is 29 percent (Lemon 1987).

By allowing black union registration the government hoped to limit membership to urbanized workers, to bar multiracial unions, and foreclose union political activity. But the government has failed to achieve these goals, since the unions have organized migrant labor and workers across racial lines, and have established political programs (Greenberg 1987:65).

To avoid South Africa's international isolation, Botha's government attempted to develop new regional relations through the creation of a Constellation of Southern African States (CONSAS). CONSAS could prove of economic benefit to South Africa by continuing to serve as sources of cheap labor but also as new markets for manufactured goods, durable and nondurable, necessary to a country that has experienced a decline in working-class purchasing power and anticipates a 35 percent level of unemployment by the year 2000 (Kibble and Bush 1986; Davies and O'Meara 1988:73). If CONSAS was to succeed, Pretoria had to defeat the attempt by bordering African states to reduce economic dependence on South Africa through the Southern African Development Coordination Conference (SADCC), which aimed at developing a regional system of economic development by coordinated economic policies by South African black states.[24] To reduce the border states' ability to achieve these economic objectives, South Africa took economic action that undermined the border states' economies, such as refusing to employ migrant labor from these countries and turning to Bantusan labor reserves instead.

In addition to economic sanctions, Pretoria took direct and indirect military actions against some border states in order to destabilize their economies and to discourage such governments from providing refuge for the Southwest African Peoples Organization (SWAPO)[25] and ANC. Botha's government engaged in direct military action by using reconnaissance commandos for hit-and-run operations against railways and oil refineries as well as ethnic battalions stationed on the borders of the neighboring states for raids or support of local dissident groups. Pretoria gave direct aid to dissident groups within the border states to create continued economic instability. Lesotha, Mozambique, and Angola have borne the brunt of these assaults (O'Meara 1986).[26] Such regional strategies had some limited success but such destabilization attempts did not destroy the effectiveness of SWAPO or the ANC. And the economic costs to the government increased year-by-year (O'Meara 1983:61).

Since the Constellation met with resistance from African border states, the South African government next proposed a Confederation of Southern African States. This Confederation was to be comprised of white South Africa and the "independent" Bantustans. Within the confederation the states were to be autonomous but could share common passports and confederal nationality (Davies, O'Meara, and Dlamini 1988, vol. 1:199).

By the time that Botha left office it had become obvious to much of the National Party leadership that cosmetic apartheid reforms were not sufficient to resolve the internal and external contradictions that were producing the interpenetration of economic, social, and political crises. The conjunctive moments initiated to handle earlier crises had only exacerbated the conflict between the government and the nonwhite groups. Cosmetic reforms were creating new problems for the government rather than resolving old ones. Botha's "total strategy" had failed to win nonwhite political support for the government, establish labor peace, stamp-out the anti-apartheid opposition, or create self-supporting Bantustans where surplus African populations could live away from white areas. The cost of the security forces increased year by year. The Broederbond leadership now recognized that the prospects for maintaining Afrikaner power by means of the apartheid system was problematic. They began to work within the Nationalist government to convince state leadership to initiate the legal processes that would destroy apartheid and replace it with a multiracial system in which whites still might retain some measure of political power.

Frederick de Klerk replaced Botha as head of the National Party in February 1989 and became acting president in August 1989 when Botha resigned. In the September elections de Klerk was elected president of South Africa though his National Party's overall majority was reduced in the legislature.[27] Both the far-right Conservative Party[28] and the moderate Democratic Party gained seats at the expense of the National Party (Battersby 1989b).

Under de Klerk's leadership the National Party appears ready to enter into negotiations with black leaders concerning black political and economic demands. The Nationalist government has met many of the demands that the ANC stipulates must be fulfilled before it will negotiate with de Klerk. In February 1990, de Klerk legalized the ANC, PAC, and the South African Communist Party. Restrictions on other anti-apartheid groups were lifted (Battersby 1990c). On 11 February 1990, the South African government released Nelson Mandela, the ANC leader, from prison (Battersby 1990d).

But the government has not met all the ANC's demands. While de Klerk has pointed to the fact that Pretoria has granted freedom to 933 political prisoners, the ANC claims that there are 1,292 political prisoners who should be released (Battersby 1991h). The ANC also wants the government to expedite the return of political exiles. In the fall of 1991 the United Nations negotiated an agreement with Pretoria for the return of an estimated 40,000 political exiles (Battersby 1991b, 1991c, 1991f; Ville-Vicencio 1990).[29] While the ANC has met the South African government's demand that it give up its intention of continuing its armed struggle, the ANC has sanctioned strikes and protest marches as a necessary means of keeping pressure on the government to continue its reforms and to win support from the grass-roots black youth within the ANC who want radical action continued. But the government argues that this is a form of armed struggle that ANC must give up before negotiations can proceed (Battersby 1990l, 1990m, 1990r, 1990s, 1990t). But within ANC, youth and military circles want to continue mass action—even insurrection—to ensure a transfer of power rather than a power-sharing compromise (Battersby 1991d, 1991f).

Moreover, up to the fall of 1991 at least, the ANC and the government remained at odds over the procedures through which a new constitution should be drawn up, how the distribution of power between white and nonwhite citizens was to be achieved, and the nature of economic reform. The ANC wanted an interim government representing all the major parties to elect a constitutional assembly that would draw up and endorse a new constitution. But the Nationalist leadership opposed the election of an interim government until a new constitution was agreed upon by a constitutional assembly (Battersby 1990r), though it now seems willing to seek a compromise with the ANC on this issue. It is also doubtful that the government will support ANC demands for an electoral system based on one-person-one-vote.

As of fall 1991, the ANC plan for economic reform also differed from that of the government. The ANC plan involved the nationalization of the mines, banks, monopoly industries, and the parastatals as well as the rapid reduction of racial inequality in housing, health, and education in order to boost the living standards of blacks and other nonwhite populations. By contrast, the government was seeking to bring about economic progress by means of deregulation and privatization of the economy. Government and business leaders stress the role of the private sector in bringing about the redistribution of wealth and income as well as overcoming inequality in housing, health, and education (Battersby 1990j).

However, the Afrikaner government has already started the process of dismantling apartheid. In February 1990 it abolished the Separate Amenities Act, which allowed local governments to bar blacks from parks, libraries, swimming pools, civic centers, buses, and public toilets. Then in February 1991, de Klerk, in his "manifest for a new South Africa," called for the elimination of the last vestiges of the apartheid laws: the Groups Areas Act, the Land Act, and the Population Registration Act (Battersby 1991c). The Group Areas Act segregated neighborhoods by race, the Land Act limited blacks to 13 percent of the country's territory, and the Population Registration Act classified all citizens into racial groups. Indeed, by June 1991 these three laws had been abolished (Battersby 1991k).

The de Klerk government's efforts to abolish the apartheid system reflects the power that the reformers (*verligtes*) within the Broederbond have gained over the anti-reform factions (*verkramptes*). The reformers receive support from the professional groups, intelligentsia, the top echelon of the civil service, and the heads of the large corporations. The reform opponents find support from some teachers, some of the clergy,[30] and most of the political bureaucracy (Adelman 1985:20).

To preserve white power and prevent civil war, middle-class reformers in the Bond want the government to forge a coalition of blacks including rural traditionalists, homeland elites, and the urban middle class that, by being given new rights and privileges, will have a stake in peaceful change. Current Bond leadership seeks a political settlement with black leaders that would reform the political system in such a way as to enable Afrikaners to retain significant power. Recently the Bond has formulated a plan of action aimed at giving all racial groups, including the black majority, a political role at all levels of government with decision-making on a consensual basis, meaning that decisions have to be approved by the majority in each group. Such "concurrent majorities" would give the white minority a veto power (Laurence 1989). Under this system there would be a two-house legislature with members of the lower house elected by all the voters, irrespective of race, while the upper house or senate would be dominated by whites with its members being selected along ethnic and regional lines. The upper house could veto or put a brake on legislation that would injure the whites (Rotberg 1990b; Battersby 1991m). Preservation of the privileged status quo of whites is obviously intended. Recent National Party proposals for a new constitution reflect Bond influence on the South African government's negotiating position.

In a period of transition, such as that which South Africa is now experiencing, when centralized authority tries to rearrange power relationships, the fragile nature of state authority is demonstrated. The earlier configurations of dominant class and/or class factions that supported the government have become unglued. To resolve the crises that threaten the replication of the existing power structure, the government initiated conjunctive moments that split the coalition of classes and/or class factions because such reforms favor one class and/or faction over others. As the coalition dissolved new fault lines between the central authority and its new opponents have appeared at which conflicts within the political and ideological subsystems have emerged.

Civil service bureaucrats feel especially threatened by reforms that have led to a real decline in public sector pay once salary equalization policies were implemented by the government. Civil servants also fear the new job competition from Coloureds and Asians (Charney 1987:16). Included in the groups of *verkramptes* are the small-scale capitalists, who wish to maintain access to cheap labor, and Afrikaner labor unions that oppose relaxation of racial job barriers (Kibble and Bush 1986:219; Carter 1980:92; Lipton 1985:306–9, 322–23; Davies and O'Meara 1988:74; Magubane 1984:216; Adelman 1985:20). Small-scale farmers also oppose the reform policies because such programs threaten their access to cheap black labor supplies and the repressive labor system they have previously used to control their black workers (Charney 1987:16).

In negotiating new power relations state authorities seek to weaken the power of opposition groups by encouraging divisions between the dominated classes and/or races. As we have seen, the Afrikaner government has encouraged if not fostered such divisions within the African population and between the blacks and other nonwhite groups. In this transition period fault lines are occuring within and between the nonwhite races. While the nonwhite populations are united in their opposition to apartheid, different groups have different agendas for change. The political agendas of the following groups differ: the black middle class from that of the working-class Africans, youthful radicals from middle-aged populations, and the tribal (Bantustan) chiefs from the urban-based leadership. The Coloured, black African, and Asian populations as distinct racial groups also have specific political objectives unique to their particular ethnic units (Thompson 1990). Recently the ANC has become involved in a violent conflict with its rival the Zulu-based Inkatha Movement in Natal and in the Johannesburg area (Battersby 1990h, 1990p).[31] Blacks have also attacked Indians and their property in Durban, increasing tensions between these races there (Thompson 1990).[32] But as of spring 1991, black leaders were making efforts to overcome these divisions, which sap the power of the anti-apartheid movement.[33] In September 1991 the National Party, the ANC, and the Inkatha Freedom Party signed an accord which set up mechanisms to resolve black violence while making the police accountable to the community (Battersby 1991n).

Divisions within the black and white communities make compromises between the ANC and the government of de Klerk difficult. If the ANC leadership gives up its constitutional objective of one-person-one-vote, it may estrange its more militant black supporters. On the other hand, if the de Klerk government does not find a constitutional way to protect the rights of the white minority within the new multiracial political system, there is a possibility that the right-wing white parties may gain power, reestablish apartheid, and plunge the country into a racial civil war.

CONFLICTS WITHIN THE BROEDERBOND

Secret societies constitute structural moments that become foci of contradictions within social formations. As in the past, so today, the internal tensions within the Bond reflect the nature of the conflicts within the wider society.[34] *Verkramptes'* discontent with government-reform policies led to a wave of resignations from the Broederbond in 1981. These resignations forced the Broederbond leadership to reverse the decision made in 1972 to expel right-wing members (Lipton 1985:314). The Broederbond leadership made a temporary peace with the right wing of the secret society. Conservatives took over the leadership of the FAK and the Afrikaner Studentebond (ASB) (Charney 1987:15).

In 1984 the Nationalist supporters took back control of the Bond, ousted the far right from the FAK executive, and also took control of the *Ruiterway* (Youth Brigade) and the ASB (Charney 1987:25).

The struggle between the *verligte* (reform) and *verkramptes* (reactionary) factions within the Bond continues. The capture of the Bond leadership by the *verligte* faction in 1984 led to the formation of *Toekomsgesprek Bond* and the *Africaner Volkswag* (AV), a new cultural body, by the ousted *verkrampters*. These organizations will compete with the Broederbond and the FAK, respectively (Charney 1987:17). Joining these groups were the leaders of the Herstigte Nasionale Party (HNP), which favors the return to apartheid based on the 1966 principles of the Nationalist Party, and the *Afrikaner Weerstandbeweging* or Afrikaner Resistance Movement (AWB), a semi-terrorist organization formed in 1979 and led by Eugene Terreblanche. In 1980 it formed a political party, *Blanke Volksstaat Party* (White People's State Party), which has organized a militia (*stormvalke*) to resist reforms through armed struggle.[35] The AV hopes to extend its influence within the South African government in a manner similar to the Broederbond FAK (Davies, O'Meara, and Dlamini 1988, vol. 2:433–34).

Members of such right-wing groups are responsible for the organization of vigilante bodies such as the *Blanke Veiligheid* (BV), which represses anti-apartheid activists in rural communities and mining towns (Battersby 1990e). The AWB seems bent on violent resistance to de Klerk's efforts to destroy apartheid. Many members of the AWB are ex-military personnel who are now serving in the defense forces and the police (Dunn 1990).

While some of the right-wing groups are willing to fight to the finish against the multiracial reforms, other conservatives are sympathetic to the idea of creating a white homeland. Some right-wing leaders want to create an independent Afrikaner state (to be called Orandia) by incorporating the northern Cape province, which would include a west coast port and an industrial complex. Blacks would be excluded. However, some Boer state advocates would create a white homeland out of the old Boer republics of Transvaal, the Orange Free State, and Vryheidin in northern Natal province where the three million Afrikaners would have full political rights and would dominate the twelve million blacks who would have no political voice (Battersby 1990o; 1991i).

The Bond position on reform has undermined its cohesion and influence. It has not been able to enforce its new policy on Afrikaners as a unified group. Public exposure of its activities and disputes has to some extent demystified the Bond. While still powerful, the Broederbond operates more today as a think tank rather than as a conspiracy (Uys 1989:214). Even so, it remains an important political tool by which the present government can gain support for its multiracial reforms, since Broederbond members still retain important positions in Afrikaner economic, governmental, social, and religious organizations through which the Bond can influence Afrikaner opinion on political issues.

<h3 style="text-align:center">SUMMARY</h3>

In tracing the history of the Broederbond in South Africa, I have pointed to its role in dealing with the crises faced by the Afrikaners. Such crises were precipitated by structural contradictions at various points in South African history, which were manifested by conflicts at the fault lines produced by these contradictions. The day-to-day events that constitute the surface relations between actors and/or collectivities cannot be understood without an adequate understanding of the dialectical processes at work in South African society. As the South African social formation evolved, two primary contradictions emerged. The first involved conflicts between the economic and political interests of the Afrikaners and the British and the Afrikaners and the blacks (as well as other nonwhites). These economic and political conflicts were reinforced by ideological differences over racial issues. The Broederbond initiated various conjunctive moments to make sure that the resolution of these conflicts would be in the Afrikaners' favor. We can view the Broederbond as a subsystem that was overdetermined by other structural moments which were in contradiction with each other but, in turn, as an overdetermining subsystem itself. The Broederbond's success in implementing such changes had a profound impact on all subsystems within the South African social formation, thereby transforming white-nonwhite and Afrikaner-British relations in the process. Obviously, then, such structural contradictions have not operated independent of human agents. The conflicts produced by these contradictions have led groups to mobilize their political forces. Those groups with sufficient power resources, such as the Afrikaners, began to impose structural changes on the less powerful. But the overdeterminant impact of the Afrikaner-dominated political structure was to have "composite effects" on the other subsystems such that new contradictions emerged.

A second basic contradiction resulted from the success of the Bond via the Nationalist government policies in improving the economic and political power of the Afrikaners through its support of apartheid structures. The apartheid system began to create barriers to economic development beneficial to white South African capitalists. This system was also directly responsible for increased political instability, which discouraged foreign investment and undermined the profitability of Afrikaner industry. As a result new fault lines appeared within the Afrikaner population and between the Afrikaners and the nonwhite groups. In its role as a "think-tank" for the Afrikaner government, the Broederbond has formulated a series of new reform policies that have been legislated by the Botha and de Klerk administrations to deal with the new crises.

Thus, the Bond has played a significant role in the construction, deconstruction, and reconstruction of the subsystems that make up the South African social formation. Viewed in this way, the Broederbond has been responsive to the dialectical forces at work in South African society. The Bond has responded to the structural contradictions within the South African social formation insofar as it has created crises that threaten economic and political power of the Afrikaners. But, in turn, the subsystem changes, initiated directly or indirectly by the Broederbond, have brought new problems to the white elite, forcing the Bond to initiate new reforms to preserve Afrikaner power. In this sense the Bond has constituted a subsystem focus that has been overdetermined by dialectical changes in other subsystems, and has had an overdeterminant impact on other structural moments, in turn.

Contradictions within the political economy of the emerging state of South Africa precipitated the structural moments, planned and unplanned, that placed Afrikaners in a position of economic and political inferiority. This inferior status led to the conflicts between Afrikaans- and English-speakers, Afrikaner and foreign capital (mainly British), and Afrikaner and black populations. The secret Broederbond served as one form of collective effort—the most successful—by the Afrikaner middle classes to improve their own economic and political positions as well as those of other Afrikaner classes. But to do so they had to limit or diminish the economic and political power of blacks (and other nonwhites), and to a certain extent, the

English-speaking populations. The National-Christian ideology gave the rationale for the apartheid policies advocated by the Bond and the history of their oppression by the British made the Afrikaner feel morally obligated to limit British power in South African society. Yet the success of the Bond in gaining power and implementing its racist and anti-British goals brought the Bond into conflict with some of the same economic interest groups that it and the Nationalist Party had helped put in power.

Today the Bond leadership supports the radical reforms of the present Nationalist regime, but the expulsion of the anti-reform faction has lost the Broederbond support from among the classes that gave it its original power base. By seeking more political power for the blacks and other nonwhites, the Bond is generating new forces of change that may ultimately undermine Afrikaner dominance, if not white power in a more general sense.

The deteriorating economic and political position of the Afrikaner (Boer) population preceding and following the Anglo-Boer War (1889–1902) reflected both a conscious effort by the British to pursue their national interests in South Africa as well as some of the unanticipated consequences of gold and diamond mine expansion. The discovery of these mineral resources within the territory of the newly formed Afrikaner republics led to unforseen damage to the Afrikaner rural economy. Mines siphoned labor from rural areas or bought up Boer farms for their own subsistence production. In this way the Afrikaner rural economy was disrupted.

Dominated by British capital, the growing mining industry found the Afrikaner Republics to be a barrier to expansion of the mining companies. But since the areas of economic growth were within the political boundaries of the Afrikaner states, the British felt their future position in South Africa seriously threatened. This primary contradiction generated a series of secondary conflicts at fault lines between the Afrikaner and British communities. Ultimately, to maintain their power in South Africa, the British were forced to destroy Afrikaner political power in those republics. This was the basic structural contradiction in South Africa which led to overt conflict, eventually leading to the Anglo-Boer War. This war further devastated the Afrikaner population, thus reinforcing the structural discontinuity between English-speakers and Afrikaans-speakers.

The general poverty that afflicted the Afrikaners, along with the overt discrimination against them by English-speakers in government, education, and at the workplace, created the series of confrontational issues that precipitated the political struggles within the newly formed Union of South Africa. Competition between mining and white farmers for cheap black labor, along with the poor-white fear of African job competition added further to the political divisions. British discrimination against the small Afrikaner middle class limited its advance in government, mining, manufacturing, and commerce.

The middle-class Afrikaners who organized the Broederbond and formulated its goals developed a program that appealed to all Afrikaner classes: white labor, white farmers, and the petite bourgeoisie. The Bond's general objective was to promote Afrikaner economic mobility and increase Afrikaner political power at the expense of the black population and of English-speaking groups as well.

Until the National Party came to power, the Bond had no formal power. Secrecy was a vital element in its expansion of control over the Afrikaner population. By constantly reinforcing basic Bond values within the organization and by secret infiltration of Afrikaner groups not directly under Bond control, this secret society was able to expand its power even in the face of a powerful opposition. The Bond began to operate in those social spaces where the structural moments were more vulnerable to transformation, namely white labor, schools, churches, business sectors, and white farmers. When the Bond helped put in power the National Party in 1948, it found a legitimate power base from which to bring about transformations through legislation, thus initiating new conjunctive moments in South African society. Shortly after they came to power, the Nationalists enacted 150 new laws giving a strong legal basis to the apartheid system, which the Broederbond strongly supported. Afrikaner success was paid for by black poverty and oppression. And with a republic status for South Africa, English-speakers lost influence over governmental policy although they retained a strong economic presence in spite of an increase in the percentage of Afrikaners involved in business, banking, and industry.

But as is often the case in such circumstances, changes in the political subsystem may give rise to changes in other subsystems which, in turn, come into contradiction with the first subsystem producing new conflicts. In this case the apartheid system itself came to form a barrier to the successful reproduction of the modern South African political economy and the stability of its political structure. These new contradictions were manifested in increased black militancy and by the attacks on apartheid by the white business sector.

The success of the National Party at improving the economic position of the Afrikaner whites and the general South African economy at the expense of the blacks led, however, to new contradictions that began to generate the politics of economic and social reform. These new contradictions were the result of composite effects that resulted from the successful economic policies of the Nationalist administration. The growth of monopoly capitalism and the increased capitalization of production in commerce, industry, and mining has increased the demand for black skilled labor and black managers. But apartheid laws have restricted black job mobility and quality education. Thus, monopoly capital has come to oppose aspects of the apartheid system, still supported by some factions within the Broederbond. Such racist policies still gain support from rural whites, petite bourgeoisie, white labor, and lower-level bureaucrats. To preserve white power and prevent civil war, reformers in the Bond want to include blacks in government but in such a way as to preserve the privileged status of the white minority. The proposed new constitution would prevent a majority group from dominating. But even these reforms threaten the privileges of some sectors of the Afrikaner population.

Efforts by the South African state to replace apartheid with some form of multiracial democracy have initiated a process that is already having an impact on the various subsystems that make up the South African social formation. But attitudes toward the reform process reflect the structural faults that have emerged within both the Afrikaner and black groups. These ideological differences, in part, reflect the different structural positions that class and class factions occupy in each ethnic or racial group. While multiracialism now serves the interests of white big business and the professional classes, Christian-Nationalism still defines the rationale for the political agendas advocated by the rural white farmers, the white small-scale businessmen, white labor, and lower-level white bureaucrats. In the black community political ideologies, with their corresponding political agendas, have divided the population along the following lines: middle class versus working class, youth versus middle age, and urban leadership versus Bantustan leadership. Thus, the South African case serves to illustrate the fact that neither the ruling class nor its opposition is ever totally successful in developing a unifying ideology sufficient to prevent fissures in the dominating and dominated classes.

The split between reformers and conservatives has created divisions within the Afrikaner population, which have weakened Bond influence to some extent within their natural constituency. Yet, Bond power is still formidable and its opposition to any but cosmetic reforms makes the possibilities for resolution of structural contradictions in modern South African society still remote. Thus, the new fault lines defined by the new structural contradictions have produced and will continue to produce conflict as blacks find new social spaces, opened by government reforms, in which to bring change through union activity, popular revolt, and other anti-apartheid political bodies.

7

The Dialectics of Secret Society Power

An analysis that solely concerns itself with secret society objectives, rituals, and structures cannot provide an adequate understanding of the political activities of secret societies within states. Nor do theories that are based on positivist principles provide us with sufficient insights into the historic role of secret societies. Positivist theories generate secret society typologies in which each form of the secret society is explained as a result of mechanical responses to special sociopolitical variables that are considered necessary and/or sufficient conditions for the appearance of such secret orders (Erickson 1981; Lyman 1964; Gist 1940).

A dialectical framework, as proposed in this book, being consistent with realistic principles of science, is a source of more fruitful analytical insights. According to a realist, an epistemologically adequate scientific explanation must be based on a search for the underlying structural mechanisms whose operation accounts for the surface phenomena. Specific moments within a social system are manifestations of the underlying structural processes that characterize the totality of elements and relationships of the total system as an entity of analysis. Parts cannot be analyzed independently from the whole. A dialectical framework requires that secret societies be studied as one manifestation of a common underlying structural process that is disclosed throughout the totality of social relations.

At any point in time the subsystems (or structural moments) within a social formation interact in complex ways to produce the social totality and are produced by it in turn. The dynamic aspect of the social formation that produces systemic changes results from the structural contradictions that occur when subsystems work toward opposite goals. Primary contradictions take place at three points in the structures of social formations (Zeitlin 1980). The extrasocial environmental capacities and the external political parameters come into opposition to the socioeconomic pressures to increase productive capacity. A second point of contradiction is between the achieved level of productive forces and the existing social organization of production that places restrictions on the productive forces. Lastly, there is a basic contradiction between the relations of production and the prevailing superstructure, that is, the political, legal, and ideological subsystems (Sztompka 1979).

All these subsystems are mutually interrelated, but they are also mutually overdetermining and overdetermined. The economic structures are not absolutely primary nor are the political and ideological subsystems absolutely secondary. Because of the mutual constitutedness of structural moments (or subsystems), movement and change in one structure will bring about change in other structures, which react back on the first subsystem bringing about further change in it. The sources of such change are structural contradictions that generate actions by social agents (individuals and groups) as their opposed interests trigger conflicts between them.

Each social formation, however, is part of a larger interactive system (social system). Internal contradictions can be generated and/or exacerbated by external structural processes as, at any historic moment, social formations become enmeshed in wider political and economic relationships and their prevailing contradictions (e.g., international, regional).

It is at the structural fault lines that the primary contradictions produce conflict. The repercussions of the basic contradictions can be detected through the tensions, frictions, and conflicts between social agents or the groups they represent, at these fault lines. Such structural contradictions create the conditions that motivate classes or groups to interfere, undermine, and/or jeopardize the position or interests of other classes or groups. Continued conflict of this sort at the fault lines produces antagonistic attitudes and ideologies among these groups or classes. The clash of these polarized viewpoints may lead to conjunctive moments of which secret society activity is one manifestation (Allen 1975; Sztompka 1979).

From the dialectical perspective "human culture is hyperadaptive: human beings in communities and groups transform their 'environments' through their cultural self-constructions and whereas their 'environments' are other classes, ethnic groups, kinship groups and so on, as well as the 'natural' conditions of human history, they transform one another and themselves in the course of dialectical opposition and struggle" (Nonini 1985:55). Secret societies are one visible demonstration of this dialectical opposition and struggle.

To understand the dialectics of secret society power we must answer four basic questions: Under what circumstances do secret societies become involved in the conflicts within social formations and what are the sources of these conflicts? How does the nature of these conflicts define the political role of the secret society? As the dialectics of interaction between the state and secret society unfold, what are the long-term consequences for the secret society itself? In the face of opposition by the state and/or other opponents, how do secret societies maintain their power?

Secret societies constitute sites at which secondary contradictions make themselves manifest. The conflicts in which secret societies become involved are the result of structural contradictions within a social formation at some point in its history. Secret societies promote the interests of individuals, groups and/or classes that come into conflict at the fault lines produced by the structural contradictions. The structural fault lines at which secret societies pursue political action serve to define the nature of the political struggle in which the secret societies are involved and thus their general political goals.

A brief review of the political role of the secret societies studied in this book again demonstrates that they constitute loci at which structural conflicts appear. In my first case study I discussed how serious economic problems forced the Americo-Liberian state to seek new sources of revenue by extending governmental control over the hinterland chiefdoms. This expansion was also provoked by Liberian fears that the French and the English might annex territory claimed by Liberia if Liberia did not demonstrate that it could exert effective control in the hinterland. These policies put the Americo-Liberian government into direct conflict with hinterland polities such as the Kpelle chiefdoms. The Poro-organized military resistance to these state attempts at extending its hegemony over the hinterland chiefdoms was an overt manifestation of the contradictory interests between the Liberian state and most of the Kpelle.

The studies on the Ottoman Bektashi and Chinese White Lotus sects, as well as the Malaysian Triads, provide further illustrations of how secret societies become involved in the conflicts engendered by structural contradictions. The Bektashi sect came into conflict with the Ottoman state. To consolidate and maintain control over their vast empire the Ottoman rulers relied on a substantial bureaucratic class and a powerful military force called the Janissaries who were equipped with modern weapons. Eventually the Janissaries came to subvert the military and economic interests of the

Ottoman sultans. By the early nineteenth century the stagnating Ottoman economy made it undesirable for the sultans to continue their support for a large Janissary corps, most of whose members now lacked military training and who also opposed the military reforms that the sultans felt were necessary to modernize the Ottoman army.

Because of this opposition and because the Janissaries intrigued against particular sultans and vezirs, one Ottoman ruler eventually eliminated the Janissary corps by killing vast numbers of them. This purge of the Janissaries gave the orthodox Sunni priesthood an opportunity to repress the heterodox Shiite Bektashi as well. Many Janissaries were members of the Bektashi sect. Therefore, sect leaders and members were considered allies of a corps that was a threat to the sultan's power.

In Malaysia emerging structural contradictions put the British colonial government into conflict with the Chinese Triad secret societies, which the British had once tolerated. World market conditions that resulted in a decline in the demand for the Malay products led to new contradictions within the Malay political economy that forced secret societies into a fierce struggle with one another over the control of economic operations in mining and on the plantations. The British feared that such secret society "wars" would discourage foreign investment. The Triads' control over Chinese labor also denied European enterprises a source of cheap labor. Therefore, the British enacted ordinances aimed at suppressing the secret societies. Secret societies could no longer operate openly and were forced to go underground, operating through front organizations.

The White Lotus sects in Ch'ing China provided individuals and groups hostile to state authority with a source of political support and protection. Efforts by the Ch'ing state to solve crises produced by structural contradictions within the Manchu empire worked to the disadvantage of the peasantry and other class segments. To establish control over their vast empire the Ch'ing created a large bureaucracy of underpaid scholar-officials, exempt from land and labor taxes, which carried out state mandates and extracted economic surpluses from the population. Scholar-officials diverted resources owed the state to their own use. For this and other reasons the Ch'ing state lost revenues and was forced to impose new tax levies that merely increased peasant resistance.

White Lotus sectarianism was one response to these crises. The millennial messages transmitted to the followers of the White Lotus sects constituted a threat to Ch'ing rule. The Ch'ing rulers were active in the suppression of the White Lotus sects, whether or not the sects actually organized rebellions.

Of the secret societies discussed in this book the Broederbond has had the most success in achieving power at the state level. The Bond was formed to serve the interests of the South African bourgeoisie class within an oppressed Afrikaner minority. British capital, finding that the Boer Republics formed a barrier to the expansion of their mining interests, encouraged the British government to eliminate them. The military destruction of these Republics created a potential for Afrikaner interclass unity, which the Bond was able to exploit. The Bond emerged as a secret society representing the interests of the Afrikaner middle class, allied classes, and class segments that were opposed to the dominance of British capital. The postwar discrimination against Afrikaners by the dominant English-speaking group merely reinforced the anti-British ideology that the Boer War had produced. But because some early Afrikaner governments sought to create an alliance with British interests, the Broederbond became their political enemy.

Through the National Party the Broederbond was successful in improving the economic position of the Afrikaner middle class and its class allies. But this economic progress for the whites, achieved by apartheid policies, was paid for by African poverty and the oppression of the nonwhites.

Of course the political activities of secret organizations are not necessarily circumscribed by the realities of state power nor solely determined by the apparent limitations on secret society resources. Secret orders do not always orchestrate their activities in terms of objective structural limits and positions. Subjective evaluations strongly influence their means and ends. Belief in the coming of a millennium in which existing state leadership will be destroyed may spur secret society revolts regardless of the prevailing state power. For example, in most instances revolts led by the White Lotus were motivated more by the sects' ideology (which predicted the imminent arrival of a new era in which the corrupt government would be overthrown and replaced by sect members), than by any practical political wisdom.

Thus, relations between state and secret society have varied not only from state to state but also over time within each state. Under some historic circumstances secret societies operate as centers of resistance to governmental authority, but later either come to establish a dominant influence over state leadership or to help reinforce state hegemony over local regions. In other cases the government, while initially tolerating secret society activities because these secret orders proved useful to state interests, later attempted to regulate and/or destroy them. Other secret societies, through the whole history of their relations with the state, have served as foci of countervailing power against state authority.

Within the state, attempts by secret societies to utilize and manipulate existing sociopolitical structures may lead to unanticipated consequences for the state authorities and/or the secret societies themselves. Secret society members evaluate and respond to crises in ways that further their objectives and interests. But the long-term effects of such secret society action programs may have composite effects unanticipated by the secret society, effects that in a direct way limit or expand secret society power. Secret society reaction to such composite effects or the political consequences of such supraintentional processes may result in changes in secret society goals and/or structures. The case studies discussed in this book provide evidence for this.

Poro-led resistance to America-Liberian government expansionism in the Kpelle hinterland made the Liberia state fearful of Kpelle secret society power. But rather than suppress the Poro, the state merely restricted its activities and co-opted it as a political organization subject to state law but useful in giving support to local government chiefs and central state leaders. Thus, the long-term impacts of Liberian state hegemony over the Kpelle chiefdoms have forced the Poro to focus its concerns on ritual matters and legal adjudication rather than on political resistance to state authority.

Shifting political relations between the states and secret societies create new, unanticipated survival problems for the secret orders. Within the Ottoman empire, for example, the close association that the Bektashi sect had with the powerful Janissary corps at first benefitted the Bektashi in spite of their heterodox religious beliefs. But when the Ottoman purged the Janissaries, the Bektashi suddenly faced disaster themselves because the Ottoman sultans, who were orthodox Sunni Muslims, considered the Bektashi not only political enemies (because of their association with the Janissaries) but religious enemies as well. In response to the Ottoman attempts to destroy them, the Bektashi sects turned themselves into a secret order using information control as a power resource to protect themselves.

And, in a similar fashion in Malaysia, the Triad secret societies, whose activities within the Chinese communities were initially tolerated by the British colonialists, suddenly faced government repression because, as we have seen, the secret societies' control over Chinese labor and the frequent wars they fought with one another now constituted political and economic threats to British interests. As a result of the attempts by the colonial and postcolonial governments to destroy them, Triad societies have made structural changes and have sought control over new client groups in order to survive.

By contrast to the Poro, the Bektashi, and the Triads (in Malaysia), the White Lotus sects, since they professed a religious ideology that challenged the authority of the Ch'ing state, were under constant threats from the state. But the diffuse structure of White Lotus organization enabled the sects to survive government efforts to destroy them. Many White Lotus sects remained undetected by the government until or unless they organized rebellions. Once the sects became involved in such collective efforts they were less successful in protecting their members from government retribution. Government loyalists living in close proximity to sect members soon learned of the sects' plans and reported them to state authorities, thus enabling the government to arrest key leaders and disrupt the rebel plans. And the loyalty of the nonsectarian troops who joined the rebellion was not assured, especially when the rebels faced military defeats. But even in defeat the White Lotus sects survived by reorganizing under new leadership.

The Poro, Bektashi, White Lotus, and Malaysian Triads represent secret orders which, at least at some point in their histories, have been forced to devise survival strategies as a result of unanticipated and/or unpredictable government repression. The Broederbond of South Africa also faced such government hostility, but, unlike these other four secret orders, the Bond was able to gain a powerful influence within the state itself. The Bond did so once it helped elect the South African National Party as the ruling party within which the Bond had a strong representation. Through its secret activities the Broederbond was able to place the Afrikaner white minority into a position of economic and political power.

Yet in helping put the Afrikaners into power through the system of apartheid the Bond has helped create a superstructure that has come into contradiction with the requirements of an expanding, modern economy. Modern South African capitalist corporations now need skilled African labor and African managerial talent. Apartheid policies have prevented the development of such a supply of skilled black labor.

The apartheid system also has precipitated continual, varied, widespread, and often violent anti-apartheid opposition movements that have contributed to the political instability that threatens white rule. The security costs for the government entailed in keeping the opposition groups in check has become immense. Economic sanctions by South Africa's trading partners also have hurt the South African economy.

This powerful opposition to the apartheid system has forced the Bond to encourage the National Party to support abolishment of apartheid laws. But Bond support for racial reform has provoked internal dissension. The Bond has lost the support of rural whites, small-scale businessmen, and white laborers who believe the retention of apartheid is in their interests.

A dialectical theory of power, then, enables us to conceptualize the dynamics of secret society power within the context of the social system and its evolving contradictions. The trajectories of secret society development cannot be understood except as part of the field of conflict produced by the system contradictions. The power strategies employed by the secret societies reflect the degree of support or resistance to the secret societies. The unfolding patterns of actions and reactions between the secret societies and other power agents will determine, at any one time, the relative power of the secret society within the system.

The consistency, duration, and intensity of opposition to secret society activity varies, depending on the historical circumstances. To the extent that the dominant class or group finds the secret society a useful mechanism to serve its interests, the greater the freedom the secret society has in carrying on its activities. And the greater the threats that the secret society presents to ruling-class interests, the more intense the attempts by the ruling groups to suppress it. Emerging systemic contradictions may require changes in the political role of secret orders. Consequently the extent of its political threat to ruling interests will change as well.

Secret society concealment triggers a chain of interactive and reactive actions. The pattern of secret society concealment and disclosure reflects the dynamics of conflict process over time. The more intense the conflict the greater the efforts by the secret societies to conceal information from their antagonists. In cases where the secret society poses a political threat to the state, the government may carry out espionage against it. Secret societies react to threats of such espionage by enhanced security or counterespionage. In this way threats by the state encourage the secret society to set rigid group boundaries and to institute strict codes of group loyalty. By indoctrinating new members into codes of secrecy and loyalty, the secret society has tried to minimize the flow of information to its enemies. Failure of these information-control strategies have threatened the power, if not the very existence, of the secret orders.

Successful information control will not necessarily enable the secret society to maintain and/or expand its power, though it is vital to its protection. To extend its power the secret society must control and/or influence the actions of nonmembers or place its own members within the government itself. The secret societies will minimize state opposition to the extent to which their organizations serve the interests of the ruling party, governing body, or ruling-class factions. By contrast, secret societies that serve as foci of state opposition for dissident classes or groups provoke hostile state actions. Under these circumstances the secret society operates as a source of countervailing power to state authority by serving the interests of opposition groups.

Thus, in certain historical circumstances there is a dialectical struggle for autonomy (space) between the secret society and the state. Resistance to state authority by the secret society creates insecurity among the state leadership. Governments then respond with coercion against the secret orders. Such repressive measures provoke, in turn, insecurity among secret society leadership and secret societies respond with the development of new power resources to protect their own autonomy (space).

The Broederbond illustrates the outcome of this dialectical power relationship between the state and secret society. Because of efforts by the early South African government to undermine Bond power and more recent attacks by its enemies, the Broederbond continues to place a veil of secrecy over membership, officers, activities, meeting places, and operations. Through selective recruitment and constant membership surveillance the Broederbond leaders try to maintain membership adherence to the strict Bond codes of loyalty and security. Watchdog committees supervise the conduct of members in carrying out Broederbond policies within the various political, religious, economic, and social organizations in which they are members.

Secrecy is also an important power resource enabling Bond leadership to infiltrate its members into all important institutions of South African society. As influential members of educational, religious, professional, labor, business, and political organizations, Bond members spread their nationalistic doctrine.

For reasons somewhat similar to those of the Broederbond the Bektashi implemented secrecy structures when the Ottoman empire attempted to repress the sect. The principle secrecy strategy was dissimulation, the cover-up of the Bektashi heterodox beliefs by claiming adherence to Muslim orthodoxy. The Bektashi made sure that only loyal followers learned of their true anti-Sunni religious doctrines. Such Sufist religious ideology was only transmitted to the faithful novice under threats of fearful penalty if this knowledge was transmitted to outsiders.

Like the Broederbond and the Bektashi, the Malay Triads maintained their power by exerting control over many aspects of their members' lives. During initiation the novice learned the detailed Triad laws governing a member's behavior, including the nature of punishments for disclosure of the society's secrets. The importance of secrecy was further dramatized when, during initiation, the initiates recited an oath of secrecy whose violation would result in their death.

In the early period the Triads inducted many prominent Chinese leaders in Malaysia and Singapore. These individuals enabled the Triads to collect useful intelligence about potential government actions against their organizations.

Once extensive government repression forced the Triad lodges to go underground, the older Triad leadership lost control to the new leaders of the front organizations that the Triads set up for protection. Many of the new leaders headed extortion gangs which operated independently of the older Hung leadership. Lacking anything but a minimal form of ritual indoctrination, members of these gangs show less identification and loyalty to these secret gangs.

Like the Triads, the White Lotus sects evolved a well-developed system of protection in the face of state persecution. Unlike the Triads, the White Lotus sects did not protect themselves through oaths of loyalty and threats of punishment for the violation of the sect's rules. By making the converts privy to the cult doctrine and by providing the converts with spiritual solace as well as the skills for discipline and self-sufficiency, the White Lotus created ties of devotion and dependency that assured great loyalty.

The White Lotus sects were organized in ways that made it difficult for the Ch'ing to identify, much less suppress, them. A sect consisted of several scattered groups of believers organized into a loose chain of teachers and disciples. Members along the chain usually did not know each other, though their leaders might know them.

Once a sect began to organize actual rebellion the government had a greater chance to detect the sect and its activities. To maintain the loyalty of the rebel forces, most of whom were not White Lotus members, the sect leaders were forced to develop new power strategies stressing the benefits that loyal followers would gain in the new society and the punishments for those who betrayed the rebellion. But sect-led rebellions destroyed the veil of secrecy surrounding secret society leadership, making it easier for the government to detect and arrest sect leaders and their disciples.

My previous analysis has already shown that the Poro and Sande, once the Kpelle chiefdoms were incorporated within the modern Liberian state, found most of their traditional power extensively circumscribed by the state. Nonetheless, information-control strategies are still important power resources for these secret orders, enabling them to carry out their political and religious roles within the local communities. The secrecy surrounding the initiations and Kpelle fear of the secret society leaders' medicine powers has enabled the Poro and the Sande to limit the flow of information concerning their initiation activities as well as the nature of political deliberation by the Poro councils. As members of the inner council of the Poro, elders of the dominant lineages still control critical historical knowledge that prevents other descent groups from successfully challenging the dominant lineages' land claims and, thus, the basis for much of their political authority. Through their secret knowledge of rituals and traditional medicines the secret society leaders can act as religious brokers, utilizing their secret knowledge of the supernatural forces to cure or prevent illness.

The analysis presented in this book has demonstrated that to understand the political role of secret societies in state systems we must know something about how they arose and developed and how they fit into the larger context or system. A dialectical analysis enables us to do this because such an interpretive framework begins with the whole, the system, and then proceeds to examination of the part to see where it fits and how it functions (Ollman 1986). This manner of analysis contrasts with that of the nondialectical approach, in which one starts with a supposedly independent part or subsystem and, through establishing connections between the parts or subsystems, tries to reconstruct the whole. Our analysis of secret societies has stressed how such secret organizations reflect the underlying processes or forces characteristic of state systems.

Given an analytical framework that proceeds from the whole to the part, dialectical research tries to understand how systemic contradictions account for the incompatible development of different elements within the same relation—that is, between elements that are also dependent on one another. Dialectical relations involve moments that mutually presuppose and mutually negate one another within the same relationship, thus constituting a unit of opposites (Vyakkerev 1982). Viewed in this way such an analysis of contradictions enables us to explain the dynamic properties of social relations because changing subsystems both support each other and block, undermine, and interfere with each other, thus eventually transforming the total system.

Overt conflict is a reflection of these structural contradictions, the underlying processes or forces responsible for the appearance of strains, tensions, dislocations, or imbalances. Thus, the political conflict at the structural fault lines in which secret societies, among other groups, become involved are reflections of the underlying primary structural contradictions that manifest themselves throughout the state system in complex ways. For example, to understand the nature of Broederbond conflict, first with the early South African government and later with the Bond's former class allies, we must come to understand the emerging structural contradictions within the South African political economy and how they are manifested as moments of conflict among class, class fractions, and racial and ethnic groups. In a like fashion the conflict between the Poro-led chiefdoms and the expanding America-Liberian state, the Bektashi and the Ottoman sultans, the Triads and various Malaysian governments, and the White Lotus sects and the Manchu (Chi'ing dynasty) cannot be adequately understood without an analysis of the underlying antinomies within each of the state systems that gave rise to these secret orders.

Through dialectical analysis we can discover the structural limits on solutions to crises faced by a state system, short of its total transformation. Within those limits the power strategies employed by the state and the secret society reflect the recursive analysis by their respective agents, which is conditioned but not totally determined by ideological and normative factors.

But as we have seen attempts by agents of both the secret society and the state to manipulate the power resources available to them to attain their goals may produce long-term consequences that undermine the power of either or both groups. In attempting to reproduce existing structures the state may trigger secret society resistance which, under certain historic circumstances, transforms existing power relations. And, in a like fashion, in reacting to state controls a secret society may initiate internal transformations that bring about basic change in secret society organization. This study of secret society and state relations reinforces the more general observation that there is a dialectic between structure and practice. Moments initiated by social actors do not always take place the way the agents suppose they will. Over time, structures that appear to be reproduced are, in actuality, transformed.

Dialectical analysis, then, enables us to better understand, in each historic instance, the nature of the state processes under which secret societies arose, the particular structural fault lines at which a secret society is in conflict with the government or other groups, how these conflicts transform the secret societies themselves (as well as their power relations with particular class and class fractions) and how the existence of such secret societies affects and/or, is affected by the inherent processes and forces promoting or undermining state power.

Notes

1. Definitions of the term *secret society* have varied from those that are too inclusive to those that are too exclusive (Hazelrigg 1969:324; Gist 1940:20; Wedgewood 1930:132; Bhutani 1962:3; Simmel 1906:441). Inclusive definitions would place corporations in the category of secret societies. Corporations guard commercial secrets but are not secret societies. Exclusive definition would eliminate most secret orders from the category of a secret society. Mak's (1981:8) definition is less exclusive but placed undue stress on oath taking as an essential criteria differentiating secret societies from other secret groups. This definition would exclude many groups from the secret society category, such as religious sects, merely because they did not administer oaths to initiates. But the differentiation between sects and secret societies is often arbitrary. If a sect is a type of religious group formed in protest against another religious group, then, in many circumstances it may take the form of a secret society in order to protect itself from attacks by its opponents (Warner 1964:624). All associations with special initiation rituals, which through oaths or *other mechanisms* impose secrecy norms on members, should be considered secret societies.

2. There have been many descriptive studies analyzing the history of secret society development in specific countries. However, these studies have not offered a theoretical framework suitable for comparative studies (Chesneaux 1971, 1972, 1973; Comber 1959; Davis 1971; Little 1948, 1949, 1965, 1966; Lyman 1970; Mak 1981; Roberts 1972; Webster 1908; Simmel 1906, 1950). Simmel comes closest to developing such an analytical framework but only identifies key secrecy strategies rather than relates these processes to the changing role of secret societies in an evolving social system. Simmel makes no attempt to develop a theory suitable for a diachronic analysis of secret society development.

3. A dialectical method, based on a realist ontology and epistemology, constitutes the most meaningful basis for explaining various historic instances of secret society activities within states. Realists argue that social reality consists not of things but relations, and rejects dualism and atomism. Dialectical analysis suggests that relata are both separate and interdependent and also opposite and identical (Rivano, 1981:28). Discovery of a regular conjunction of externally related events or things does not constitute the basis for causal explanation of phenomena. This world of external (pseudo-concrete) phenomena operate on the surface of real, essential processes (Kosik 1976:2). Such surface phenomena both

reveal and conceal the essences. Essential processes are mediated by the surface phenomena, only revealing aspects of themselves through fetishized praxis. Knowledge seeks to overcome the mystification of appearances and move beyond them (Sayers 1985:30).

Reality-as-it-is (things-in-themselves) pass into social relations (social phenomena) and are manifest and revealed, in part, in these relations (Sayers 1985:37). But social relations require interpretation to reveal information about underlying structural mechanisms (reality-as-it-is). While social relations affect and alter how social agents perceive the world, at the same time they reflect and reveal reality for us (Sayers 1985:133).

Contrast this view with that of the positivists, who assume that the observable level of social relations constitutes the essential structure of those relations and that the structure of these relationships results from norms that constitute rules that are both restrictive and determinative (Wilson 1982:112).

An adequate scientific explanation must identify the underlying structural mechanisms (Benton 1977; Harre 1972; Manicas 1982; Craib 1984). Such mechanisms, upon being stimulated, produce effects. The total system is a manifestation of such essential structural mechanisms. The nature of the mechanisms is determined by the internal constitution of the system. This may involve the idea of a Hegelian totality in which a simple essence or dominant principle (or mechanism) comes to pervade the entire society or may, in a contrary fashion, involve a simple part (economic) determining relations among all the parts of the system (Burawoy 1979:17).

Having identified and described such internal mechanisms, we can only assess their power to bring about certain outcomes, not the probability that they will do so (Wilson 1982, 1983; Harre 1972; Secord 1986:199). The generative mechanisms characteristic of social systems have the power to produce effects under certain conditions. Unexercised causal power is nonetheless real (Collier 1989:12–13). Such generative mechanisms are causally responsible for the phenomena we experience but cannot directly observe. For a realist, reality is not a series of events we experience. The appearance of the world cannot be confused with the reality of the world (Isaac 1987:46; Collier 1989:12–13).

In contrast, positivists believe that through repeated tests of causal hypotheses they can formulate universal abstract laws of social behavior. This is because scientific observation can be made free from temporal and contextual associations (Gergen 1968). But as Isaac suggests "realism rejects the understanding of causality as a constant conjunction and scientific explanation as a prediction of empirical regularities" (1987:46). Realists do not search for universal laws.

Realists accept the ontological argument that "reality-as-it-is" differs from "our-conception-of-reality." Our theoretical concepts do not actually represent "reality-as-it-is" but only an approximation of these entities. The fit between our scientific ideas and reality itself is a very rough correspondence (Rescher 1987). What counts as relevant and proper is partly determined by the theoretical paradigm. Scientific observations are "theory impregnated" (Knorr-Cetina and Muklay 1983:4). Such scientific accounts are mediative, not straightforward, representations of external reality (Woolgar 1983:244). Thus, thought and reality, the subjective and objective, constitute a dialectical unity. These opposites interact and interpenetrate, each being transferred into the other in the course of knowledge development (Sayers 1985). Theories are products of history itself, since they are the consequences of the combined practical and analytical efforts of all the historic actors (Albert and Hahnel 1978:89). Theory formation is constituted and determined by all other aspects of social reality (Resnick and Wolff 1982:37).

By contrast idealists assume that social actors are purposeful and creative molders of their own environment. Rules are open to continual reinterpretation. There is no "reality-as-it-is." Reality is the product of the social actors' mutual construction. Thus social reality is an outcome of the social actors' sustained interpretive efforts. Intentions and actions are not cause and effect. Intention and action are two aspects of the same thing. Therefore, agent causality is stressed by idealists. Links between events are made by reference to the actors' intentions (Wilson 1983:106–21).

In contrast, positivism ignores the role of human agency. Since social science has modeled itself on the scientific enterprise in physics and chemistry, where no human agency plays a role, positivists assume human agency is an irrelevant concept as it applies to human society. From the viewpoint of positivist social science, social structure seems to be governed by principles independent of the goal-directed activity of individuals (Porpora 1985:220–21).

However, realists assume that the same internal mechanisms have different consequences in different historic circumstances (Bhaskar 1979:43; Boudon 1986:101). Human agents "in some sense must be able to do other than they do do" (Flew 1985:90). Their behavior is not "inexplicably necessitated" (Porpora 1985:222). Thus, the aim of realist social science is not to develop categories of universal applicability. Such abstract analysis merely formalizes manifest properties of life. A realist social science aims at enlarging our capacity to perform specific analysis by means of establishing the distinctiveness of structures and/or social systems, suggesting the main lines of development of these systems and/or structures, and determining which are the essential processes for change within each system and/or structure (Wilson 1982:170; Sayer 1987).

4. Braudel (1972:26) argues that conscious history—the history of events—proves illusory. But Braudel suggests that significant history is unconscious history that determines the dynamic process beyond the "flashes of light." Unconscious history is "richer than the flashing surface that our eyes are used to seeing." But penetrating to this hidden level "is difficult and chancy."

5. This dialectical concept of opposition differs from the empiricist "dualistic" concept. Dualism conceptualizes the world as based on either/or distinctions. Identity and difference are absolute opposites that entirely exclude each other. But from the dialectical perspective concrete identity includes difference. Opposition exists in concrete unity, in which opposite elements contradict, interfere, interpenetrate, and pass into each other (Sayers 1980b).

6. Cunningham conceptualizes the dialectical contradiction in the following way:

> A thing (anything) is composed of features (or parts) which promote its continued existence and of other features which militate against its continued existence. The latter features militate against its continued existence in that they are causally related to the former features in such a way

as to tend, in some respects, toward their destruction. In this way the two sorts of features are opposites. At the same time, however, the two sorts of features constitute a unity in that they also interact in at least one of three ways: (a) the one sort of feature plays a role in bringing the other into existence; (b) in some respects the one sort of feature sustains the continued existence of the other; (c) the two sorts in some respects sustain the continued existence of one another. (1982:60–61)

7. Yet we must remember that structural contradictions do not inevitably breed conflicts. This is because actors (or collectivities) are not always aware that they have divisive interests at stake and/or are not able or motivated to act on their divisive interests (Giddens 1984:199).
8. Decisions taken by human groups (a synthesis of individual decisions) have a greater impact in situations of societal crisis (Lukacs 1978:171).
9. There are two forms of consciousness: spontaneous and philosophical. Philosophical consciousness is more contemplative, interpretive, and introspective while spontaneous consciousness is more flexible, pragmatic, adaptive and less conditioned by principle (Sumner 1979:17–19).
10. It is for this reason, in spite of the fact that social agents' actions are not completely necessitated, that diachronic propositions concerning the possible unintended consequences of patterned social actions, in particular, historic circumstances, can be made (Flew 1985:103–4).
11. According to the Marxian perspective, thought processes are both an outcome and a reflection of the material elements while at the same time they are opposed to the material relations and react back on them. Belief systems develop that contradict the economic and environmental subsystems and have influence on them (Sayers 1980a:89).
12. Within the Marxian tradition there are differing views on the overdeterminant role of the ideological subsystem within the social formation. Althusser (1970) argues that the legal-political and ideological superstructures are responsible for the reproduction of the relations of production. Ideology, then, functions to reproduce the conditions of production, making existing patterns seem natural and universal. Ideology is never a source of movement in the social formation. Of course, the manner in which the ideology produces a submissive population varies with the social formation.

 By contrast Poulantzas (1973) argues that the dominant ideology is a product of class struggle. It incorporates many ideological elements from the dominated classes. Factions within the dominant class also contribute different elements to the prevailing ideology. In any case the dominant ideology disguises the real contradictory interest of class and class factions.

 While both Althusser and Poulantzas perceive social agents as having limited knowledge about the institutions that are responsible for social reproduction, Therborn (1980) views the social agent as a creative actor in ideological formation. Through the acquisition of new skills social actors come into conflict with the traditional forms of subjugation. Social agents come to evaluate the dominant ideology by assessing whether it supports institutions that are advantageous or disadvantageous to them in comparison to other beliefs that sanction other social structures (see Boswell, Kiser, and Baker 1986 for further discussion of these and other views on ideology).

13. My conception of system boundaries differs from that of Mann, who claims that in no sense are societies unitary, that is there are no instances in which we can find a "single bounded society in geographical or social space" (1986:1). Allen (1975:269) takes a similar view when he suggests that the limits of society can only be gauged by the spread of its repercussion effects and by the reciprocal contradictions that they generate. While societal boundaries are not always clear-cut, nonetheless, in my view, societies can still be distinguished at some levels, whether political, cultural, or economic.

14. The *state* as public power embodies offices and rules that carry out the authority of the state. The term *government* refers to a person or persons who exercise public power at a particular point in time. Government carries the authority of the state, a continuous authority that is above any particular government and the people it governs. The *administration* or *political bureaucracy* is the totality of persons or bodies who are discharging government responsibilities (Vincent 1987:20–31).

15. Empires are polities dominated by a state whose control has expanded beyond the borders of its original territorial framework. The shift of independent polities to client or subordinate provinces is central to the growth of empires (D'Altroy 1981:2).

16. A class faction (sometimes called fraction) is a segment of either the producing or nonproducing classes whose specific interests in some respects are divergent from the interests of their class allies. Such factions are social ensembles within a class which represent distinct economic interests and which constitute social forces capable of political action. Thus class segments or factions are differentiated by their locations in the process of production and surplus appropriation (Zeitlin 1980; Poulantzas 1973).

17. Distinction between legitimate authority and coercive authority should be made. In the first case, authority rests on the fact that most members of the society accept the rulers' power as legal, just or rightful (Vincent 1987:38). Such authority might be based, for example, on divine right as a legitimate basis for the fact the leaders ought to be obeyed. In the second case most members of the society would change rulers if they could, but they still obey the leaders out of fear of the consequences if they do not do so or because they have no alternatives (Easton 1958:180–81). Cohen (1988a) has suggested that acceptance of authority may range from grudging acceptance to more wholehearted enthusiasm.

18. Power agents are individuals or organized groups which, at different times, can produce effects or suffer consequences or both (Cartwright 1959).

19. Isaac (1987) has argued that such concepts of social power rest on empiricist assumption. They imply conjunctive causation since A's power over B suggests A's behavior causes B's behavior or A's mobilization of bias suggests A's decision or action causes B's behavior. However, I look on these power relationships as patterned regularities, whether asymmetrical or symmetrical, which are surface manifestations of underlying structural mechanisms. To understand the nature of these power structures we must develop abstract models that enable us to relate the effect of system contradictions on power relationships which are essential to the reproduction of a given social formation. We must investigate how emerging political relationships that result from these contradictions enhance or restrict the ability of social agents to exercise social power.

20. Authorities do not command complete obedience by subordinates. In authority

structures there is not an absence of resistance but only its legitimization (Rus 1980). Thus, authority relations involve the institutionalization of induction and resistance. Or as Rus describes the relationship "induction and resistance are permitted and limited in advance" (1980:10). Subordinated actors take a calculated attitude toward authoritative commands, finding subtle ways to resist if self-interest dictates (Olsen 1970; Giddens 1981).

21. If a leadership's secret decisions or nondecisions result in circumstances that bring negative consequences to societal members, even though they might not know the cause, the people may challenge the authorities. This is especially true when such concealed decisions help perpetuate a system of inequality. Under these conditions some people "will question whatever legitimizations are offered, some will be moved to resentment and some will resist. Counter power movements, though not directed at specific decision-makers, may undermine the leaders' ability to control the situation, thus modifying the power relation" (Turk 1982:254).

CHAPTER 2: THE PORO AND SANDE SECRET SOCIETIES AMONG THE KPELLE OF LIBERIA

1. Shifting cultivation (slash-and-burn, or *swidden*) is a type of horticulture, most common in the tropics, in which short periods of cultivation of a plot alternate with long periods of fallow.

2. Until World War II domestic rice production satisfied Liberian demands. But the displacement of labor to mining, construction, and plantation employment has led to a decline in rice production relative to national needs. As a result, in the 1980s Liberia imported 70 percent of its marketed rice (Whitaker 1985:158).

3. By the early 1980s the average subsistence household of five to seven members cultivated about three acres of upland rice and one to two acres of other crops. One out of five households had a small section of land (one-half to one acre) on which coffee or cacao trees were grown to provide a cash income (Whitaker 1985:156).

4. The *loi-namu* (landowner) gave his important immigrant chiefs a wife, usually a sister or brother's wife. Through this marriage the landowner's "sister" became the mother of the newcomer's children and, by extension, the mother of the newcomer's expanding descent group as a whole. In this way the landowner's lineage assumed the position of "mother's brother" to the newcomer's lineage, which became "sister's son" to the landowner's lineage. This "nested" structure was extended as the newcomers, in turn, received and incorporated, through wife-giving, latecomers in their areas. These recent immigrant lineages became "sister's sons" to them in turn (Murphy and Bledsoe 1987:128).

5. Support for the American Colonization Society not only came from white Americans who wished to correct the injustices done to blacks by slavery but also from other whites who looked on the increasing population of freed blacks within the United States as a threat to white interests (Rinehart 1985:8).

6. Congoes were recaptured Africans. This group comprised over 5,000 Africans that had been seized from slavers in Atlantic waters by the American navy, mostly between 1845–62, and settled near or in Americo-Liberian communities.

They were granted the same political and civil rights as settlers (Akpan 1985:9). The Congoes were eventually absorbed by the lower strata of the Americo-Liberians through intermarriage (Kaplan 1985:102).

7. Political power was concentrated within twelve families that formed factions and alliances within the True Whig Party (TWP). All leaders with the TWP belonged to the Masonic Order. As members of the Masonic Lodge, the Americo-Liberian leaders worked out political deals and compromises outside the formal government channels (Rinehart 1985:32). Of the 20,000 descendants of the nineteenth-century settlers, there were only about 2,000 that could be classified as elite or sub-elites (Kaplan 1985:104).

8. Britain also came into conflict with Liberia over Liberia's attempt to collect duties on imports and exports. These custom duties were a principle source of revenue for the Liberian government. Trade was limited to customs ports (Rinehart 1985:17).

9. Early resistance throughout the nineteenth century had been confined to coastal Vai, Dei, Bassa, Kru, Grebo, and the Southeast Gola groups. As the Liberian government moved to extend control in the hinterland, the government policies of forced labor, taxation, and expropriation of land led to revolts by the Grebo and Kru, Boroba, Grebo, Gola, and Bandi-Jokwele Kpelle among others (Abasiattai 1987).

10. Not long after the Republic of Liberia was formed in 1847, the government proclaimed that all Liberian land was to be public property subject to the sale to Liberian citizens, for the government use, or for grants to missions or foreign corporations with the major exceptions being African village sites and their adjoining farmlands (Akpan 1985:10).

11. Kpelle chiefs made followers incur debts that they couldn't pay. This forced the debtor to give a member of his household as security for the debt or loan. Some of these pawns worked off the debt in a short time, while others worked the rest of their lives without liquidating the family debt. A wealthy family's desire for labor or reproductive rights was paramount in its acquisition of pawns and slaves (Bledsoe 1980). Americo-Liberians also raised tribal children who had been placed with them as pawns by their parents, for which the parents received some compensation (Kaplan 1985:113).

12. All Poro tribes but the Mano were northwest of the Saint John River. Of the remaining six tribes the Basse, Gio, and Kru had versions of the Poro (Kaplan 1985:94, 114).

13. Bellman (1979) describes a major "devil" who is responsible for assisting in adjudication of disputes between Poro chapters. He is recognized as the political head of an area's Poro lodge. I suspect that this formal role for a regional *Zo* was imposed by the Americo-Liberian government on the hinterland. Normally Poro leaders resolved disputes between their respective chiefdoms or districts or, on occasion, turned to some prominent *Zo* to help resolve inter-Poro conflicts.

14. *Sale* refers to a substance, utterance, or action which possesses unusual powers. Owners of the most powerful *sale* and leaders of secret societies are called *Zoes* (Murphy 1980:197).

15. There seems to be considerable disagreement about the number and nature of the ranks within the Poro. Harley (1941) suggests there were ninety-nine levels. Bellman (1984) mentions only thirteen ranks within the Poro priesthood. Bell-

man suggests that the highest ranking Zoes belong to *Balasilangamu* Society (Sheep-Adorn Devil Society) within the Poro (paralleled by the *Zohii* for the highest ranking priestesses in Sande). Within this group are members from specific families associated with the body called *lalou* (lay inside of). *Balasilanga-mu Zoes* perform various roles including serving as liaisons with the town, protecting the bush school from intruders, training initiates, meting out punishments, adjudicating disputes within the Poro and between the Poro and its allied secret societies, and transmitting government requests to the Poro. Initiates to the Poro join the *Ngwalpiye* association.

16. Women are a source of lineage strength. Women provided labor on Kpelle farmlands. And such farmlands were sources of Kpelle wealth. The more wives a man had, the more land he could bring into production and therefore the more wealth he could acquire (Gibbs 1965:215).

17. Other Kpelle secret societies included the Snake Society (*Kali sale*) whose *Zoes* cured snake-bite victims. The Thunder (or Lightning) Society had medicine to control thunder, lightning, and rain. The Iron Society (*Kawli sale*) served the community by protecting it from the water dream spirit (Bellman 1984; Murphy 1978).

18. Today the Kpelle still fear the potential physical sanctions of the Poro but their fear of supernatural punishment has dropped away (Stakeman 1986:216).

19. It is likely that the Liberian Poro operated like the "war Poro" and "peace Poro" in Sierra Leone. The secrecy surrounding Poro activities allowed the organization to make war preparations without the enemy suspecting military preparations were underway. The "peace Poro" provided the inter-chiefdom structure through which negotiations could take place when both sides wanted a cessation of conflict (Barrows 1976:70–71).

20. Unlike the Liberian Poroes, the Sierra Leone Poroes have become involved in the modern political process. Poroes have given support to the Sierra Leone Peoples Party (SLPP) which became a dominant political movement in the 1950s. This party was closely allied to local chiefs. In some chiefdoms the Poroes conducted a terrorist campaign against the SLPP's major rival, the All Peoples Congress (APC), a political party organized by middle-class professionals, traders, and some skilled workers which opposed the political dominance of the chiefs under the SLPP (Barrows 1976:128; Kilson 1966:256:57).

21. The Liberian-American-Swedish Mineral Co. is a joint venture accounting for one-half of the Liberian annual iron-ore output (Whitaker 1985:174).

CHAPTER 3: THE OTTOMAN BEKTASHI

1. Warriors of the faith were called *ghazis*. It was their sacred duty to extend the Islamic territory at the expense of lands inhabited by non-Muslims. The *ghazi* emirates were products of the *ghazi* raids against Byzantium. The *emirs* or chiefs led the warrior bands that conquered various districts. Such *ghazi* leaders became the founders of dynasties (Itzkowitz 1980:6–12).

2. The education of the Christian children was spartan, intensive, competitive, and selective. Not all the students became Janissaries. Some became palace gardeners or seamen. Those with the most ability staffed the imperial administration. They

would rise to become governors of provinces, members of the sultans' council of state, the president of the council, or even the grand vezir (Toynbee 1974:25–26). Suleiman's eight grand viziers were all Christians brought to Turkey as slaves. But the *ulema*, the judges, and the teachers were sons of Turkish fathers, reared on the Koran (Severy 1987:574).

3. The prophet Muhammed could have no successor. On his death his closest companions made Abu Bakr the *Khalifa* (successor or deputy). Many of Muhammed's followers condemned Abu Bakr as a usurper, claiming that Ali Ibn Abi Tabib, the husband of Muhammed's daughter, Fatima, was the rightful successor. Those who accepted the legitimacy of the early caliphs came to be known as Sunni. Opponents, who were followers of Ali and his descendants, were known as Shi'a (Lewis 1985).

4. Some dervish orders such as the *Khalwati* accommodated to their middle- and upper-class followers. The *Khalwati* dervishes adopted many orthodox views. They dampened their previous political activism. *Ulema* criticism of them was muted (Martin 1972).

5. By the eighteenth century prominent *ulema* had become members of the Otto-man ruling class and had therefore attained positions of power and privilege. They were exempt from taxation, on death their personal estates could not be subject to state confiscation, and they could pass on these estates to their heirs. High ranking *ulema* families supervised vast religious endowments (*evkaf*) and held high political posts (Chambers 1972).

CHAPTER 4: WHITE LOTUS SECRET SOCIETY ACTIVITY DURING THE CH'ING DYNASTY

1. The Ming dynasty reigned from A.D. 1368 to 1644. After seventeen years of civil war, the former peasant rebel Chu Yuan-Chang forced the Yuan dynasty from the dragon throne of China. The term *ming* may refer to the Confucian term translated as "bright, clear, discerning," or to the more heretical Manichaean belief which postulates the triumph of light (*ming*) over darkness of the Yuan dynasty. In A.D. 1351 the White Lotus Society started a series of revolts. These early rebel movements were, in part, motivated by the Manichaean belief that predicted the end of the old order and the beginning of a new millennium of peace and prosperity. Later rebel movements attempted to establish dynasties of the more traditional Confucian sort. Both movements spawned other move-ments, one of which was led by Chu Yuan-Chang, which overthrew the Yuan dynasty (Dardess 1976).

2. The annual cost of the military force rose from 500,000 *taels* of silver in the late fifteenth century to nearly four million taels in the early seventeenth century (Chan 1982:127).

3. During the early Ming period taxes had been paid in goods, grain, tea, charcoal, silk cloth, and services (corvee labor on irrigation works, transport, postal service, and menial work in government offices). Cash played only a modest role in the tax system. The Single Whip reforms enabled the government to commute material, grain, and labor levies to taxes in silver (Goldstone 1988:113).

4. Late Ming rebellions began in Northern Shensi province. This was an area where

local bandits and outlaw Ming troops, who had deserted their units, sought asylum. The power of rebellions waxed and waned depending on local conditions. Most of the Ming rebels had a predatory and highly militaristic ethos, quite at variance with the values of the ordinary peasant. The rebels never championed agrarian reforms (Dardess 1972).

5. The Manchu success in occupying Beijing and the surrounding towns was, in part, due to the fact that the *khan* (*Dorgon*) welcomed Ming officials into his new regime (Wakeman 1985, vol. 2:416).

6. In some areas such as Southeast China, Southern Fujian, Eastern Guangdong, and Taiwan, fights (*xiedou*) between land-owning clans brought considerable disruption. These armed fights growing out of disputes over land, boundaries, water rights, and so forth turned into long-term feuds or vendettas, which not only included clansmen on both sides but mercenaries and bandits that became involved in these clan wars (Zurndorfer 1983:314).

7. The Mongols had to be controlled, otherwise the Manchu homeland would have been threatened. To do this the Manchus had to conquer Tibet to safeguard their control of Turkestan and Mongolia. Thus, they had to secure an area that had little economic value to them at considerable expenditure of government funds (Eberhard 1966:289).

8. Li Tzu-Ch'eng's forces captured Peking (Beijing) in April 1644 just before the Manchu armies moved into the city. Li's success as a rebel leader rested on the presence of famine in Honan, disintegration of the Ming armies, and Li's ability to overwhelm walled cities. Li turned his bandit gang into a peasant movement (after 1641). Li was eventually driven from Beijing by the Manchu and subsequently he and his army were destroyed (Dardess 1972).

    Chang Hsien-Chung, in the first phase of his rebellion, which lasted till 1643, was primarily interested in acquiring plunder. His gang's activities extended from Shensi into Kiangsu. After 1643 he seems to have pursued the goal of setting up an independent state. Eventually, in January 1644, he invaded Szechwan, capturing Chungking in July 1644, and occupied Chengtu in September 1644. At Chengtu, Chang set up a civil administration that minted money, held official exams, and established a *pao-chia* system. Because of the resistance to Chang organized by Ming officials, he started a campaign of terror in the province, which eventually was responsible for about one million deaths. The failure of the Chengtu administration motivated Chang to plan an invasion of Shensi, in the course of which he was killed by the Manchus and his forces destroyed (Parsons 1970).

9. For example, local officials had to pay expenses of escorts on which they depended for protection on journeys and they had to pay for their own private secretaries (Lui 1979:314).

10. Because clerks and runners knew the local dialects and customs, magistrates depended on them for work in their offices and as messengers. Such underlings' official stipends were no better than a peasant's income (Lui 1979:24–26).

11. Kazumi (1984) suggests that there was a qualitative difference between economic and social struggles and political and religious movements. Peasants who became involved in religious movements went through an ideological transformation that changed the nature of the struggle from one based solely on economic considerations to one which aimed at a millennial metamorphosis.

12. Orthodox Pure Land advocates emphasized a divine intervention that would give their followers a blissful rebirth, while other sects stressed salvation from the catastrophe that would overcome nonbelievers (Harrell and Perry 1982: 288–90).
13. Earlier dynasties had been concerned with White Lotus Society activities. As early as A.D. 1257 government edicts called for the suppression of the White Lotus Society and related sects (Overmyer 1972:48).

CHAPTER 5: CHINESE SECRET SOCIETIES IN MALAYSIA

1. Negrito, proto-Malay, and other hunters and gatherers preceded the Malays to the peninsula. These "Sakai" populations withdrew to the hills and had little contact with the later Malay immigrants. Malay contacts with the Sakai consisted of a little trade and some slave raiding (Gullick 1988:7).
2. The Portuguese captured Malacca in A.D. 1511 and made it a strongpoint of their maritime empire. Then the Dutch captured Malacca in A.D. 1641 from the Portuguese. The Dutch, who promoted trade with the Malay states, became the dominant European power of the Malacca Straits. The British took Malacca in A.D. 1795 (Gullick 1988:8).
3. Up until 1860 dry-padi cultivation was more important than wet-padi production in most of the Malaysian peninsula. Only in the northern states did wet-padi production become established after its introduction from Siam. This was because there was an extensive river plain suitable for cultivation. The unavailability of vast areas of flat land and a good water supply for irrigation made dry-padi cultivation better suited for most of the Malaysian environment.
4. Each traditional sultanate constituted a state (called *negri* by the Malays). Each *negri* encompassed the basin of a large river or, sometimes, a group of adjacent rivers, forming a block of land extending from the coast inland to the central watershed. A ruler (called *Sultan, Raja, Yang-Di-Pertuan*), a member of a royal patrilineage, was vested with supernatural power and high prestige. States were divided into districts (*jajahan* or *daerah*) whose chiefs were drawn from aristocratic lineages that had long-established connections with the districts. In turn the districts were divided into villages (*kampong*) led by a headman who served as a channel of communication between the villages and district chiefs (Gullick 1988:20–22; Butcher 1979:5).
   The *negri* were unstable units. A sultan was in firm control of his royal district but not over the other districts within his sultanate. Often the Malay state broke up as a result of civil wars. Nonetheless the sultan did serve as a focus for state integration. Charters for the titles of district chiefs had to be confirmed by the sultan. Without such a charter and consequent recognition of their power, such titles were of little value. Thus chiefs were driven by their political needs to preserve the sultanate. Chiefs did not fight wars with each other to become sultans but to acquire enough state power to control the legitimate sultan. Ultimately, the sultan preserved the unity of the state through his symbolic role (Gullick 1988:133–37).
5. The Communist Party in China was organized after a split in the ranks of the Kuomintang. The Kuomintang was organized in about 1894 by Sun Yat-Sen. It

succeeded in overthrowing the Manchu dynasty in 1912 and established a Chinese republic. The Malayan Communist Party was established in 1930 short-ly after the left and right wings of the Kuomintang split (Comber 1957).

6. The Alliance Party constituted a union of class factions who had a common interest in preserving the capitalist order in Malaysia. These "administocrats" or statist petite bourgeoisie mediated between the interests of foreign capital, fac-tions of local capital, the upper strata of the peasantry, and the urban petite bourgeoisie on one hand, and the dominated classes (the working class, lower strata of the peasantry, and the urban workers) on the other (Jomo 1988:271). These statist capitalists controlled capital accumulation by virtue of their hold on state power. They were powerful ruling-party politicians, senior bureaucrats, as well as politically connected businessmen, predominantly though not exclusively Malay (Jomo 1988:268). See Hui (1988) for an alternative view.

7. The National Front was formed following a loss of support by voters in the 1969 elections for the parties participating in the Alliance Party and the subsequent race riots in May 1969 (Jomo 1988:254). The parties that undermined the Alliance were the Pan Malayan Islamic Party (PMIP), which argued that Chinese and Indians in Malaya should return to their homelands, the Democratic Action Party (DAP) that advocated that the Malay privileges should be eliminated, and the Progressive Party (PP) that ran on a multilingualism program (Rabushka 1973:35–37).

8. The United Front dominated by the United Malay National Organization (UNMO) established a New Economic Plan (NEP). NEP moved the Malaysian government from a passive to an active role in the promotion of Malaysian capitalism. The state became the medium for capital accumulation. The govern-ment made direct and indirect subsidies to business, held wages and production costs low, and gave business tax incentives (Jomo 1988:237).

But the identification of the state with the interests of the Malays has under-mined its legitimacy in the eyes of other ethnic groups. Protests by non-Malay and foreign capital have forced the state to temper its policies. The Malay businessmen have voiced their dissatisfaction over competition from state enter-prises. These protests have forced the state to trim back the role of state corporations (Hui 1988).

9. Between 1851 and 1860, 23 percent of the total British tin consumption was met by Malayan exports. Over the next decade the peninsular exports of tin more than doubled in tonnage (Jomo 1988:142). Even so the largest single source of government revenue for the British in Malaysia from 1874 until World War II was not tin or rubber but opium. During half of this period 40 to 60 percent of Straits Settlements revenue was from opium (Jomo 1988:171).

10. The colonial government favored European capital at the expense of the local populations by appropriating land from Chinese and Malay owners and issuing this land to European businessmen at low cost. The British supported the price of tin when the world price dropped and also lowered the export rates on tin. In addition the government provided many infrastructural facilities (Jomo 1988:171).

11. With the expansion of the European-owned tin sector there was a decline in Chinese employment in the mines. The percentage of Chinese working in tin

mines declined from 96 percent in 1911 to about 81 percent before World War II, and to 61 percent by the early 1960s (Jomo 1988:174).

12. The growth of Chinese and Indian labor in Malaysia led to a corresponding increase in the demand for rice. The demand was so great that by 1890 rice imports were necessary. They constituted 35 percent of the total imports (Jomo 1988:56). This was one reason why the colonial government encouraged Malay peasants to produce food for local consumption. But a more compelling reason was to discourage peasants from turning to cash crop production, thus keeping such export production in the hands of the British capitalists (Jomo 1988:57).

13. The colonial government helped British capital gain a monopoly on rubber production by providing infrastructural facilities, alienating the best land from local populations, and undertaking state financed botonic research. The government helped rubber plantations to get labor from India at low cost (Jomo 1988:199). Nonetheless, many Malay peasants have found ways to establish small-scale rubber production (Jomo 1988:63).

14. But in some Straits Settlements there was an early decline in Chinese emigrants who had their fares paid. While 36.7 percent of Chinese emigrants arriving at Singapore and Penang in 1881 had their fares paid, this proportion fell to 10.9 percent by 1890 (Jomo 1988:168).

15. Even though the colonial government condemned the system of labor indentureship, a 1910 government commission, while painting a terrible picture of the lot of indentured laborers, nevertheless recommended extending the use of indentured labor to the largely British-owned rubber industry which was in great need of workers at the time (Jomo 1988:163).

16. Trade guilds had little relation to the Chinese secret societies in Malaya but were important economic associations for the Chinese. They furnished mutual aid and provided training for apprentices as well as regulated wages for carpenters, builders, blacksmiths, tanners, shoemakers, tailors, and barbers (Freedman 1960:41).

17. A number of Chinese secret societies also named their societies *kongsi*, possibly the more localized and economically oriented ones (Wong 1979).

18. The indirect rule system started in Malacca in the late sixteenth century when Malacca was under Spanish rule. The system was adopted by the British, who extended it to Penang in 1786 and to Singapore in 1819. The *kapitan* system was abolished in 1825. It was replaced by the *T'ing Chu* (master of the temple) system in Malacca and Singapore. The *T'ing Chu* was a leader elected by prominent Chinese connected with the temple (Mak 1988b:234). The T'ing Chu system was abolished in 1901. As a consequence there was a leadership gap in the Chinese community. Later associations and guilds supplied leadership with a minimum of government interference until the 1940s (Douglas and Pedersen 1973:33).

19. The Malay rulers benefitted from the Chinese development of the tin-mining industry because the Malay sultans agreed to the arrangement only when they were paid a large commission by the Chinese mine owners (Jomo 1988:157).

20. Mak (1975b) has suggested that where political rule over the Chinese immigrants was direct, there was no sign of secret societies (except in Burma), but where Chinese secret societies existed there was some form of indirect rule.

21. The name of the Triad society is often represented symbolically in the society's ritual by an equilateral triangle that depicts the harmonious blending of heaven, earth, and humanity (Comber 1957:2).

22. In Singapore the nearest approach to a grand lodge was that of the Kuang Hui Chao I Hsing Ta Kung Szu in 1870. Members of the Cantonese, Hokkien, and Teochew dialect groups participated in society rituals, probably at different times, in this lodge. Disagreements between these groups eventually led to their splitting into different sections (Comber 1962:35). Up to 1890 the Ghee Hin branches may have been part of one organization. The nine branches met twice yearly for rituals in a house called the "mother temple" (Freedman 1960:35–36).

23. Wynne (1941) has argued that there are two distinct and rival secret societies in China, the Triads and the Han Liu Society, from which the rival Malaysian secret societies stem. There is little evidence to support this idea. The Han Liu is but an alias dicta of the Triads (Comber 1957:1). The rivalries of secret societies in Malaysia does not grow out of traditional conflicts between their parent societies in China but because of clashes over economic interests in Malaysia itself.

    One version of traditional history explaining Triad origins suggests that the Triad society was founded by five monks of Shao Lin Monastery in Fukien Province who escaped when the monastery was sacked by order of the Manchu emperor, Yung Ching, despite the fact that some years earlier the monks had been successful in driving out the Mongol forces that threatened the Manchu throne. As a result the Triad society has always proclaimed an ideology that was hostile to the Manchu rule (Comber 1957:1–7). Tai (1977) disputes this explanation of Triad origins. He suggests that the phrase *wu-tzu* (five founders) refers to the five Confucians virtues of benevolence, integrity, etiquette, wisdom, and sincerity but not to actual human beings. According to Tai the Triad society was founded in the year 1767 by a monk named Hung Erh in Kuanyin Temple of the Chang Chou district (Fukien Province).

24. The pseudo-brotherhood-type secret societies admitted candidates based on sex, speech, and territorial criteria. The pure-brotherhood model was not this restrictive (Mak 1985:144–45).

25. Experts on Triad society ritual each know only parts of the total traditional ceremony. Ceremonial practices vary in details from lodge to lodge (Comber 1961:40). For another description of Triad initiation see Purcell (1948:55–57).

26. The Malays formed secret societies that were often allied with the Chinese secret societies. The White and Red Flag societies were two of the most prominent Malay secret orders. The White and Red Flag societies were suppressed in the Straits Settlement by the 1882 Ordinance but were not included in the suppression ordinance of 1890. Even after the Chinese secret societies were subject to increased suppressive measures, the Malay societies freely operated as underground organizations (Wynne 1941:425).

27. Aside from passing ordinances aimed at regulating and/or banning secret societies the colonial government also tried to eliminate Chinese control of labor through debt-bondage. The Truck Enactment of 1908 barred debt-bondage of mine labor and gave the workers the option of receiving cash instead of consumption items as part of their wages. Wages paid in opium was forbidden. The prices on goods sold to workers under the truck system were fixed by the government (Jomo 1988:170).

28. An amendment to the Societies Law was passed in 1882 to deal with Muslim Red and White Flag secret societies and to prevent British subjects and persons of non-Chinese descent from belonging to a Chinese secret society.

    Along with the Societies Ordinance of 1890 a Chinese Advisory Board was installed in the Straits Settlements. This board included eight leaders of the Chinese community distributed among the dialect groups. It served as a legal alternative to the now-illegal secret societies by arbitrating disputes within the Chinese community.

29. Dr. Sun Yat-Sen was a senior Triad member and so were other important figures in the Republican government. The Triads became a powerful lobby in the political and civic affairs of the New China. The Triads were so prominent in the republican government that ambitious people in the military, private business, and political life sought their assistance in order to advance their careers.

    Later General Chiang Kai-Shek made certain Triad societies the strongarm of his Kuomintang Party by giving them unlimited criminal control as well as a prominent position in his government. The Green Gang Society helped Chiang eliminate the communist-led labor unions in Shanghai. Under Chiang's government the Triads infiltrated the police and military (Posner 1988:32–34).

30. Christian converts had always been a threat to secret society power. The anti-Chinese Roman Catholic riots of 1851 in Singapore led by the Ghee Hok society stemmed as much from secret society competition with Christian religious groups over converts as it did from the basic Han society hostility to revealed religion (Wynne 1941).

31. Some of the older Triad societies enrolled members from several dialect groups. For example, five of the nine branches of the Ghee Hin society, accounting for about one-half the members, enrolled recruits from single-dialect associations. But the four other branches were heterogeneous for dialect membership (Freedman 1960:36).

CHAPTER 6: THE BROEDERBOND OF SOUTH AFRICA

1. The pass law system governed the movement of Africans throughout South Africa. Africans over the age of sixteen were required to carry a passbook proving that they were entitled to be, remain to work, or reside in white areas. The passbook holder's employer's signature had to be renewed each month to prove that the holder was still employed. A black African that failed to produce a passbook would land in prison, and one who failed to prove his or her right to be present in a white area was ordered to return to his or her homeland ("endorsed out") (Meredith 1988:127).

   Enforced segregation was secured through the 1927 Immorality Act, which forebade extramarital sex between black Africans and whites, and the 1923 Urban Areas Act, which confined Africans to segregated townships and locations and regulated the number of pass-bearing Africans who would have access to urban areas (Horwitz 1967:205).

2. Of course there had been black and liberal white resistance to apartheid from the very beginning of the union. As early as 1935 an All-African Convention demanded the extension of the Cape franchise to all of South Africa. The African

National Congress endorsed universal franchise in 1943 and by 1949 was advocating strikes, boycotts, and other forms of civil disobedience to achieve black freedom (Carter 1986:349).

3. President Smuts used the army and air force to suppress the 1922 strike. In the conflict, 153 miners died, and more than 500 were wounded (Meredith 1988).

4. Organizers of Young South Africa were responding to the street fight between English-speaking patriots and Afrikaner nationalists that followed a speech on April 13, 1918, by Dr. Malan at Johannesburg City Hall in which Malan called on Afrikaners to rally to the Republican banner and convert the Union into an independent Republic outside the British empire (Bloomberg 1989:65).

5. Within the Dutch Reformed Church (NGK) there were leaders who did not always follow the Broederbond line. In December 1966, for example, leading figures of the NGK who attended a World Council of Churches Conference in Johannesburg accepted the conference declaration that criticized South Africa's apartheid policies. However, the Bond forced the NGK to recant their support of the anti-apartheid statement and forced the leaders who had supported it from the church (Meredith 1988:88).

6. The Afrikaner Nasionale Studentebond (Afrikaans National Students Association [ASB]) was organized in 1933, and by 1935 had branches in all Afrikaner universities. Until schisms emerged within the Broederbond in the 1980s the ASB maintained a solid front for the support of apartheid among the Afrikaner students. In 1986 *verligte* (reformers) left the ASB. Since the ASB decline, far right students have increased their support of the Afrikaanse Studente Federasie (Afrikaans Students Federation) which supports white supremacist policies (Uys 1989:227–230).

7. *Ossewabrandwag* (Brigade of Ox-Wagon Sentinels or OB) was a paramilitary, ultra-nationalist mass movement formed in 1939. Its main aim was the establishment of a Nazi-Calvinist Republic in South Africa. The secret military arm of the OB, the *stormjaers* (stormtroopers) was modeled on the Nazi SS during World War II. The *stormjaers* launched a campaign of terror and sabotage, blowing up post offices, cutting telephone lines, and carrying out assassinations. At its peak OB claimed 250,000 members including the paramilitary *stormjaers* (Bloomberg 1989:169–183; Uys 1989:211).

8. The Bond also provides study loans for members' children or takes donations to families of deceased members (Bloomberg 1989:34).

9. This strong religious element governing the Bond mission is reflected in the Broederbond meetings, which are held in a religious atmosphere that reflects the Bond's Calvinist values. All brethren who attend are expected to wear dark clothing. Dominating all discussions is the notion that the Bond members are a religious elite chosen for a civilizing mission in South Africa (Bloomberg 1989:38).

10. The National Party draft constitution issued in January 1941, before its parliamentary victory, reveals the Christian-Nationalist principles on which the National Party based its political, social, and economic agenda:

> "1. The Republic would be an independent sovereign state outside the Empire.
> 2. It would be an Afrikaner-dominated *volk* state.

3. Ideologically, the state would be Christian-Nationalist and recognise the sovereignty of God. All moral creeds, such as liberalism, socialism and secularist doctrines, are forbidden.
4. The state would be totalitarian. All media, and certain important aspects of the means of production and distribution, would be state-controlled.
5. All British symbols would be effaced and replaced by Afrikaner symbols: the Head of State would become the President; the old Transvaal flag, the *Vierkleur*, would replace the Union Jack and the Union Flag; the national anthem would be 'Die Stem.'
6. Considerable authority is vested in the President, who is elected for five years. He has the power to appoint and dismiss the Prime Minister and Cabinet, and is responsible to God alone.
7. A corporate element is introduced into the machinery for electoral representation; in addition to Parliament, there is a Community Council with advisory powers composed both of official nominees and elected spokesmen for various social institutions, spheres of activity, occupations and interest groupings.
8. Non-whites are strictly segregated and encouraged to develop separately, although not in such a way as to disturb the availability of labour." (Bloomberg 1989:178–79)

11. By 1962 every branch of the state apparatus including civil service, judiciary, police, and army was controlled and staffed by Afrikaners: of the 46 top civil servants, 42 were Afrikaners; of the nation's 318 diplomats, 315 bore Afrikaner surnames; of the 11 Appeals Judges, only 2 were of English descent. No English names at all were to be found in the senior military and police lists (Bloomberg 1989:441).
12. Since 1924 South African administrations have made direct investments in parastatal corporations which have provided the foundation for industrial growth. Such parastatals include ISCOR (iron and steel), FOSKOR (phosphates), SASOL, ARMSCOR (military equipment), SENTRACHEM (chemicals), and NATREF (oil refining) (Lemon 1987:150).
13. The African National Congress (ANC) is the leading force for the national liberation struggle in South Africa. The ANC aims to forge a broad nonracial movement of elements in South Africa pledged to overthrow the apartheid state. The ANC was formed in 1912. It was first named the South African Natives National Congress. Led by Western-educated black professionals, it followed a policy of nonviolence for fifty years. The ANC leaders preferred negotiations with the government of South Africa rather than armed resistance. But after the massive government crackdown on the ANC and other black resistance organizations following the Sharpeville killings (1960), ANC began to expand its underground cell networks, adopting armed struggle as its principal tactic. The armed struggle was to be carried out by its military wing the Umkhonto we Sizwe ("The Spear of the Nation"). The failure of the Umkhonto to disrupt the South African economy through sabotage and the effectiveness of the government penetration of ANC underground cells led the ANC to establish external command posts in sanctuary states of Zambia, Tanzania, and Angola. In the sanctuary states the Congress eventually developed a complex infrastructure

enabling it to train, house, feed, employ, educate, and organize about 13,000 exiles. The ANC reorganized its underground cell networks in South Africa and through Umkhonto began guerrilla war. The frequency of bombings, raids, and political assassinations in South Africa rose approximately 62 percent between 1976–86. The 1976 Soweto riots and their aftermath brought more black support to the ANC. To capitalize on this support the ANC encouraged the formation of the United Democratic Front (UDF) and the Congress of South African Trade Unions (COSATU). These organizations have given the ANC access to a huge number of blacks in the townships and on the shop floors (Davis, O'Meara, and Dlamini 1988:283; Davis 1987). By 1986, 700 community bodies were affiliated with UDF including civic organizations, union groups, labor unions, youth leagues, and religious councils, all of which engaged in anti-apartheid activity. Organized in 1985, COSATU constituted the largest single union alliance in the nation's history. COSATU's agenda is broadly coincident with that of ANC (Davis 1987).

14. The Pan African Congress (PAC) was launched in a convention at Soweto on 6 April 1959. The PAC considered anti-apartheid protest a "black-only affair." It opposed the multiracial anti-apartheid movement advocated by ANC. It also opposed the involvement of communists in the anti-apartheid cause. In the post-Soweto period PAC has not played a significant role in the armed resistance to apartheid. PAC has been unable to prevent the South African government from decimating the leadership through arrest. It has also been weakened by factional disputes (Davis 1987).

The other main rival of ANC is the Inkatha Freedom Party, a Zulu-based cultural and political movement. Inkatha's roots go back to 1922. It was founded by King Solomon Ka Dinizulu to preserve Zulu culture. The modern form of Inkatha was established in 1975 when Chief Gatsha Buthelezi revived the earlier organization. Membership was restricted to blacks, mostly Zulus, until July 1990, when Inkatha was made open to all races. Inkatha has been the source of Buthelezi's power as chief of the KwaZulu Bantustan. Members of the organization hold all the seats in the KwaZulu rubber-stamp legislature. While Inkatha rejects apartheid, it nonetheless, has opposed the ANC policy of armed struggle against the South African state and its socialist economic philosophy (Davies, O'Meara, and Dlamini 1988:387–95).

15. In some cities there has been a catastrophic unemployment rate among blacks. For example in Port Elizabeth where Ford, General Motors, and Volkswagen drastically reduced production because of the collapse of the local market, the black unemployment rate has reached 56 percent (Thompson 1987).

16. COSATU has made greater efforts in recent years to improve wages for its members. For example, on 21 August 1987, COSATU started its campaign for a living wage. Over 350,000 mine workers along with 20,000 postal workers, 15,000 chemical workers, and 4,000 mill workers went on strike (Magubane 1990:336–37).

17. The Anglo-American Corporation is the largest and most powerful South African–based conglomerate and multinational. Anglo owns 69 percent of the total capital invested in the South African mining industry. It has a major presence in agriculture, insurance, finance, property, press, and service sectors. The South African National Life Assurance Company (SANLAM) is a leading

Afrikaner insurance and financial conglomerate with strong ties to key factions within the Nationalist Party. The Barlow Rand Group is a big conglomerate with substantial mining and industrial interests. The Rembrandt Group is mainly a tobacco and liquor conglomerate with substantial industrial and mining interests (Davies, O'Meara, and Dlamini 1988, vol. 1:65–93).

18. Over a forty-year period from 1946, the African population has increased from 7.8 million to nearly 25 million. By the year 2000 the size of the African population could grow to 35 million, which would make it seven times the size of the white population (Meredith 1988:226).

19. The United Democratic Front now plans to disband in order to give total support to the ANC in its negotiations over reform with the South African government.

20. Township unrest increased during 1984–86 when the masses unleashed an offensive against "collaborators," "black police," "spies," and "informers." Many of these were killed or forced to flee or resign from their jobs (Murray 1989; Saul and Gelb 1986; Lipton 1985). The first cycle of violence broke out within the townships around the industrial centers of the Vaal Triangle in Southern Transvaal. The center of violence then spread to the townships of the Eastern Cape eventually shifting to the mining towns of the Eastern Rand and Soweto. These riots stemmed from various local issues (Meredith 1988).

21. Transkei serves as an example of such "independent" Bantustans. It was granted self-government in 1962. Transkei has a flag, national anthem, legislative assembly, cabinet, and ministers of finance, justice, education, agriculture and forestry, roads, and public works. But the South African government retains control over internal security, defense, railways, currency, banking, immigration, post and telegraph, customs, etc. Pretoria has retained the right to veto legislation, cut off funds and revote Transkei's constitution (Meredith 1988:96).

22. In the 1980s, one-third of the Bantustan labor force worked in white areas as migrants, another one-third worked as commuter labor and the remaining one-third was either employed in the homeland or unemployed (Meredith 1988:152).

23. Between 1983 and 1988 the number of workers belonging to registered trade unions increased from 1.3 million to 1.7 million. But several hundred thousand black workers belong to unregistered unions (Davies, O'Meara, and Dlamini 1988, vol. 2:457). The multiracial Trade Union Council of South Africa (TUG-SA) dissolved itself in 1986 due to unresolved disaffection of liberal and conservative member unions (Davies, O'Meara, and Dlamini 1988, vol. 2:250–52). Black independent unions have formed two different confederations, the Federation of South African Trade Unions (FOSATU) and the Council of Unions of South Africa (CUSA). The confederations differ on questions of support to the resistance movements and on the desirability of registration (MacShane, Plant, and Ward 1984, 111–18). CUSA federated with the Azanian Congress of Trade Unions (AZACTU) in 1986, which in 1987 adopted a new name, The National Council of Trade Unions (NACTU). This federation stands for worker control and black working-class leadership in South Africa (Davies, O'Meara, and Dlamini 1988, vol. 2:463–64). In 1985, twelve affiliates of FOSATU joined the newly organized Congress of South African Trade Unions (COSATU) along with other democratic unions. COSATU aims at promoting union unity and

advocates a form of militant trade unionism (Davies, O'Meara, and Dlamini 1988, vol. 2:458–62).

24. SADCC states include Angola, Botswana, Lesotho, Malawi, Mozambique, Swaziland, Tanzania, Zambia, and Zimbabwe.

25. Southwest African Peoples Organization (SWAPO) was a revolutionary movement which aimed at liberating Namibia from South African rule. It appears that SWAPO has finally achieved its objective. On 27 December 1988, Angola, Cuba, and South Africa reached an agreement on a plan to end the thirteen-year-old war in Namibia. In exchange for Cuba's gradual withdrawal of troops from Angola, South Africa will withdraw all its troops by 1 November 1994, and accept the United Nations' independence plan (Campbell 1989). A new constitution was drawn up in January 1990. The first president is to be chosen on the basis of simple majority in the National Assembly. All laws passed by the Assembly will be subject to review by the upper house, the National Council. The constitution provides for a directly elected president limited to two five-year terms. The Assembly will be elected on the basis of proportional representation. The constitution abolishes capital punishment and sanctions affirmative action programs to redress the legacy of apartheid. In November 1989, SWAPO won the national election with 41 out of the 72 seats in Namibia's new constitutional assembly. The white-led Democratic Turnhall Alliance won 21 seats with smaller parties sharing the rest (Wren 1989). On 21 March 1990, Namibia became an independent state after seventy-four years of South African rule (Battersby 1990b).

26. The devastation caused by the South African–backed contra war in Mozambique provides one example. This proxy war has driven a million Mozambicans from their communities and resulted in over 250,000 killed or wounded. The whole economy of Mozambique has been damaged (Campbell 1989:6).

27. The National Party won 94 seats in a 166-seat white house of Assembly and polled about 48 percent of the national vote. The Conservative Party with 31 percent of the national vote gained 16 seats (total 39 seats) and the moderate Democratic Party gained 13 seats (total 33 seats) with 21 percent of the national vote. While the National Party retained its support in the Cape province it lost heavily to the CP candidates in rural areas of the Transvaal and Orange Free State provinces. The DP found strength in the urban areas of Johannesburg and Cape Town (Battersby 1989b).

28. Among Afrikaner voters there has been increased support for right-wing parties formed by *verkrampte* leaders who have split from the National Party, such as Albert Hertzog who formed the HNP in 1969 and Andries Treurnicht who formed the Conservative Party in 1982 (Lipton 1985:54). In 1985 there was a 200 percent increase in Afrikaners voting for such ultra-right parties (Kibble and Bush 1986:220). This voting trend seems to have continued in the 1987 elections (Battersby 1987a:3).

   The HNP Party favors a return to a fully fledged apartheid system based on the 1966 National Party principles. The CP has opposed National Party plans for "power sharing" and attempts at "limited" integration (Davies, O'Meara, and Dlamini 1988, vol. 1:149–52).

29. President Frederick de Klerk plans to dismantle the Security Management Sys-

tem set-up by Botha and replace it with a system under civilian control. It appears these reforms are the first step toward ending the forty-two-month-old state of emergency (Battersby 1989e).

30. But the head of the Dutch Reformed Church, Johan Heyns, has attacked apartheid policies of the government. In 1986 the church adopted a declaration in which it declared that apartheid was a "scriptural error," branded racism a sin, and declared the church in favor of a system based on social justice and equality "before God" (Battersby 1989d). The DRC has 90 percent of the senior government officials as members and 70 percent of the legislators. The Nederduits Hervormde Kerk and the right-wing splinter church, the Afrikaner Protestante Kerk, do not support this new DRC policy change (Battersby 1990q).

31. The Afrikaner government has sought support from Bantustan chiefs to support it in its future negotiations with the ANC. But now the chiefs in Transkei, KaNgwane, and Lebowa have sought alliance with the ANC. There is a struggle between pro- and anti-ANC forces in Ciskei, Bophuthatswana, Venda, Gazankulu, and Natal (Battersby 1990f). In Natal savage fighting has taken place between the Zulu-based Inkatha (see note 14) and the ANC loyalists. As a result of such clashes there have been almost 4,000 persons killed and 70,000 or more displaced from their homes (Battersby 1990h; 1990i).

In January 1991, ANC Deputy President Nelson Mandela and Inkatha Freedom Party (IFP) leader Chief Buthelezi met to seek an end to the violence between supporters of their two parties. Buthelezi opposes the ANC call for an interim government and elected constitutional assembly to form a new constitution. IFP also rejects the ANC call for continued economic sanctions. Through these positions he can give powerful support to the government in future negotiations. Efforts by the two leaders has so far failed to end the fighting as of April 1991 (Battersby 1991g, 1991b; Laurence 1990b).

There is new evidence suggesting that the government's South African Defense Force has trained black mercenaries, who have been used to fan ethnic conflict between the ANC and the IFP supporters (Battersby 1991j). The de Klerk government also secretly helped finance two major Inkatha rallies (Wren 1991). The government has given financial aid to other anti-ANC organizations (Laurence 1991). In these ways the de Klerk government may be attempting to divide the black population and, thereby, weaken the ANC's bargaining power.

32. Africans have attacked Indians in Durban and destroyed their property. There has been a history of tensions between Asians and Africans in Durban because Indians are better educated, control much of the trade, and hold a high percentage of the white collar jobs both in the government and private business (Thompson 1990).

33. There have been recent efforts by the ANC and the PAC to form a new alliance in order to work together to force an end to apartheid (Battersby 1990r).

34. The Bond has always had tempestuous relations with its own right-wing elements. Initially, for example, the Broederbond tried to heal the schism with such groups as the pro-Nazi *Ossewabrandwag* (OB). In 1941 the Bond set up a Peoples Front composed of all Christian-Nationalist and pro-Republican bodies. But this unity effort failed and by January 1942 the Bond and the OB were in violent opposition to each other. Until 1948 the OB continued to attack the

parliamentary system. But with the Nazi defeat in Germany the OB went into decline. The Bond helped integrate former OB members into the National Party (Bloomberg 1989:161–82).

35. The Afrikaner Weerstandbeweging (Afrikaner Resistance Movement) states that it is maintaining a military readiness so it can intervene if the white reformist government rule collapses and whites need armed protection. AWB parades with uniforms, its marshals carry holstered pistols, its leaders use the rhetoric of violence and its structure is highly authoritarian. The real menace of the AWB is its white vigilantism and the havoc it could cause in race relations (Uys 1989:211).

References

Abasiattai, M. B. 1987. "Resistance of the African Peoples of Liberia." *Liberia-Forum* 3:53–69.

Abercrombie, N., and B. S. Turner. 1978. "The Dominant Ideology Thesis." *British Journal of Sociology* 29:149–70.

———. 1980. *The Dominant Ideology Thesis*. London: Allen & Unwin.

Adelman, S. 1985. "Recent Events in South Africa." *Capital and Class* 26:17–30.

Adkins, Jr., E. H. 1962. "Malaya Controls its Criminal Societies." Michigan State University Vietnam Advisory Group.

Akpan, M. B. 1985. "Gola Resistance to Liberian 'Rule' in the Nineteenth Century, 1835–1905." *Liberia-Forum* 1:5–26.

Albert, M., and R. Hahnel. 1978. *Unorthodox Marxism*. Boston: South End Press.

Alderson, A. D. 1956. *The Structure of the Ottoman Dynasty*. Oxford: Clarendon Press.

Alexander, G. 1983. *Silent Invasion*. London: MacDonald.

Allen, V. L. 1975. *Social Analysis*. London: Longman.

Althusser, L. 1970. *Reading Capital*. London: New Left Books.

Andaya, B. W., and L. Y. Andaya. 1982. *A History of Malaysia*. New York: St. Martin's Press.

Anderson, P. 1974. *Lineages of the Absolutist State*. London: New Left Books.

Archer, M. S. 1988. *Culture and Agency*. Cambridge: Cambridge University Press.

Arkush, R. D. 1990. "Orthodoxy and Heterodoxy in Twentieth-Century Chinese Peasant Proverbs." In *Orthodoxy in Late Imperial China*, edited by K. C. Liu, 311–31. Berkeley: University of California Press.

Aronoff, M. J. 1980. "Ideology and Interest: The Dialectics of Politics." In *Political Anthropology Yearbook I*, edited by M. J. Aronoff, 1–29. New Brunswick, NJ: Transaction.

Atmore, A., and S. Marks. 1974. "The Imperial Factor in South Africa in the 19th Century: Toward A Reassessment." *Journal of Imperial and Commonwealth History* 3:105–39.

Atsushi, S. 1984. "The Origins and Structure of Gentry Rule." In *State and Society in China*, edited by L. Grove and C. Daniels, 335–85. Tokyo: University of Tokyo Press.

Atwell, W. 1988. "T'ai-Chiang, T'ien-Chi and Ch'ung-chen Reigns, 1368–1644." In *The Cambridge History of China: The Ming Dynasty, 1368–1644, vol. 7, part 1*, edited by F. W. Mote and D. Twitchett, 585–640. Cambridge: Cambridge University Press.

Au-Yong, W. 1972. "Suppression of Secret Societies in Singapore." *I.P.C.T.O.*

Report and Resource Material Series No. 4, 158–68. U.N.A.F.E.

Bachrach, P., and M. S. Baratz. 1963. "Decisions and Nondecisions: An Analytical Framework." *The American Political Science Review* 53:632–42.

————. 1970. *Power and Poverty: Theory and Practice*. New York: Oxford University Press.

Barnes, J. R. 1974. "A Short Note on the Dissolution of the Dervish Orders in Turkey." *Muslim World* 64:33–34.

Barrows, W. 1976. *Grassroots Politics in An African State*. New York: Africana Publishing Co.

Basserman, P. 1968. *Dialectical Sociology*. Boston: Porter Sargent.

Battersby, J. D. 1987a. "It's to Be Gradual Change, Botha Says." *New York Times*, 8 May, 3.

————. 1987b. "Sanctions." *Africa Report* 32:4–10.

————. 1989a. "Black Nationalists Broaden Support." *The Christian Science Monitor*, 5 July, 4.

————. 1989b. "S. African Vote Gives Reformers a Majority." *The Christian Science Monitor*, 8 September, 1–2.

————. 1989c. "S. Africa Opens Door to Negotiations." *The Christian Science Monitor*, 12 October, 4.

————. 1989d. "Pricking the Afrikaner Conscience." *The Christian Science Monitor*, 14 October, 14.

————. 1989e. "S. Africa Downgrades Military Role." *The Christian Science Monitor*, 1 December, 4.

————. 1990a. "S. Africans Vow Intensified Struggle." *The Christian Science Monitor*, 19 January, 4.

————. 1990b. "Namibia Forges New Constitution." *The Christian Science Monitor*, 1 February, 1.

————. 1990c. "Pretoria Opens Door to Dialogue." *The Christian Science Monitor*, 5 February, 3.

————. 1990d. "Mandela Release: Watershed for South Africa." *The Christian Science Monitor*, 12 February, 1.

————. 1990e. "Mandela Takes Tough Stance for Bargaining." *The Christian Science Monitor*, 16 February, 1.

————. 1990f. "Blacks Demand Right in S. African Homelands." *The Christian Science Monitor*, 9 March, 1–2.

————. 1990g. "Probe Damages Militia Credibility." *The Christian Science Monitor*, 15 March, 4.

————. 1990h. "Natal Violence Set Stiff Test for ANC Leadership." *The Christian Science Monitor*, 4 April, 1.

————. 1990i. "Whites Organize against Blacks." *The Christian Science Monitor*, 12 April, 3.

————. 1990j. "S. Africa Balances Equality, Growth." *The Christian Science Monitor*, 31 May, 5.

————. 1990k. "Zulus Form New Multiracial Party to Broaden Support." *The Christian Science Monitor*, 17 July, 1.

————. 1990l. "Role of ANC Militia Clouds Talks." *The Christian Science Monitor*, 25 July, 3.

———. 1990m. "S. African Communists Maintain Armed Conflict." *The Christian Science Monitor*, 31 July, 4.

———. 1990n. "S. Africa Accord Signals Move to Joint Rule." *The Christian Science Monitor*, 8 August, 1.

———. 1990o. "Afrikaners Propose White Homeland in S.A." *The Christian Science Monitor*, 9 August, 5.

———. 1990p. "South Africa Calls for End to Nation's Killing Fields." *The Christian Science Monitor*, 24 August, 6.

———. 1990q. "South Africa's Churches Move Toward Conciliation." *The Christian Science Monitor*, 13 November, 6.

———. 1990r. "ANC Tack Tests S. Africa Dialogue." *The Christian Science Monitor*, 30 November, 8.

———. 1990s. "ANC Shifts its Tactics to Force New Concessions." *The Christian Science Monitor*, 11 December, 7.

———. 1990t. "ANC Leaders Feel Force of Grass Roots Discontent." *The Christian Science Monitor*, 17 December, 6.

———. 1991a. "Mandela Meets Buthelezi Amid Hope to End Black Strife." *The Christian Science Monitor*, 29 January, 1.

———. 1991b. "S. Africa Black Leaders Call for End to Violence." *The Christian Science Monitor*, 31 January, 6.

———. 1991c. "South Africa Leader Calls for End of Apartheid, Outflanks Political Rivals." *The Christian Science Monitor*, 4 February, 6.

———. 1991d. "Mandela's First Year of Freedom." *The Christian Science Monitor*, 11 February, 4.

———. 1991e. "De Klerk Resists Calls to Reopen Death Squad Inquiry." *The Christian Science Monitor*, 12 February, 5.

———. 1991f. "The Word from Johannesburg." *The Christian Science Monitor*, 19 February, 3.

———. 1991g. "Pretoria Welcomes Sanctions Move." *The Christian Science Monitor*, 19 April, 8.

———. 1991h. "Pretoria's Failure to Free Prisoners Brings Protest." *The Christian Science Monitor*, 2 May, 1.

———. 1991i. "Afrikaners Plan White Homeland." *The Christian Science Monitor*, 9 May, 6.

———. 1991j. "South African Military Is Said to Spark Unrest." *The Christian Science Monitor*, 18 June, 1.

———. 1991k. "Pretoria Ends Apartheid System." *The Christian Science Monitor*, 19 June, 1.

———. 1991l. "S. African Accord Advances Peace." *The Christian Science Monitor*, 19 August, 4.

———. 1991m. "S. Africa's Ruling Party Draws Fire." *The Christian Science Monitor*, 9 September, 6.

———. 1991n. "South Africans Sign Historic Peace Accord." *The Christian Science Monitor*, 16 September, 6.

Beattie, H. 1979. "The Alternatives to Resistance: The Case of T'ung Ch'eng." In *From Ming to Ch'ing*, edited by J. Spence and J. E. Willis, Jr., 239–76. New Haven: Yale University Press.

Bellman, B. L. 1979. "The Social Organization of Knowledge in Kpelle Ritual." In *The New Religions of Africa*, edited by J. Rosette, 39–56. Norwood, NJ: Ablex Publishing Company.

———. 1984. *The Language of Secrecy*. New Brunswick, NJ: Rutgers University Press.

Benton, T. 1977. *Philosophical Foundations of Three Sociologies*. London: Routledge & Kegan Paul.

———. 1984. *The Rise and Fall of Structural Marxism*. New York: St. Martin's Press.

Best, K. 1991. "The Continuing Quagmire." *Africa Report* 36:39–41.

Bhaskar, R. 1979. "On the Possibility of Social Scientific Knowledge and the Limits of Naturalism." In *Issues in Marxist Philosophy, Vol. 3: Epistemology Science and Ideology*, edited by J. Mepham and D. Hillel-Ruben, 107–39. Atlantic Highlands, NJ: Humanities Press.

Bhuntani, S. 1962. "Secret Society Systems among the American Indians and the Africans." Masters thesis, University of North Carolina at Chapel Hill.

Birge, J. K. 1937. *The Bektashi Order of Dervishes*. Hartford, CT: Hartford Seminary Press.

Bledsoe, C. H. 1980. *Women and Marriage in Kpelle Society*. Stanford: Stanford University Press.

Bloch, M. 1977. "The Past and the Present in the Past." *Man* 12:278–92.

———. 1985. "From Cognition to Ideology." In *Power and Knowledge*, edited by R. Fardon, 21–48. Edinburgh: Scottish Academic Press.

Bloomberg, C. 1989. *Christian-Nationalism and the Rise of the Afrikaner Broederbond in South Africa, 1918–1948*. Bloomington: Indiana University Press.

Blythe, W. L. 1950. "The Interplay of Chinese Secret and Political Societies in Malaya." *Eastern World* 4 (March): 14–15 and 5 (April): 10–13.

———. 1969. *The Impact of Chinese Secret Societies in Malaya*. London: Oxford University Press.

Bodie, B., and P. Birnbaum. 1983. *The Sociology of the State*. Chicago: University of Chicago Press.

Boswell, T. E., E. L. Kiser, and K. A. Baker. 1986. "Recent Developments in Marxist Theories of Ideology." *The Insurgent Sociologist* 13:5–22.

Boudon, R. 1979. *The Logic of Social Action*. London: Routledge & Kegan Paul.

———. 1986. *Theories of Social Change*. Berkeley: University of California Press.

Bowen, J. A. 1973. "The Republic of Liberia." In *The History of West Africa*, vol. 2, edited by J. F. A. Ajayi and M. Crowder, 308–43. New York: Columbia University Press.

Braudel, F. 1972. "History and Social Sciences." In *Economy and Society in Early Modern Europe*, edited by P. Burke, 11–42. New York: Harper and Row.

Brown, J. P. 1968. *The Dervishes*. London: Frank Cass and Co. Ltd.

Brumfiel, E. M. 1983. "Aztec State Making: Ecology, Structure and the Origin of the State." *American Anthropologist* 85:261–84.

Buckley, W. 1967. *Sociology and Modern System Theory*. Englewood Cliffs, NJ: Prentice Hall.

Bundy, C. 1979. *The Rise and Fall of the South African Peasantry*. Berkeley: University of California Press.

Bunting, P. 1964. *The Rise of the South African Reich*. Harmondsworth: Penguin.

Burawoy, M. 1978. "Contemporary Currents in Marxist Theory." *American Sociologist* 13:50–64.

———. 1979. "Contemporary Currents in Marxist Theory." In *Theoretical Perspectives in Sociology*, edited by S. G. McNell, 16–39. New York: St. Martin's Press.

Butcher, J. C. 1979. *The British in Malaya, 1880–1941*. Kuala Lumpur: Oxford University Press.

Callinicos, A. 1983. *Marxism and Philosophy*. Oxford: Clarendon Press.

Campbell, H. 1989. "The Military Defeat of the South Africans in Angola." *Monthly Review* 40:1–15.

Cape, J. 1967. *South Africa*, 2d ed. New York: Praeger.

Carchedi, G. 1987. *Class Analysis and Social Research*. Oxford: Basil Blackwell.

Carneiro, R. L. 1970. "A Theory of the Origin of the State." *Science* 169:733–38.

———. 1978. "Political Expansion as an Expression of the Principle of Competitive Exclusion." In *Origins of the State: The Anthropology of Political Evolution*, edited by R. Cohen and E. R. Service, 205–24. Philadelphia: Institute for the Study of Human Issues.

Carnoy, M. 1984. *The State and Political Theory*. Princeton, NJ: Princeton University Press.

Carter, G. M. 1959. *The Politics of Inequality*. New York: Praeger.

———. 1980. *Which Way Is South Africa Going?* Bloomington: Indiana University Press.

———. 1982. "South Africa: Growing Black-White Confrontation." In *Southern Africa: The Coming Crisis*, edited by G. Carter and D. O'Meara, 93–120. Bloomington: Indiana University Press.

———. 1986. "The Republic of South Africa: White Political Control Within an African Continent." In *Africa*, 2d ed., edited by P. M. Martin and D. O'Meara, 343–57. Bloomington: Indiana University Press.

Cartwright, D. 1965. "Influence, Leadership and Control." In *The Handbook of Organizations*, edited by J. G. March, 1–47. Chicago: Rand McNally and Co.

Chambers, R. L. 1972. "The Ottoman Ulema at Tanzimat." In *Scholars, Saints and Sufis*, edited by R. Keddie, 33–46. Berkeley: University of California Press.

Chan, A. 1982. *The Glory and the Fall of the Ming Dynasty*. Norman: University of Oklahoma Press.

Chan, H. 1969. "The White Lotus Maitreya Doctrine and Popular Uprisings in Ming and Ch'ing China." *Synologica* 10:211–33.

Charney, C. 1987. "The National Party, 1982–1985: A Class Alliance in Crisis." In *The State of Apartheid*, edited by W. G. James, 5–36. Boulder, CO: Lynne Rienner.

Cheng, H. 1950. "The Network of Singapore Societies." *Nam-Yau Hsueh Pao* 6:10–12.

Chesneaux, J. 1971. *Secret Societies in China*. London: Heinemann.

———. 1972. "Secret Societies in China's Historical Evolution." In *Popular Movements and Secret Societies in China, 1840–1950*, edited by J. Chesneaux, 22–46. Stanford, CA: Stanford University Press.

———. 1973. *Peasant Revolt in China, 1840–1949*. New York: Norton.

Chiang, T. 1983. "The Salt Trade in Ch'ing China." *Modern Asian Studies* 17:197–219.

Ch'u, T'. 1962. *Local Government in China Under the Ch'ing*. Cambridge: Cambridge University Press.

Chu, Y. R. 1967. "An Introductory Study of the White Lotus Sect in China's History with Special Reference to Peasant Movements." Ph.D. dissertation, Columbia University, New York.

Clutterbuck, R. 1973. *Riot and Revolution in Singapore and Malaya, 1945–1968*. London: Faber and Faber.

Cohen, R. 1988. "Legitimacy, Illegitimacy and State Formation." In *State Formation and Political Legitimacy*, edited by R. Cohen and J. D. Toland, 69–83. Series: *Political Anthropology*, vol. 6. New Brunswick, NJ: Transaction.

Collier, A. 1989. *Scientific Realism and Socialist Thought*. Hertfordshire: Harvester and Wheatsheal.

Comaroff, J. L. 1982. "Dialectical Systems: The History of Anthropology, Units of Study and Questions of Theory." *Journal of the Southern African Studies* 8:143–72.

Comber, L. 1957. *An Introduction to Chinese Secret Societies in Malaya*. Singapore: Donald Moore.

———. 1959. "Chinese Secret Societies of Malaya." *Monograph of the Association for Asian Studies*, no. 6. Locust Valley, NY: Augustin.

———. 1962. *The Traditional Mysteries of Chinese Secret Societies in Malaya*. Singapore: Eastern Universities Press, Lt.

Cowgill, G. L. 1988. "Onward and Upward with Collapse." In *The Collapse of Ancient States and Civilizations*, edited by N. Yoffee and G. L. Cowgill, 244–76. Tucson: University of Arizona Press.

Craib, I. 1984. *Modern Social Theory*. New York: St. Martin's Press.

Crowell, W. 1983. "Social Unrest and Rebellion in Jiangnan During the Six Dynasties." *Modern China* 9:319–54.

Cunningham, F. 1982. "Dialectical Contradictions: Some Conjectures." In *Dialectical Contradictions: Contemporary Marxist Discussions*, edited by E. Marquit, P. Moran, and W. Truitt, 59–66. Series: *Studies in Marxism, vol. 10*. Minneapolis: Marxist Educational Press.

D'Altroy, T. N. 1981. "Empire Growth and Consolidation: The Xauya Region of Peru Under the Incas." Ph.D. dissertation, University of California at Los Angeles.

Daraul, A. 1961. *A History of Secret Societies*. New York: Citadel Press.

Dardess, J. W. 1972. "The Late Ming Rebellions: Peasants and Problems of Interpretation." *Journal of Interdisciplinary History* 3:103–17.

———. 1976. "The Transformations of Messianic Revolt and the Founding of the Ming Dynasty." *Journal of Asian Studies* 24:539–58.

Davenport, T. R. H. 1977. *South Africa*. New York: MacMillan.

Davies, R. H., and D. O'Meara. 1988. "The State of Analysis of the Southern Region: Issues Raised by the Southern African Strategy." *Review of African Political Economy* 29:64–76.

Davies, R. H., D. O'Meara, and S. Dlamini. 1988. *The Struggle for South Africa*, vols. 1, 2. London: Zed Books Ltd.

Davis, F. 1971. *Primitive Revolutionaries of China*. Honolulu: University Press of Hawaii.

Davis, S. M. 1987. *Apartheid's Rebels*. New Haven: Yale University Press.

d'Azevedo, W. L. 1962a. "Some Historical Problems in the Delineation of a Central West Atlantic Region." *Annals of the New York Academy of Sciences* 96:512–38.

———. 1962b. "Continuity and Integration in Gola Society." Ph.D. dissertation, Northwestern University, Evanston, IL.

———. 1962c. "Uses of the Past in Gola Discourse." *History* 3:11–34.

———. 1969. "A Tribal Reaction to Nationalism." *Liberian Studies* 1:1–21, 2:43–63.

———. 1973. "Mask Makers and Myth in Western Liberia." In *Primitive Art and Society*, edited by A. Forge, 127–50. London: Oxford University Press.

DeGeorge, R. T. 1985. *The Nature and Limits of Authority*. Lawrence: University Press of Kansas.

DeGroot, J. J. M. 1863. *Sectarianism and Religious Persecution in China*, vols. 1, 2. Taipei, Taiwan: Literature House.

———. 1963. *Sectarianism and Religious Persecution in China*, vols. 1, 2. Taipei, Taiwan: Literature.

De Kock, W. J. 1968. *History of South Africa*. New York: South African Government Information Service.

Douglas, S. A., and P. Pedersen. 1973. *Blood, Believer and Brother: The Development of Voluntary Associations in Malaya*. Paper in International Studies, Southeast Asian Series, no. 29. Athens, OH: Ohio University Center for International Studies.

Dowse, R. E., and J. A. Hughes. 1972. *Political Sociology*. London: John Wiley and Sons.

Doyle, M. W. 1986. *Empire*. Ithaca, NY: Cornell University Press.

Dunham, D. L. 1990. *History, Power, and Ideology*. Cambridge: Cambridge University Press.

Dunn, R. 1990a. "S. Africa Whites Prepare to Fight." *The Christian Science Monitor*, 27 April, 4.

———. 1990b. "Some Gold Mines in Deep Trouble." *The Christian Science Monitor*, 10 May, 19.

DuPlessis, J. S. 1981. "The South African Republic." In *Five Hundred Years: A History of South Africa*, edited by C. F. J. Muller, 256–96. Pretoria: Academica.

Easton, D. 1958. "The Perception of Authority and Political Change." In *Authority*, edited by C. J. Friedrich, 170–96. Cambridge: Harvard University Press.

Eberhard, W. 1966. *A History of China*. Berkeley: University of California Press.

Eisenstadt, S. N., M. Abitbol, and N. Chazan. 1988. "The Origins of the State Reconsidered." In *The Early State in African Perspective*, edited by S. N. Eisenstadt, M. Abitbol, and N. Chazan, 1–27. Leiden: E. J. Brill.

Ekholm, K. 1981. "On the Structure and Dynamics of Global Systems." In *The Anthropology of Pre-Capitalist Societies*, edited by J. S. Kahn and J. R. Llobera, 241–61. London: MacMillan Press.

Ekholm, K., and J. Friedman. 1979. "Capital, Imperialism and Exploitation in the Ancient World." In *Power and Propaganda, Mesopotamia*, vol. 7, edited by M. T. Larsen, 41–58. Copenhagen: Akademisk Forlag.

Ellen, R. 1982. *Environment, Subsistence and System*. Cambridge: Cambridge University Press.

Elster, J. 1985. *Making Sense of Marx*. Cambridge: Cambridge University Press.

———. 1989. *Nuts and Bolts for Social Science*. Cambridge: Cambridge University Press.

Engel, K. 1990. "Apartheid and the Schools." *The Christian Science Monitor*, 2 August, 19.

Erickson, B. H. 1981. "Secret Societies and Social Structure." *Social Forces* 60:188–208.

Fairbank, J. F. 1967. "The Nature of Chinese Society." In *Imperial China*, edited by F. Schurmann and O. Schell, 36–66. New York: Random House.

Faure, D. 1979. "Secret Societies, Heretic Sects and Peasant Rebellions in 19th Century China." *Hsiang Kong Chung* 5:188–206.

Feuerwerker, A. 1975. *Rebellion in 19th Century China*. Center for Chinese Studies. Ann Arbor: University of Michigan.

———. 1976. *State and Society in 18th century China: The Ch'ing Empire in Its Glory*. Center for Chinese Studies. Ann Arbor: University of Michigan.

Fiori, G. 1970. *Antonio Gramsci—Life of a Revolutionary*. London: New Left Books.

Flew, A. 1985. *Thinking About Social Thinking*. Oxford: Basil Blackwell, Ltd.

Foucault, M. 1977. *Discipline and Punishment*. New York: Vintage Books.

———. 1980. *Power/Knowledge*. Harmondsworth: Penguin.

Freedmen, M. 1960. "Immigrants and Associations: Chinese in 19th Century Singapore." *Comparative Studies in Society and History* 3:25–48.

Freedmen, M., and M. Topley. 1961. "Religion and Social Realignment among Chinese in Singapore." *The Journal of Asian Studies* 21:3–24.

Freund, B. 1984. "Forced Resettlement and the Political Economy of South Africa." *Review of African Political Economy* 29:49–63.

Friedman, J. 1976. "Marxist Theory and Systems of Total Reproduction." *Critique of Anthropology* 7:3–17.

Fulton, R. M. 1968. "The Kpelle Traditional Political System." *Liberian Studies* 1:1–19.

———. 1969. "The Kpelle of Liberia: A Study of Political Change in the Liberian Interior." Ph.D. dissertation, University of Connecticut, Storrs.

———. 1972. "The Political Structure and Functions of the Poro in Kpelle Society." *American Anthropologist* 7:1218–33.

Gailey, C. W. 1985. "The State of the State in Anthropology." *Dialectical Anthropology* 9:65–87.

———. 1987. *Kinship to Kingship*. Austin: University of Texas Press.

Gamble, C. 1981. "Social Control and the Economy." In *Economic Archaeology*, edited by A. Sheridan and G. Bailey, 215–30. BAR International Series, 96. Oxford: Oxford University Press.

Garnett, L. M. J. 1912. *Mysticism and Magic in Turkey*. London: Pitman and Sons, Ltd.

Gergen, K. 1968. "Correspondence Versus Autonomy in the Language of Understanding Human Action." In *Metatheory in Social Science*, edited by D. W. Fiske and R. A. Shweder, 136–62. Chicago: University of Chicago Press.

Gernet, J. 1972. *A History of the Chinese Civilization*. Cambridge: Cambridge University Press.

Gibb, H. A. R., and J. H. Kramers. 1953. "Bektashi." In *The Short Encyclopedia of Islam*, 61–75. Ithaca: Cornell University Press.

Gibbs, Jr., J. L. 1965. "The Kpelle of Liberia." In *People of Africa*, edited by J. L. Gibbs, Jr., 197–240. New York: Holt, Rinehart and Winston.

Giddens, A. 1979. *Central Problems in Social Theory*. Berkeley: University of California Press.

———. 1981. "Time and Space in Social Theory." In *Current Perspectives in Social Theory*, vol. 2, edited by S. McNell and G. H. Howe, 3–13. Greenwich, CT: JAI.

———. 1984. *The Constitution of Society*. Berkeley: University of California Press.

Gilsenen, M. 1976. "Lying, Honor and Contradiction." In *Transaction and Meaning*, edited by B. Kapferer, 191–219. Philadelphia: Institute for the Study of Human Issues, Inc.

Gist, N. P. 1938a. Structure and Process in Secret Societies. *Social Forces* 16:349–57.

———. 1938b. "Dogma and Doctrine in Secret Societies." *Society and Social Research* 23:121–30.

———. 1940. *Secret Societies: A Cultural Study of Fraternalism in the United States*. Columbia, MO: The University of Missouri Studies, no. 15.

Gledhill, J. 1981. "Time's Arrow: Anthropology, History, Social Evolution and Marxist Theory." *Critique of Anthropology* 16:3–30.

Gledhill, J., and M. J. Rowland. 1982. "Materialism and Socio-economic Process in Multilinear Evolution." In *Ranking Resources and Exchange*, edited by C. Renfrew and S. Shennan, 144–49. Cambridge: Cambridge University Press.

Glick, C., and S. Hong. 1947. *Swords of Silence*. New York: McGraw-Hill.

Godelier, M. 1986. *The Mental and Material*. London: Verso.

Goldstone, J. A. 1988. "East and West in the Seventeenth Century: Political Crises in Stuart England, Ottoman Turkey and Ming China." *Comparative Studies in Society and History* 30:103–42.

Gramsci, A. 1971. *Selections from the Prison Notebooks*, edited by Q. Horace and G. Nowell-Smith. London: Lawrence and Wishart.

Greenberg, S. B. 1987. "Resistance and Hegemony in South Africa." In *The State of Apartheid*, edited by W. G. James, 51–73. Boulder, CO: Lynne Rienner.

Griswold, W. J. 1966. "Political Unrest and Rebellion in Anatolia, 1605–1609." Ph.D. dissertation, University of California, Los Angeles.

Gullick, J. M. 1988. "Indigenous Political Systems of Western Malaya." *London School of Economics Monographs on Social Anthropology No. 17*. London: The Athlone Press.

Haas, J. 1982. *The Evolution of the Prehistoric State*. New York: Columbia University Press.

Habermas, J. 1975. *Legitimization Crisis*. Boston: Beacon.

Hampshire, S. 1982. *Thought and Action*. Notre Dame, IN: University of Notre Dame Press.

Harley, G. W. 1941. "Notes on the Poro in Liberia." Peabody Museum Papers, vol. 19, no. 2. Cambridge, MA.

———. 1950. "Masks as Agents of Social Control." Papers of the Peabody Museum of American Archaeology and Ethnology, vol. 39. Cambridge, MA.

Harre, R. 1972. *The Philosophies of Science*. Oxford: Oxford University Press.

Harrell, S., and E. J. Perry. 1982. "Syncretic Sects in Chinese Society." *Modern China* 8:283–303.

Harrison, D. 1981. *The White Tribe of Africa*. Berkeley: University of California Press.

Harsch, E. 1989. "Living Dangerously." *Africa Report* 34:56–60.

Hawkes, T. 1977. *Structuralism and Semiotics*. Berkeley: University of California Press.

Hazelrigg, L. E. 1969. "Reexamination of Simmel: The Secret and the Secret Society: Nine Propositions." *Social Forces* 47:323–30.

Heckethorn, C. 1965. *Secret Societies of All Ages and Countries*, vol. 1, 2. New Hyde Park, NY: Universal Books.

Heilbroner, R. L. 1980. *Marxism: For and Against*. New York: W. W. Norton.

Heng, P. K. 1983. "The Social and Ideological Origins of the Malayan Chinese Associations." *Journal of Southeast Asian Studies* 13:290–311.

Heyd, U. 1970. "The Later Ottoman Empire in Rumelia and Anatolia." In *The Cambridge History of Islam*, vol. 1, edited by P. M. Holt, A. K. S. Lambton, and B. Lewis, 354–73. Cambridge: Cambridge University Press.

Hindess, B. 1982. "Power, Interest and the Outcome of Struggles." *Sociology* 16:498–511.

Hindess, B., and P. Hirst. 1977. *Mode of Production and Social Formation*. London: MacMillan.

Hochschild, A. 1990. "Pretoria's Need for 'Loyal Natives.'" *The Christian Science Monitor*, 13 November, 18.

Horwitz, R. 1967. *The Political Economy of South Africa*. New York: Praeger.

Houghton, D. H. 1971. "Economic Development, 1865–1965." In *The Oxford History of South Africa, Vol. 2: South Africa, 1870–1966*, edited by M. Wilson and L. Thompson, 1–49. Oxford: Clarendon Press.

Hsiao, K. C. 1960. *Rural China: Imperial Control in the 19th Century*. Seattle: University of Washington Press.

Huband, M. 1970. "Doe's Last Stand." *Africa Report* 35:47–49.

Hui, L. M. 1988. "Contradictions in the Development of Malay Capital: State, Accumulation and Legitimation." In *Sociology of Developing Societies: Southeast Asia*, edited by J. G. Taylor and A. Turton, 19–32. New York: Monthly Review Press.

Inalcik, H. 1970a. "The Emergence of the Ottomans." In *The Cambridge History of Islam*, vol. 1, edited by P. M. Holt, A. K. S. Lambton, and B. Lewis, 263–92. Cambridge: Cambridge University Press.

———. 1970b. "The Rise of the Ottoman Empire." In *The Cambridge History of Islam*, vol. 1, edited by P. M. Holt, A. K. S. Lambton, and B. Lewis, 295–323. Cambridge: Cambridge University Press.

———. 1970c. "The Heyday of the Decline of the Ottoman Empire." In *The Cambridge History of Islam*, vol. 1, edited by P. M. Holt, A. K. S. Lambton, and B. Lewis, 324–53. Cambridge: Cambridge University Press.

Isaac, J. C. 1987. *Power and Marxist Theory*. Ithaca, NY: Cornell University Press.

Islamoglu, H., and C. Keyder. 1977. "Agenda for Ottoman History." *Review* 1:31–35.

———. 1981. "The Ottoman Social Formation." In *The Asiatic Mode of Production*, edited by A. M. Bailey and J. Llobera, 301–24. London: Routledge & Kegan Paul.

Israel, J. 1979. *The Language of Dialectics and the Dialectics of Language*. Copenhagen: Munksgaard.

Itzkowitz, N. 1980. *Ottoman Empire and the Islamic Traditions*. Chicago: University of Chicago Press.

Jakubowski, F. 1976. *Ideology and Superstructure*. New York: St. Martin's Press.

James, L. 1986a. "Oui Wankpa's Fatal Gamble." *Africa Report* 31:47–49.

———. 1986b. A "Seven-Cornered Solution." *Africa Report* 31:31–33.

James, W. G., and A. du Pisanie. 1987. "End of a 'New Deal': Contradictions of Constitutional Reform." In *The State of Apartheid*, edited by W. G. James, 37–50. Boulder, CO: Lynne Rienner.

Jessop, B. 1982. *The Capitalist State*. New York: New York University Press.

Jomo, K. S. 1988. *A Question of Class*. New York: Monthly Review Press.

Jones, A. B. 1973. "The Republic of Liberia." In *The History of West Africa*, vol. 2, edited by J. F. A. Ajayi and M. Crowder, 308–43. New York: Columbia University Press.

Kaplan, I. et al. 1985. "The Society and Its Environment." In *Liberia*, edited by H. D. Nelson, 73–138. Foreign Area Studies Handbook: U.S. Government Printing Office.

Karpat, K. 1973. "An Inquiry into the Social Formation of Nationalism in the Ottoman State: From Social Estates to Classes, from Millet to Nation." Research Monographs No. 34. Woodrow Wilson School of Public and International Affairs. Princeton, NJ: Princeton University.

———. 1974. "The State of Ottoman History." In *The Ottoman State and Place in World History*, edited by K. H. Karpat, 71–106. Leiden: E. J. Brill.

Kaslow, A. 1990. "Apartheid System Takes Its Toll." *The Christian Science Monitor*, 11 January, 8.

Kaufman, H. 1988. "The Collapse of Ancient States and Civilizations as an Organizational Problem." In *The Collapse of Ancient States and Civilizations*, edited by N. Yoffee and G. L. Cowgill, 219–43. Tucson: University of Arizona Press.

Kazumi, K. 1984. "The Other Side of Rent and Tax Resistance Struggle: Ideology and the Road to Rebellion." In *State and Society in China*, eds. L. Grove and C. Daniels, 215–44. Tokyo: University of Tokyo Press.

Keat, R. 1981. *The Politics of Social Theory*. Chicago: Chicago University Press.

Keat, R., and J. Urry. 1975. *Social Theory as Science*. Boston: Routledge & Kegan Paul.

Kibble, S., and R. Bush. 1986. "Reform of Apartheid and Continued Destabilisation in Southern Africa." *The Journal of Modern African Studies* 24:203–27.

Kilson, M. 1966. *Political Change in a West African State*. Cambridge: Harvard University Press.

Knorr-Cetina, K., and M. Mulkay. 1983. "Introduction: Emerging Principles in the Social Studies of Science." In *Science Observed*, edited by K. D. Knorr-Cetina and M. Mulkay, 1–17. Beverly Hills: Sage Publishers.

Koon, H. P. 1988. *Chinese Politics in Malaysia*. Singapore: Oxford University Press.

Kosik, K. 1976. *Dialectics of the Concrete*. Dordrecht, Holland: D. Reidel Publishing Co.

Krader, L. 1968. *Formation of the State*. Englewood Cliffs, NJ: Prentice Hall.

Kuhn, P. A. 1970. *Rebellion and Its Enemies in Late Imperial China: Militarization and Social Structure, 1796–1864*. Cambridge: Harvard University Press.

Lapidus, I. M. 1975. "Hierarchies and Networks: A Comparison of Chinese and Islamic Societies." In *Conflict and Control in Imperial China*, edited by F. Wakeman, Jr., and C. Grant, 26–43. Berkeley: University of California Press.

Lardner, Jr., T. 1990. "An African Tragedy." *Africa Report* 35:13–16.

Lasswell, H., and A. Kaplan. 1950. *Power and Society*. New Haven, CT: Yale University Press.

Laurence, P. 1989. "Secret Afrikaner Society Could Regain Influence in South Africa." *The Christian Science Monitor*, 17 July, 4.

———. 1990a. "Marked for Murder." *Africa Report* 25:22–25.

———. 1990b. "Comrades and Capitalists." *Africa Report* 35:39–42.

———. 1991. "The Credibility Gap." *Africa Report* 36:44–48.

Legassik, M. 1985. "Southern Africa in Crisis: What Route to Democracy." *African Affairs* 84:587–602.

Legros, D., D. Hunderfund, and J. Shapiro. 1979. "Economic Base, Mode of Production and Social Formation; A Discussion of Marx's Terminology." *Dialectical Anthropology* 4:243–49.

Lemon, A. 1987. *Apartheid in Transition*. Boulder, CO: Westview Press.

Levins, R., and R. Lewontin. 1985. *The Dialectical Biologist*. Cambridge: Harvard University Press.

Levy, A. 1971. "The Ottoman Ulema and the Military Reform of Sultan Mahmud II." *Asian and African Studies* 7:13–39.

Lewis, B. 1970. "Some Reflections on the Decline of the Ottoman Empire." In *The Economic Decline of Empires*, edited by C. M. Cipolla, 215–34. London: Methuen and Co., Ltd.

———. 1985. "The Shia." *New York Review of Books*, 15 August, 7–10.

Liebenberg, B. J. 1981. "Botha and Smut in Power, 1910–1924." In *Five Hundred Years: A History of South Africa*, edited by C. F. J. Muller, 385–410. Pretoria: Academica.

Liebenow, J. C. 1969. *Liberia: The Evolution of Privilege*. Ithaca: Cornell University Press.

———. 1987. *Liberia*. Bloomington, IN: Indiana University Press.

Lincoln, Y., and E. G. Guba. 1985. *Naturalistic Inquiry*. Beverly Hills: Sage.

Lipton, M. 1985. *Capitalism and Apartheid*. Totowa, NJ: Rowman and Allanheld.

Little, K. L. 1948. "The Poro Society as an Arbitor of Culture." *African Studies* 7:2–15.

———. 1949. "The Role of the Secret Society in Cultural Specialization." *American Anthropologist* 51:199–212.

———. 1951. *The Mende of Sierra Leone: A West African People in Transition*. London: Routledge & Kegan Paul, Ltd.

———. 1965. The Political Function of the Poro, Part 1. *Africa* 35:350–53.

———. 1966. The Political Function of the Poro, Part 2. *Africa* 36:62–71.

Liu, K. C. 1990. "Introduction: Orthodoxy in Chinese Society." In *Orthodoxy in Late Imperial China*, edited by K. C. Liu, 1–24. Berkeley: University of California Press.

Lowenkopf, M. 1976. *Politics in Liberia*. Stanford, CA: Hoover Institute Press.

Lui, A. Y. 1979. "Corruption in China During the Early Ch'ing Period." Center of Asian Studies. Occasional Papers and Monographs No. 39. University of Hong Kong.

Lukacs, G. 1968. *History and Class Consciousness*. Cambridge: MIT Press.

———. 1978. *Marx's Basic Ontological Principles*. Translated by D. Fernbah. London: Merlin Press.

Lukes, S. 1974. *Power: A Radical View*. London. MacMillan.

———. 1979. "On the Relativity of Power." In *Philosophical Disputes in Social Science*, edited by S. C. Brown, 243–59. Atlantic Highlands, NJ: Humanities Press.

Lyman, S. M. 1964. "Chinese Secret Societies in the Occident: Notes and Suggestions for Research in Sociology of Secrecy." *The Canadian Review of Sociology and Anthropology* 1:79–102.

———. 1970. "The Asian in the West." Social Science and Humanities Publications No. 4. Desert Research Institute, Reno and Las Vegas: University of Nevada.

MacKenzie, N., ed. 1967. *Secret Societies*. New York: Collier Books.

MacShane, D., M. Plant, and D. Ward. 1984. *Power!* Boston: South End Press.

Magubane, B. 1978. "The 'Native Reserves' (Bantustans) and the Role of The Migrant Labor System in the Political Economy of South Africa." In *The World As a Company Town*, edited by A. E. Indris-Sovern and M. R. Vaugh, 255–93. The Hague: Mouton.

———. 1984. "The Mounting Class and National Struggles in South Africa." *Review* 8:197–231.

———. 1990. *The Political Economy of Race and Class in South Africa*. New York: Monthly Review Press.

Mak, L. 1975a. "Chinese Secret Societies in Ipoh Town, 1945–1969." Department of Sociology Working Papers No. 42. University of Singapore.

———. 1975b. "The Kongsi and the Triad." *Southeast Asia Ethnicity and Development Newsletter* 3:47–57.

———. 1980. "Rigidity of System Boundary Among Dialect Groups in Nineteenth Century Singapore: A Study of Inscription Data." *Modern Asian Studies* 14:465–487.

———. 1981. *The Sociology of Secret Societies*. Oxford: Oxford University Press.

———. 1983. "Subcommunal Participation and Leadership Cohesiveness of the Chinese in 19th Century Singapore." *Modern Asian Studies* 17:437–53.

———. 1985. "Chinese Secret Societies: Criminologically Defined." *Bulletin of the Institute of Ethnology* 59:143–61.

———. 1988a. "Solidarity Models: A Sociological Framework for Comparative Criminal Organization." Working Papers, No. 87. Singapore: Department of Sociology, National University of Singapore.

———. 1988b. "Chinese Secret Societies in the 19th Century Straits Settlements." In *Early Chinese Immigrant Societies: Case Studies from North America and British Southeast Asia*, edited by L. T. Lee, 231–43. Singapore: Heinemann Asia.

Manicas, P. T. 1982. "The Human Sciences: A Radical Separation of Psychology and Social Sciences." In *Exploring Human Behavior*, edited by P. F. Secord, 155–73. Beverly Hills: Sage.

Mann, M. 1968. "The Autonomous Power of the State: Its Origins, Mechanisms and Results." In *States in History*, edited by J. H. Hill, 109–36. Oxford: Basil Blackwell.

———. 1986. *The Sources of Social Power, Vol. I: A History of Power From the Beginning to A. D. 1760*. Cambridge: Cambridge University Press.

Martin, B. C. 1972. "A Short History of the Khalwati Order of Dervishes." In

Scholars, Saints, and Sufis, edited by N. R. Keddie, 275–305. Berkeley: University of California Press.

Marx, K. 1904. *Critique of Political Economy*. Translated by N. I. Stone. Chicago: Charles H. Kerr.

———. 1961. *Economic and Philosophic Manuscripts of 1874*. Translated by M. Milligan. Moscow: Foreign Language Publishing House.

———. 1963. In *Selected Works*, edited by V. Adorafsky. New York: International Publishers.

———. 1964. *Economic and Philosophic Manuscripts of 1844*. Edited by D. J. Struik. New York: International Publishers.

———. 1971 (1857). In *The Grundrisse*, edited by D. McCellan. New York: Harper and Row.

———. 1975(1857). "Introduction to the Grundrisse." In *Karl Marx Texts on Method*, translated and edited by T. Carver, 47–87. New York: Barnes and Noble.

Marx, K., and F. Engels. 1970. In *The German Ideology*, edited by C. J. Arthur. New York: International Publishers.

———. 1975. In *Collected Works*. New York: International Publishers.

Masatoshi, T. 1984. "Popular Uprising, Rent Resistance and Bond Servant Rebellion in Late Ming." In *State and Society in China*, edited by L. and C. Daniels, 165–214. Tokyo: University of Tokyo Press.

Maud, R. 1974. "The Future of an Illusion: The Myth of White Meliatism in South Africa." In *South Africa: Economic Growth and Political Change*, edited by A. Leftwich, 287–318. New York: St. Martin's Press.

Means, G. P. 1976. *Malaysian Politics*. London: Hodder and Stroughton.

Meldrum, A. 1990. "The Assassination Bureau." *Africa Report* 35:42–44.

Meredith, M. 1988. *In the Name of Apartheid*. New York: Harper and Row.

Meszaros, I. 1972. *Lukacs' Concept of the Dialectic*. London: Merlin Press.

———. 1987. "Customs, Tradition, Legality: A Key Problem in the Dialectic of Base and Superstructure." In *Social Theory and Social Criticism*, edited by W. Outhwaite and M. Mulkay, 53–82. Oxford: Basil Blackwell.

Michael, F. 1965. *The Origin of Manchu Rule in China*. New York: Octagon Books.

Miliband, R. 1990. "Counter-Hegemonic Struggles." In *The Socialist Register*, edited by R. Miliband, L. Panitch, and J. Saville, 346–65. London: Merlin Press.

Milkman, R. 1979. "Contradictions of Semi-Peripheral Development: The South African Case." In *The World-System of Capitalism: Past and Present*, edited by W. Goldfrank, 267–84. Beverly Hills: Sage.

Miller, D., and C. Tilley. 1984. "Ideology, Power and Prehistory: An Introduction." In *Ideology, Power and Prehistory*, edited by D. Miller and C. Tilley, 1–16. Cambridge: Cambridge University Press.

Miller, H. 1965. *A Short History of Malaysia*. New York: Frederick A. Praeger.

Mirkovic, D. 1980. *Dialectic and Sociological Thought*, Ontario: Diliton Publishers, Inc.

Muller, C. K. J. 1981. "The Period of the Great Trek, 1834–1854." In *Five Hundred Years: A History of South Africa*, edited by C. F. J. Muller, 146–82. Pretoria: Academica.

Muramatsu, Y. 1960. "Some Themes in Chinese Rebel Ideologies." In *The Confu-*

cian Persuasion, edited by A. F. Wright, 241–67. Stanford: Stanford University Press.

Murphy, W. P. 1976. "A Semantic and Logical Analysis of Kpelle Proverbs and Metaphors of Secrecy." Ph.D. dissertation, Stanford University, Stanford, CA.

———. 1980. "Secret Knowledge as Property and Power in Kpelle Society: Elders Versus Youth." *Africa* 50:193–207.

———. 1981. "The Rhetorical Management of Dangerous Knowledge in Kpelle Brokerage." *American Ethnologist* 8:667–85.

———. 1989. Letter to the author, 24 January.

Murphy, W., and C. H. Bledsoe. 1987. "Kinship and Territory in the History of a Kpelle Chiefdom (Liberia)." In *The African Frontier*, edited by I. Kopytoff, 123–47. Bloomington: Indiana University Press.

Murray, M. J. 1989. "The Popular Upsurge in South Africa, 1984–1986." *Critical Sociology* 16:55–74.

Nagata, J. 1979. *Malaysian Mosaic*. Vancouver: University of British Columbia Press.

Nakamura, J. I., and M. Matao. 1982. "Social Structure and Population Change: A Corporate Study of Tokugawa Japan and Ch'ing China." *Economic Development and Culture Change* 30:229–69.

Naohiro, T. 1984. "Rural Control in the Ming Dynasty." In *State and Society in China*, edited by L. Grove and C. Daniels, 245–77. Tokyo: University of Tokyo Press.

Naquin, S. 1976. *Millenarian Rebellion in China*. New Haven, CT: Yale University Press.

———. 1981. *Shantung Rebellion: The Wang Lun Uprising of 1774*. New Haven, CT: Yale University Press.

———. 1982. "Connections between Rebellions." *Modern China* 9:337–60.

Nattrass, J. 1981. *The South African Economy*. Capetown: Oxford University Press.

Nonini, D. M. 1985. "Varieties of Materialism." *Dialectical Anthropology* 9:7–63.

Novicki, M. A. 1990. "Obed Asamoab: A New Role for ECOWAS." *Africa Report* 35:17–20.

O'Connor, J. 1987. *The Meaning of Crisis*. Oxford: Basil Blackwell.

Ollman, B. 1986. "The Meaning of Dialectics." *Monthly Review* 38:42–55.

Olsen, M. F. 1970. "Power as a Social Process." In *Power in Societies*, edited by M. E. Olsen, 2–10. London: MacMillan.

O'Meara, D. 1977. "The Africaner Broederbond 1927–1948: Class Vanguard of Africaner Nationalism." *Journal of Southern African Studies* 3:156–86.

———. 1983. *Volkskapitalisme*. New York: Cambridge University Press.

Onraet, R. H. d. S. 1947. *Singapore: A Police Background*. London: Dorothy Crisp.

Overmyer, D. L. 1972. "Folk-Buddhist Religion: Creation and Eschatology in Medieval China." *History of Religions* 12:42–69.

———. 1976. *Folk Buddhist Religion*. Cambridge: Harvard University Press.

———. 1981. "Alternatives." *Modern China* 7:153–90.

Parenti, M. 1978. *Power and the Powerless*. New York: St. Martin's Press.

Parker-Pearson, M. 1984. "Social Change, Ideology and the Archaeological Record." In *Marxist Perspectives in Archaeology*, edited by M. Spriggs, 59–71. Cambridge: Cambridge University Press.

Parry, V. J. 1970. "Warfare." In *The Cambridge History of Islam, Vol. 2*, edited by P. M. Holt, A. K. S. Lambton, and B. Lewis, 824–50. Cambridge: Cambridge University Press.

Parsons, J. B. 1970. *The Peasant Rebellion of the Late Ming Dynasty*. Tucson: University of Arizona Press.

Patterson, T. C. 1990. "Process in the Formation of Ancient World Systems." *Dialectical Anthropology* 15:1–18.

Pearson, M. P. 1984. "Social Change, Ideology and the Archaeological Record." In *Marxist Perspectives in Archaeology*, edited by M. Spriggs, 59–71. Cambridge: Cambridge University Press.

Pickering, W. A. 1879. "Chinese Secret Societies." *Journal of the Straits Branch of the Royal Asiatic Society of Great Britain and Ireland* 3:1–18.

Pirie, G. H., C. M. Rogerson, and K. S. O. Beavon. 1980. "Covert Power in South Africa: The Geography of the Afrikaner Broederbond." *Area* 12:97–104.

Porpora, D. V. 1985. "The Role of Agency in History: The Althusser-Thompson-Anderson Debate." *Current Perspectives in Social Theory* 6:219–41.

Posner, G. L. 1988. *Warlords of Crime*. New York: McGraw-Hill.

Poulantzas, N. 1973. *Political Power and Social Classes*. London: NLB.

Press, R. M. 1990. "African Nations Send Military Force to Liberia." *The Christian Science Monitor*, 9 August, 4.

Purcell, V. 1948. *The Chinese in Malaya*. London: Oxford University Press.

Rabushka, A. 1973. *Race and Politics in Urban Malaya*. Stanford: Hoover Institution Press.

Rescher, N. 1987. *Scientific Realism*. Dordrecht: D. Reidel.

Resnick, S., and R. D. Wolff. 1982. "Marxist Epistemology: The Critique of Economic Determinism." *Social Text* 6:31–72.

———. 1987. *Knowledge and Class*. Chicago: University of Chicago Press.

Richards, J. V. O. 1973. "The Sande and Some of the Forces that Inspired Its Creation or Adoption with Some References to the Poro." *Journal of Asian and African Studies* 8:69–77.

Rinehart, R. 1985. "Historical Setting." In *Liberia*, edited by H. D. Nelson, 1–72. Foreign Area Studies Handbook: U.S. Government Printing Office.

Rivano, J. 1981. "Joachim Israel's Epistemology of the Social Science: A Review Essay." Council on International Studies, Special Studies No. 140. Amherst: State University of New York.

Roberts, J. M. 1972. *The Mythology of Secret Societies*. London: Secker Warburg.

Roseberry, W. 1984. "Why Should Marxists Take Culture Seriously?" Eighty-third annual meeting of the American Anthropological Association, Denver, Colorado.

Rossabi, M. 1979. "Muslim and Central Asian Revolts." In *From Ming to Ch'ing*, edited by J. D. Spence and J. E. Wills, Jr., 167–200. New Haven, CT: Yale University Press.

Rotberg, R. I. 1989. "The Broederbond and Progress." *The Christian Science Monitor*, 26 October, 19.

———. 1990a. Education Deficit in South Africa. *The Christian Science Monitor*, 29 January, 19.

———. 1990b. "Shared Power in South Africa." *The Christian Science Monitor*, 3 December, 9.

Roth, G. 1979. "The Manchu-Chinese Relationship, 1618–1636." In *From Ming to Ch'ing*, edited by J. D. Spence and J. Wills, Jr., 1–38. New Haven, CT: Yale University Press.

Rus, V. 1980. "Positive and Negative Power: Thoughts on the Dialectics of Power." *Organizational Studies* 1:3–19.

Saul, J. S., and S. Gelb. 1986. *The Crises in South Africa*. New York: Monthly Review Press.

Sayer, D. 1979. *Marx's Method*. Atlantic Highlands, NJ: Humanities Press.

———. 1987. *The Violence of Abstraction*. Oxford: Basil Blackwell.

Sayers, S. 1980a. "Dualism, Materialism and Dialectics." In *Hegel, Marx and the Dialectic*, edited by R. Norman and S. Sayers, 67–141. Atlantic Highlands, NJ: Humanities Press.

———. 1980b. "On the Marxist Dialectic." In *Hegel, Marx and the Dialectic*, edited by R. Norman and S. Sayers, 1–24. Atlantic Highlands, NJ: Humanities Press.

———. 1985. *Reality and Reason*. New York: Basil Blackwell, Inc.

Schatzberg, M. F. 1988. *The Dialectics of Oppression in Zaire*. Bloomington: Indiana University Press.

Scheibe, K. E. 1979. *Mirrors, Masks, Lies and Secrets*. New York: Praeger.

Schuster, L. 1989. "The New Man in the Driver's Seat." *The Christian Science Monitor*, 9 May, 9.

Schwab, G. 1947. *Tribes of the Liberian Hinterland*. Cambridge, Mass: Peabody Museum.

Scott, J. 1977. "Hegemony and Peasantry." *Politics and Society* 7:267–96.

Seah, C. M., and L. S. G. Ag ASP. 1978. "Secret Societies Today." *Police Life Annual* 2:86–93.

Secord, P. 1986. "Explanation in Social Science and in Life Situations." In *Metatheory in Social Science*, edited by D. W. Fiske and R. A. Shweder, 197–221. Chicago: University of Chicago Press.

Serfontein, J. H. P. 1978. *Brotherhood of Power*. Bloomington: Indiana University Press.

Severy, M. 1987. "The World of Suleymman, the Magnificent." *National Geographic* (November), 533–601.

Shaw, S. 1965. "The Origins of Ottoman Military Reform: The Nizam-I-Cedid Army of Sultan Selim III." *Journal of Modern History* 37:291–305.

———. 1976. *History of the Ottoman Empire and Modern Turkey, Vol. 1: The Rise and Decline of the Ottoman Empire, 1280–1808*. Cambridge: Cambridge University Press.

Shek, R. 1982. "Millenarianism Without Rebellion." *Modern China* 8:305–36.

Sibley, J. L., and D. Westermann. 1928. *Liberia-Old and New*. Garden City, NY: Doubleday.

Simmel, G. 1906. "The Society of Secrecy and the Secret Society." *American Journal of Sociology* 11:441–98.

———. 1950. *The Sociology of Georg Simmel*. Translated and edited by K. H. Wolff. New York: Free Press.

Simson, H. 1980. "The Social Origins of the Afrikaner Fascism and Its Apartheid Policy." Acta Universitutis Upsaliensis. Uppsala Studies in Economic History No 21. Stockholm: Almquist and Wiksell, Inc.

Skalnik, P. 1978. "The Early State as a Process." In *The Early State*. edited by J. M.

Claessen and P. Skalnik, 397–437. The Hague: Mouton Publishers.

Smith, L. 1987. "Muzzling the Media." *African Report* 32:58–60.

Spies, S. G. 1981. "Reconstruction and Unification, 1902–1910." In *Five Hundred Years: A History of South Africa*, edited by C. F. J. Muller, 362–84. Pretoria: Academica.

Stakeman, R. 1986. *The Cultural Politics of Religious Change*. New York: Edwin Mellen Press.

Strauch, J. 1981. *Chinese Village Politics in the Malaysian State*. Cambridge: Harvard University Press.

Suchting, W. A. 1983. *Marx: An Introduction*. New York: New York University Press.

Sumner, C. 1979. *Reading Ideologies*. New York: Academic Press.

Sztompka, P. 1974. *System and Function*. New York: Academic Press.

———. 1979. *Sociological Dilemmas*. New York: Academic Press.

Tai, H. 1977. "Origin of the Heaven and Earth Society." *Modern Asian Studies* 11:405–25.

Tainter, J. A. 1988. *The Collapse of Complex Societies*. Cambridge: Cambridge University Press.

Tartter, J. R. 1985. "Government and Politics." In *Liberia*, edited by H. D. Nelson, 195–246. Foreign Area Studies Handbook: U.S. Government Printing Office.

Therborn, G. 1980. *The Ideology of Power and the Power of Ideology*. London: New Left Books.

Thompson, L. 1987. "Before the Revolution." *The New York Review of Books* 34:20–27.

———. 1990. "South Africa: The Fire This Time." *The New York Review of Books* 37:12–18.

Tilley, C. 1981. "Economy and Society: What Relationship?" In *Economic Archaeology*, edited by A. Sheridan and G. Bailey, 131–48. BAR International Studies No. 16. Oxford: England.

Ting, C. 1982. "Chinese Immigration and the Growth of a Plural Society." In *Research on Racial and Ethnic Relations*, vol. 3, edited by C. B. Marrett and C. Leggon, 103–23. Greenwich, CT: JAI Press.

Toland, J. D. 1987. "Discrepancies and Dissolution: Breakdown of the Early Inca State." In *Early State Dynamics*, edited by H. J. M. Claessen and P. V. D. Velde, 138–53. Leiden: E. J. Brill.

Topley, M. 1961. "The Emergence and Social Function of Chinese Religious Associations in Singapore." *Comparative Studies in Society and History* 31:289–314.

Toynbee, A. J. 1974. "The Ottoman Empire's Place in World History." In *The Ottoman State and Its Place in World History*, edited by K. H. Karpat, 15–33. Leiden: E. J. Brill.

Turan, O. 1970. "Anatolia in the Period of the Seljuks and the Beyliks." In *The Cambridge History of Islam*, vol. 1, edited by P. M. Holt, A. K. S. Lambton, and B. Lewis, 231–62. Cambridge: Cambridge University Press.

Turk, A. T. 1982. "Social Control and Social Conflict." In *Social Control*, edited by J. P. Gibbs, 249–64. Beverly Hills, CA: Sage Publications.

Tygesen, P. 1991. "The ABCs of Apartheid." *Africa Report* 36:13–17.

Ulin, R. 1984. *Understanding Culture*. Austin: University of Texas Press.

Ume, K. E. 1981. "The Origin of Apartheid in South Africa: A Review." *Journal of South African Studies* 8:176–81.

Unger, J. 1975. "The Making and Breaking of Chinese Secret Societies" (review article). *Journal of Contemporary Asia* 3:89–98.

Uys, S. 1989. "The Afrikaner Establishment." In *South Africa: No Turning Back*, edited by S. Johnson, 206–39. Bloomington: Indiana Press.

Van Der Sprenkel, O. D. N. B. 1967. "The Chinese Civil Service." In *The Decline of Empires*, edited by S. N. Eisenstadt, 50–61. Englewood Cliffs, NJ: Prentice Hall.

Van Schore, M. C. E. 1981. "The Orange Free State." In *Five Hundred Years: A History of South Africa*, edited by C. F. J. Muller, 234–55. Pretoria: Academica.

Van Zyl, M. C. 1981. "States and Colonies in South Africa, 1854–1902." In *Five Hundred Years: A History of South Africa*, edited by C. F. J. Muller, 297–327. Pretoria: Academica.

Vasil, R. K. 1980. *Ethnic Politics in Malaysia*. New Delhi: Radiant Publishers.

Villa-Vicencio, C. 1990. "Options for the Future." *Africa Report* 35:29–30.

Villiers, R. D. 1971. "Afrikaner Nationalism." In *The Oxford History of South Africa, Vol. 2: South Africa, 1870–1966*, edited by M. Wilson and L. Thompson, 365–423. Oxford: Clarendon Press.

Vincent, A. 1987. *Theory of the State*. Oxford: Basil Blackwell.

Vyakkerev, F. F. 1982. "Objective Contradiction and Its Theoretical 'Image.'" In *Dialectical Contradictions: Contemporary Marxist Discussions*, edited by E. Merquit, P. Moran, and W. H. Truitt, 84–95. Minneapolis: Marxist Educational Press.

Wakeman, Jr., F. 1966. *Strangers at the Gate*. Berkeley: University of California Press.

———. 1975a. *The Fall of Imperial China*. New York: Free Press.

———. 1975b. "Introduction: The Evolution of Local Control in Late Imperial China." In *Conflict and Control in Late Imperial China*, edited by F. Wakeman, Jr., and C. Grant, 1–25. Berkeley: University of California Press.

———. 1977. "Rebellion and Revolution: The Study of Popular Chinese Movements in Chinese History." *Journal of Asian Studies* 36:201–37.

———. 1985. *The Great Enterprise*, vols. 1, 2. Berkeley: University of California Press.

Walsh, D. 1974. "The Political Economy of Africaner Nationalism." In *South Africa: Economy, Growth and Political Change*, edited by A. Leftwich, 249–85. New York: St. Martin's Press.

Wardell, M. L., and J. K. Benson. 1979. "A Dialectical View: Foundation for an Alternative Sociological Method." In *Theoretical Perspectives in Sociology*, edited by S. McNell, 232–48. New York: St. Martin's Press.

Warner, W. J. 1964. Sect. In *A Dictionary of the Social Sciences*, edited by J. Gould and W. I. Kolb, 624–25. Glencoe, IL: Free Press.

Warren, S. 1984. *The Emergence of Dialectical Theory*. Chicago: University of Chicago Press.

Webb, M. 1975, "The Flag Follows Trade: An Essay on the Necessary Interaction of the Military and Commercial Factors in State Formation." In *Ancient Civilization and Trade*, edited by C. C. Lamberg-Karlovsky and J. A. Sabloff, 155–210.

Albuquerque: University of New Mexico Press.

Weber, M. 1968. *Economy and Society*, vol. 2. New York: Bedminster Press.

Webster, D. 1975. "Warfare and the Evolution of the State: A Reconsideration." *American Antiquity* 40:464–70.

Webster, H. 1908. *Primitive Secret Societies: A Study of Early Politics and Religion.* New York: MacMillan.

Wedgewood, C. H. 1930. "The Nature and Function of Secret Societies." *Oceania* 1:124–41.

Weller, R. P. 1982. "Sectarian Religion and Political Action in China." *Modern China* 8:463–83.

Wells, D. S. 1979. "Dialectical Social Science." In *Theoretical Perspective in Sociology*, edited by S. G. McNell, 214–31. New York: St. Martin's Press.

Wells, R. 1990. "The Last of Liberia." *Africa Report* 35:21–22.

Welmers, W. E. 1949. "Secret Medicine, Magic and Rites of the Kpelle Tribe in Liberia." *Southwestern Journal of Anthropology* 5:208–43.

Welsh, D. 1975. "The Politics of White Supremacy." In *Change in Contemporary South Africa*, edited by L. Thompson and J. Butler, 51–78. Berkeley: University of California Press.

Whitaker, D. P. 1985. "The Economy." In *Liberia*, edited by H. D. Nelson, 139–94. Foreign Area Studies Handbook: U.S. Government Printing Office.

Wilkins, I., and H. Strydon. 1979. *The Broederbond*. New York: Paddington Press, Ltd.

Williams, D., ed. 1973. *Secret Societies in Ireland*. New York: Barnes and Noble.

Wilsnack, R. W. 1980. "Information Control: A Conceptual Framework for Sociological Analysis." *Urban Life* 8:467–500.

Wilson, F. 1975. "The Political Implications to Blacks of Economic Change Now Taking Place in South Africa." In *Change in Contemporary South Africa*, edited by L. Thompson and J. Butler, 168–200. Berkeley: University of California Press.

Wilson, H. S. 1980. "Nation Building, Ethnicity and the New Imperialism: Dilemmas of Political Development in Liberia." In *West African Culture Dynamics*, edited by B. K. Swartz and E. Dumett, 563–86. Hague: Mouton Publishers.

Wilson, J. 1982. "Realist Perspectives as a Foundation for Marxist Social Theory." In *Current Perspectives in Social Theory*, edited by S. G. McNell, 243–63. Greenwich, CT: JAI Press.

————. 1983. *Social Theory*. Englewood Cliffs, NJ: Prentice Hall.

Wittek, P. 1958. *The Rise of the Ottoman Empire*. Royal Asiatic Society of Britain and Ireland. London: Luzac and Co., Ltd.

Wolpe, H. 1980. "Capitalism and Cheap Labour-Power in South Africa: From Segregation to Apartheid." In *The Articulation of the Modes of Production*, edited by H. Wolpe, 289–319. London: Routledge & Kegan Paul.

Wong, T. P. 1979. "The Word Kongsi." *Journal of the Malaysia Branch of the Royal Asiatic Society* 52:102–5.

Woodside, A. 1990. "State, Scholar and Orthodoxy: The Ch'ing Academy, 1736–1834." In *Orthodoxy in Late Imperial China*, edited by K. C. Liu, 158–84. Berkeley: University of California Press.

Woolgar, S. 1983. "Irony in the Social Study of Science." In *Science Observed*, edited by K. D. Knorr-Cetina and M. Mulkay, 259–66. Beverly Hills: Sage Publishers.

Wren, C. 1989. "Namibian Rebel Group Short of Full Control." *New York Times*, 15 November, 1, 11.

———. 1991. "Scandal Threatens De Klerk and Talks." *New York Times*, 21 July, 3.

Wrong, D. 1979. *Power: Its Forms, Bases and Uses*. Oxford: Basil Blackwell.

Wynne, M. L. 1941. *Triad and Tabut*. Singapore: Government Printing Office.

Yang, C. 1961. *Religion in Chinese Society*. Berkeley: University of California Press.

Yen, C. 1986. *A Social History of the Chinese in Singapore and Malaya, 1800–1911*. Singapore: Oxford University Press.

Yoffee, N. 1988. "Orienting Collapse." In *The Collapse of Ancient States and Civilizations*, edited by N. Yoffee and G. L. Cowgill, 10–19. Tucson: University of Arizona Press.

Yong, C. F. 1977. "Leadership and Power in the Chinese Community of Singapore During the 1930's." *Journal of Southeast Asian Studies* 8:195–209.

Yoong, N. S. 1961. "The Chinese Protectorate in Singapore, 1877–1900." *Journal of Southeast Asian History* 2:89–116.

Younghusband, P. 1989. "De Klerk Puts End to Apartheid on South Africa's Beaches." *The Washington Post*, 17 November, 18.

Yuan, T. 1979. "Urban Riots and Disturbances." In *From Ming to Ch'ing*, edited by J. D. Spence and J. E. Wills, Jr., 277–320. New Haven: Yale University Press.

Yukio, Y. 1984. "Reforms in the Service Levy System in Fifteenth and Sixteenth Centuries." In *State and Society in China*, edited by L. Grove and C. Daniels, 279–310. Tokyo: University of Tokyo Press.

Zagarell, A. 1986. "Structural Discontinuity—A Critical Factor in the Emergence of Primary and Secondary States." *Dialectical Anthropology* 10:155–77.

Zeitlin, M. 1980. "On Classes, Class Conflict and the State: An Introductory Essay." In *Classes, Class Conflict and the State*, edited by M. Zeitlin, 1–37. Cambridge, MA: Winthrop Publisher, Inc.

Zurndorfer, H. T. 1983. "Violence and Political Protest in Ming and Qing China." *International Review of Social History* 28:304–19.

Index